Unaccompanied Children
From Migration to Integration

UNACCOMPANIED CHILDREN

From Migration to Integration

Edited by

Işık Kulu-Glasgow

Monika Smit

Ibrahim Sirkeci

TRANSNATIONAL PRESS LONDON

2019

Unaccompanied Children: From Migration to Integration
Edited by Işık Kulu-Glasgow, Monika Smit and Ibrahim Sirkeci

Copyright © 2019 by Transnational Press London

First Published in 2019 by TRANSNATIONAL PRESS LONDON in the United Kingdom, 12 Ridgeway Gardens, London, N6 5XR, UK.
www.tplondon.com

Requests for permission to reproduce material from this work should be sent to:
sales@tplondon.com

Paperback
ISBN: 978-1-912997-14-5

Cover Design: Gizem Çakır
Cover image: Thanks to Joel Mott, https://unsplash.com/@joelmott

www.tplondon.com

ABOUT THE AUTHORS

Roberta Lo Bianco, Clinical Psychologist; coordinator of the Migration Unit of CESIE, based in Palermo; trainer and project manager in EU and national projects addressed to UAMs, asylum seekers, refugees and migrants aiming at socio-economic inclusion; member of a scientific committee for the design of the Master: "Expert in reception processes and intercultural inclusion" in the faculty of Psychology, University of Palermo; founding member of social enterprise 'Moltivolti'; Legal tutor of UAMs; coordinator of Action 2_workshop paths of the project Ragazzi Harraga.

Georgia Chondrou is a student of European and International Studies in the University of Macedonia, in Thessaloniki, Greece. She received interdisciplinary trainings on the migration situation, focusing on the reception and the inclusion policies of different European countries. She collaborated in the 'Creative Community Leaders' project, funded by the UNHCR, that focused on supporting the inclusion of asylum seekers, refugees and migrants in Thessaloniki. She currently works as a trainer, as well as a project manager of European funded projects on topics such as socio cultural orientation and employability and entrepreneurship in the Migration Unit of CESIE, based in Palermo.

Aycan Celikaksoy, PhD, is based at Swedish Institute for Social Research (SOFI) at Stockholm University, Sweden. Her research interests include economics of the family, labour economics, immigration and integration, family structure, marriage migration, unaccompanied minors, and refugee children. Her recent project was on unaccompanied minors in Sweden, which was funded by the European Refugee Fund.

Mariglynn Edlins, Ph.D., is an Associate Professor of Human Services Administration at the University of Baltimore. Her research is focused on the interactions that occur between individuals and the public servants who implement public policy. She is particularly interested in interactions that involve children, specifically how these interactions with public servants are different for children than for adults, as well as how to improve these interactions with empathy.

Winta Ghebreab is a project manager with Nidos, the Dutch family guardian organisation. Since 2015 she has managed and implemented projects focusing on improving the resilience of unaccompanied minor asylum seekers. She has a Masters of Arts in Advanced Development Studies and Sociology of Non-Western Societies. Before Nidos she worked in development cooperation in Africa and Asia on gender equality and social development issues.

Anna de Haan is a psychologist and researcher, and she works as a project manager and advisor with Pharos, the Dutch Centre of Expertise on Health Disparities. She works within both nationwide and local projects focusing on refugee children, refugee families and unaccompanied refugee minors. Her PhD study

i

"Ethnic minority youth in youth mental health care: utilisation and dropout" focused on the disparities in the accessibility of youth care between various ethnic groups.

Yodit Jacob works as a project manager, advisor and trainer with Pharos, the Dutch Centre of Expertise on Health Disparities. The themes she works on are female genital mutilation, collaboration with cultural mediators (e.g., Eritrean key persons), the health of and accessibility of health care (e.g., birth care and mental health care) for asylum seekers and refugees, and stimulating cultural sensitive approaches in health care.

Raphael Kamp is author, policy analyst and lecturer for migration, integration and the social protection system in Germany. His book "Grenzenlos - Warum wir illegale Migration neu denken müssen" was published in Spring 2019. Moreover, he currently works as a social worker in a refugee integration project in Germany. Raphael Kamp has been working in different areas of residual youth welfare, including trauma pedagogy and emergency foster care. This also included the foster care of unaccompanied minors. He holds a Master of Science in Public Policy and Human Development with a specialization in Migration Studies from the United Nations University and Maastricht University.

Işık Kulu-Glasgow, PhD, is a researcher at the Research and Documentation Centre (WODC) of the Dutch Ministry of Justice and Security. She has been involved in many research projects on asylum, migration and integration issues, including evaluation of policy measures. Currently, she is working on topics related to unaccompanied minor asylum seekers and refugees. Recently she completed a research project regarding migration decisions and destination choices of these minors in the Netherlands. At present, she is involved in a project on the future of (ex-) unaccompanied minors in the Netherlands.

Katie Kuschminder is an Assistant Professor at Maastricht University and UNU-Merit. Her research focuses on refugees and other migrants' journeys, irregular migration, and return and reintegration. Her work has been published in International Migration, Journal of Refugee Studies, and Migration Studies as well as in popular outlets such as Euronews, NewsDeeply, and the Conversation. She regularly teaches in migration at the bachelors, masters, PhD and professional level and has delivered training for the College of Europe, Dutch Ministry of Foreign Affairs, and other country governments.

Jennica Larrison, Ph.D., is an Assistant Professor and Graduate Program Director in the School of Public and International Affairs at the University of Baltimore. Her research examines the distinctions between how migration is experienced, portrayed, and legislated. Prior to joining the University of Baltimore, she worked with the World Bank focusing on issues of migration and social protection in East Asia and Central Asia. She has a PhD from the George Washington University, a masters degree from the University of California, San Diego, and undergraduate degrees from the University of Texas at Austin.

Hilde Lidén, Dr. Polit. in Social Anthropology, NTNU Norway (2000). Lidén is a Research Professor at the Institute for Social Research (ISF), Oslo. Her research interests are transnational migration, childhood, family practices, unaccompanied minors, resettlement and integration. Her research includes rights dilemmas in national and international policies and regulations on immigration, transnational families and citizenship, from a child's point of view. Recently she has published a monograph on children and migration (Lidén, 2017) and articles in international journals, e.g. Unaccompanied Migrant Youth in the Nordic Countries (Lidén, 2019).

Trudy Mooren, PhD, works as a clinical psychologist in Centrum '45, a partner in Arq Psychotrauma Expert Group and as a senior researcher at the Department of Clinical Psychology, Faculty of Social Sciences of Utrecht University. Centrum '45 is a national institute for specialised diagnostics and treatment of psycho-traumatic problems in people with experiences of war, persecution and violence. She coordinates Arq's research program on Youth, family and trauma, and her current studies concern parent-child and family relationships in response to trauma.

Sanne Noyon, PhD (European University Institute 2017), is a migration researcher at the Research and Documentation Center (WODC) with the Dutch Ministry of Justice and Security. With expertise in the study of human behaviour, she is interested in micro-level processes involved in migration, such as how individual attitudes and preferences shape migration decisions. Her current work focuses on asylum migrants' relationship with the democratic rule of law.

Cathrine Holst Salvesen, Master in Political Science 2014. She is a Senior Advisor at the Norwegian Woman's Public Health Association and works within the field of migration and adolescence. Her master thesis Du ser det ikke før du tror det was based on qualitative analysis of how Norwegian public agencies identify unaccompanied minor asylum seekers as victims of trafficking. Salvesen contributed as a research assistant to a research project on the voices of minors who have been victims of human trafficking (Lidén and Salvesen, 2016).

Ibrahim Sirkeci is Professor of Transnational Studies, Director of Regent's Centre for Transnational Business and Management, Head of Marketing Subject Cluster, and Associate Dean for Research (Interim) at Regent's University London. Previously he worked at the University of Bristol, Atilim University, Hacettepe University and Bilkent University. He earned his PhD from the University of Sheffield. His research focuses on migration, integration, labour market outcomes, remittances and transnational marketing. He has founded Migration Letters journal with Jeffrey Cohen and Elli Heikkila in 2003 and has been a chief editor or associate editor of several other journals including Remittances Review, Transnational Marketing Journal, and Goc Dergisi. He has chaired the Migration Conference series since 2012.

Monika Smit was an assistant professor of Child and Youth Care at Leiden University where she carried out several studies on unaccompanied minor asylum seekers until 2000. From 2000-2009 she worked at the Bureau of the Dutch national rapporteur on trafficking in human beings. Currently, she heads the research division Administration of Justice, Legislations and International and aliens Affairs of the Research and Documentation Centre at the Dutch Ministry of Security and Justice, and holds an endowed chair at Groningen University on Psycho social care for unaccompanied minor asylum seekers.

Carla van Os has a background in orthopedagogy and law and has been working as a researcher and teacher at the Study Centre for Children, Migration and Law at the Faculty of Behavioural rand Social Sciences of the University of Groningen in the Netherlands, since 2014. She wrote her PhD (2018) on Best Interests of the Child assessments for accompanied and unaccompanied asylum-seeking children in the context of their asylum procedure. Before, Carla worked as a fundraiser and public information officer at the Dutch Refugee Foundation (1996-2005) and as a legal adviser on children's rights and migration at Defence for Children (2005-2014).

Eskil Wadensjö is Professor of Labour Economics at the Swedish Institute for Social Research (SOFI) at Stockholm University since 1980. He was the dean of the Faculty of Social Sciences from 1996 to 2005. He received a Ph.D. in economics at Lund University in 1972. He has authored and edited several books including *The Nordic Labour Market in the 1990's* (1996), *Immigration to Denmark. International and National Perspectives* (1999), and *The Common Nordic Labor Market at 50* (2008).

Elianne Zijlstra is working as an assistant professor at the Study Centre for Children, Migration and Law at the Faculty of Behavioural and Social Sciences of the University of Groningen in the Netherlands. She finished her PhD in 2012 on the Best Interests of the Child in decisionmaking in migration law. During her PhD research, she worked as a behavioural scientist at a youth care organisation, and she obtained her post master degree for diagnostics and treatment of children and families.

CONTENT

CHAPTER 8

Social Inclusion Processes for unaccompanied minors in the city of
Palermo: Fostering Autonomy through a New Social Inclusion Model

INTRODUCTION

Işık Kulu-Glasgow, Monika Smit, Ibrahim Sirkeci

According to the United Nations Refugee Agency (UNHCR), we are witnessing the highest displacement of the world population on record: by the end of 2017, 68.5 million people around the world have been forced to leave their homes as a result of persecution, conflict, or generalised violence. While 40 million people were internally displaced, nearly 25.4 million refugees had crossed international borders with more than two-thirds originating from five countries only: Syria, Afghanistan, South Sudan, Myanmar and Somalia. Developing regions hosted 85 per cent of the world's refugees (with Turkey, Uganda, Pakistan, Lebanon and Iran in the top-five refugee-hosting countries). In addition, about 3.1 million people were awaiting a decision on their application for asylum - about half in developing regions (UNHCR, 2018). In 2017, 1.7 million new asylum claims were submitted, with the United States of America (US) being the top destination country (with 331,700 new individual applications) followed by Germany (198,300), Italy (126,500), and Turkey (126,100) (idem).

We know that among these refugees are minors, some of whom are not accompanied by parents or other adults who are responsible for them, but our knowledge regarding the numbers of unaccompanied minors and separated children who are on the move worldwide is relatively limited. According to the International Organisation for Migration (IOM) and the United Nations Children's Fund (UNICEF) formal registration procedures in many countries, including those in Europe, do not allow for their identification (IOM/UNICEF, 2015). On the basis of the available information, UNICEF reports that since 2010, the number of children travelling alone has increased fivefold: in 2015 and 2016 a total of at least 300,000 unaccompanied and separated migrant children were recorded in some 80 countries – compared to a total of 66,000 in 2010 and 2011 (UNICEF, 2017).

In 2017, for the first time, UNHCR had reported on unaccompanied and separated children among the registered refugees.[1] They estimated cautiously that in that year minors (accompanied and unaccompanied) constituted 52 per cent of the world refugee population, an increase from 41 per cent in

---

[1] Until then the reporting was on asylum-seeking unaccompanied and separated minors (UNHCR, 2018).

2009. (UNHCR, 2018). In addition, it was (conservatively) estimated that in 2017, there were 173,800 unaccompanied and separated asylum-seeking *and* refugee children who were displaced from their homes worldwide. In the same year, 45,500 children were reported to have sought asylum on an individual basis in 67 countries. However, this number is also considered to be an underestimate, as, among other things, it does not cover figures from three important destination-countries: Russia, the US and South Africa. Although the majority of these asylum applications were made by children aged 15 to 17, a sizeable segment of the minors was aged 14 years or younger (26 per cent) (UNHCR, 2018).

In 2017, the highest number of asylum applications by unaccompanied minors and separated children were in Italy, followed by Germany. Also, Egypt, Sweden, Turkey, Greece, the United Kingdom, Tanzania, Austria, France, Zambia and the Netherlands were among top destination countries. The top three countries of origin were Afghanistan, Eritrea, and the Democratic Republic of Congo (UNHCR, 2018).

Although most unaccompanied minors do not move to Europe, in 2015, the European Union (EU) witnessed a record number of minors seeking international protection in member states (Eurostat, 2017). With almost 96,500 unaccompanied minors, this number was about eight times higher than the annual average during the period 2008-2013 (around 12,000 per year). However, more recently, the number of asylum seeking unaccompanied minors and their share among minor asylum applicants have declined considerably in the EU-countries (Eurostat 2017; 2018). UNICEF reports an increase in the share of unaccompanied or separated children among child migrants in certain European countries such as Greece, Spain, Italy and Bulgaria.[2] Similar to the global trend of asylum seekers, Afghan and Eritrean minors are the top-two nationalities who sought asylum in the EU in 2017, followed by those from the Gambia, while in 2015, Syrian minors were among the top-three nationalities (Eurostat, 2018).

These statistics make it obvious that children move in great numbers, and many do so alone. While some of the reasons which motivate them to undertake such journeys alone are similar to those of adults – e.g. wars, forced conscription, pursuing aspirations for better social and economic opportunities[3], ethnic violence, cultural differences, examples of others migrating - others are more specific to children, such as forced child marriages, lack of educational opportunities or being sent ahead to realize family reunification in another country.

Without the protection of their adult family members or relatives,

---

[2] https://www.unicef.org/eca/emergencies/latest-statistics-and-graphics-refugee-and-migrant-children

[3] Similar to adult companions, they suffer from and react to 'democratic deficit' and 'developmental (economic) deficit' (Sirkeci et al., 2017:1-2).

unaccompanied minors are considered to be the most vulnerable group of migrants who run the risk of exploitation and abuse during their flight (Hopkins & Hill, 2008; Thommessen, Corcoran & Todd, 2015; Keles et al., 2018).

Reaching their destination does not mean however that they are then less vulnerable. To start with, at arrival they may be detained by immigration authorities due to their unknown migration status which endangers the best interest of the child – there are over 100 countries which detain children for migration-related reasons (UNICEF, 2017). Once they are let in the country, they can still be under risk of exploitation due to exhaustion or lack of resources, as may have to work off debts to their smugglers (UNHCR, 2018).[4] At the same time, they are faced with specific challenges of integration on economic, social, and cultural dimensions and in many cases also face burdens of the reunification of their family. Growing anti-immigration tendencies in public opinion do not help either.

The migration process is to be considered as travel through time and space at the face of evolving and shifting insecurities[5] (often referring to vulnerabilities) at the origin, transit and destination countries. In spite of their high vulnerabilities, there is relatively little attention for unaccompanied minors in the literature on (forced) migration. This was an important reason to initiate this book. It covers different phases of the migration and integration processes of unaccompanied minors: from the decision to migrate and the migration journey, including the risk of exploitation en route, the period shortly after the arrival in the destination country, and the integration process. Via this broad scope, this book aims to contribute to the literature on child migration, and specifically on unaccompanied minors and separated children.

Most of the chapters in this book focus on unaccompanied minors who arrived in a European country in 2015, with special attention to the top-three nationalities of unaccompanied minors arriving in the EU, namely Syrian, Afghan and Eritrean minors. One of the contributions sheds light on the arrival of unaccompanied minors from Central American countries in the US to offer the readers an opportunity to compare and contrast.

Kamp and Kushminder's opening chapter explores the consecutive phases of migration and integration processes as they examine the migration journey, decision making and integration experiences of 17 Syrian born unaccompanied minors in Germany. The accounts they present show that destination country is mostly decided in Syria, and the minors' ethnicity influences the migration route, costs and duration of the journey, as well as the dangers, encountered en route. The outcome of the process is somewhat

---

[4] Globally children account for approximately 28 per cent of trafficking victims (UNICEF, 2017).
[5] See Sirkeci (2009) for en elaboration of insecurities and conflict model of migration.

disappointing: the minors are dissatisfied with their refugee status in Germany, they do not feel welcome, and expectations of family reunification could not be met. These young people not only miss the support of their core family but are burdened by the obligation to support the family members who stayed behind. Kamp and Kushminder recommend prioritisation of family-reunification for unaccompanied minors arriving in Germany.

Kulu-Glasgow, Noyon and Smit analyse the agency of 45 unaccompanied minors from the top three nationalities (Syrian, Eritrean and Afghan) of the 2015 cohort of unaccompanied minors in the Netherlands, regarding the migration decision and choice of the destination. They argue that factors at macro, meso and micro level determine the context of the migration process and the degree of agency. Their results show that the degree of agency not only differs per nationality but also in different phases of the migration process. The authors observe a continuum in the agency of unaccompanied minors about the migration decision. Concerning Afghan unaccompanied minors, the decision to migrate is mostly made by parents and/or elderly relatives, in the case of Syrian minors, this is a joint decision of the minors and their parents, while Eritrean minors decide on the departure independently, even without informing their parents.

With regard to the decision making regarding destination, the continuum is fuzzier: it is not always clear where the agency lies, and it shifts during the process. At departure, the Netherlands was the destination for most of the Syrian unaccompanied minors, for none of the Afghan minors and some of the Eritrean ones. The results show that not only deliberate choice but also coincidences determine where the minors end up.

Lidén and Salvesen concentrate on one of the risks unaccompanied minors run during their journey to and within Europe, the risk to be trafficked and exploited. Based on a national survey including the police and child welfare services on their involvement in migrant child victims and a review of 17 child victim cases in Norway, they present three scenarios which represent various ways in which unaccompanied minors are recruited into exploitative situations. The authors state that the current policy and political interest in immigration control and security in Norway as well as in other European countries prevent making the best interest of the child the decisive principle when assessing asylum cases. They recommend gaining more insight into the conditions for recruitment and exploitation, the combat intercontinental human trafficking on a national, regional and international level, and to include an overall assessment of the child's best interest while deciding unaccompanied minors' asylum requests.

The best interest of the child (BIC), not a self-evident concept in migration law, is the core topic in the chapter by Van Os and Zijlstra, who describe how the assessment of the best interest of unaccompanied minors

4

could be performed and used in the decision-making process on children's asylum applications. They provide an insight into the theoretical framework, content and procedure of the BIC assessment for recently arrived refugee children, illustrated by a case study on a recently arrived unaccompanied Eritrean girl. The BIC assessment, which comprises 14 conditions for a child's development (seven related to the family context and seven to the societal context), and the adaptation for recently arrived children, are developed by professional assessors from the Study Center for Children, Migration and Law at Groningen University in the Netherlands. The authors round their contribution off with an invitation to other countries to include the implementation of the best interest of the child principle in their migration procedures, and to join forces to study the feasibility of a universal method.

The chapter by Larrison and Edlins concerns the initial experiences of unaccompanied minors who arrived in the United States of America between 2015 and 2017. They conducted an inductive content analysis on data collected by group discussions with 24 unaccompanied minors mainly from Central America who had been resettled with family members. Their experiences varied dramatically depending upon where they were in the process, and who was responsible for their treatment. Three themes that emerged from the data appear to act as significant contributors to the unaccompanied minors' experiences: housing conditions, treatment and public servants that interacted with them. The minors seem to generally view their time in their first days in the US, while under the custody of the Department of Homeland Security (DHS), detained in locations to which they refer as, e.g. 'the icebox' or 'the dog pound', negatively. They experience their time under the custody of the Department of Health and Human Services (HHS), which has a mission to consider the best interest of the child, more positively. Conditions and individuals that do not take into account the well-being of unaccompanied minors lead to more negative experiences while conditions and individuals that do lead to more positive experiences. The authors emphasise the opportunity and need to increase policies and efforts aimed at the best interest of the child.

The following chapters focus on the integration of unaccompanied minors. Çelikaksoy and Wadensjö investigate the educational careers of unaccompanied minors and separated children in Sweden, by analysing their dropout behaviour from the educational system. Education is not only an important indicator of later economic success but also a protective factor for refugee youth that offers stability and purpose. Different from the other authors, they dispose of a large national data set - register data from Statistics Sweden - which enables them to compare the unaccompanied minors' educational situation with that of accompanied minors as well as native-born youth. Their results show that the dropout rate is influenced by gender and age at arrival: girls are less likely to drop-out compared to boys and the older the minors are at arrival, the more likely they are to drop out. Unaccompanied minors have a higher probability of dropout not only compared to the native youth but also compared to accompanied minors. In light of these findings, similar to Kamp & Kushminder, the authors draw attention to the importance of family reunification and raise their concern about the recent restrictions in family reunification policies. They advocate the investigation and understanding the specific circumstances of unaccompanied minors in order to be able to help them to stay in the educational system.

The arrival of unaccompanied minors from Eritrea has confronted professionals in the Netherlands with new challenges. Based on three studies that were recently conducted in response to these challenges, De Haan, Jacob, Mooren and Ghebreab focus on Eritrean unaccompanied minors in the Netherlands. The three studies included amongst others focus group discussions with Eritrean key persons who are professionally involved in the reception, supervision and care for Eritrean refugees, interviews with reunited Eritrean families, focus groups with Eritrean adolescents and interviews with legal guardians. These studies show that the wellbeing of Eritrean unaccompanied minors can fluctuate and largely depends on factors such as the presence and wellbeing of their family, the quality of service of professionals in the Netherlands and the social environment they live in. Misunderstanding of cultural norms is the cause of much miscommunication. The authors stress the importance of culture-sensitive methods for the integration of Eritrean youth. Active involvement of and closely working together with 'cultural mediators' or other key persons who are familiar with the background of these minors can bridge cultural gaps.

The final chapter in the book, by Lo Bianco and Chondru, concerns the introduction of a holistic local inclusion oriented model for supporting unaccompanied minors in becoming autonomous. The model is developed by a group of non-governmental organisations and associations in the city of Palermo, Italy. The aim of the so-called Ragazzi Harraga project, which started in 2017, is to strengthen, test and evaluate innovative pathways to sustain the transition of unaccompanied minors to adulthood by offering a series of educational experiences (training opportunities, work placement and independent housing solutions). The authors describe the different pillars of the – ongoing – project, reflect on the results on a set of key performance indicators, and give suggestions for wider implementation of the model. Thereby they stress the importance of co-creating projects *with*, not for unaccompanied minors. In the Ragazzi Harraga project, this was done by involving a validation group of eight unaccompanied minors who gave feedback at different stages of the project.

We would like to draw the attention of our readers to the fact that the authors preferred to use their own terminologies and abbreviations in their chapters while referring to the unaccompanied minors and separated children (unaccompanied minors, unaccompanied minor asylum seekers, refugee children, unaccompanied refugee minors or unaccompanied foreign minors).

As mentioned above, these contributions focus on one or more phases of the migration and integration processes of unaccompanied minors. Although the angles of incidence within the chapters differ, various threads running through them can be identified.

Firstly, the vulnerability of unaccompanied minors, which is mentioned in the literature, also appears in the different chapters, whether they cover the journey from the origin country to the destination country, the early phases of arrival, or the integration process. The migration policies and especially the policies with regard to unaccompanied minors in the different countries do not seem to reckon with these vulnerabilities and are criticised in almost every contribution. Especially the limited role of the best interests of the child, as described in the United Nations Convention of the Rights of the Child (article 3, section 1) (UN, 1989), is under discussion. Several contributions refer to the importance, and/or the limited possibilities of family reunification.

A final thread is related to the scale of the studies. Many of the studies in the literature on unaccompanied minors and separated children are based on research with a limited number of respondents and are of qualitative nature. However informative and valuable they are; this is also the case for most of the contributions in this book. The contribution of Çelikaksoy and Wadensjö is an exception; they have access to a large Swedish population register data set in which unaccompanied minors can be identified, a rare luxury for researchers.

That research on unaccompanied minors is overwhelmingly small scale is not surprising, regarding the fact that we are studying a particularly 'difficult to reach' and vulnerable group. Moreover, as mentioned above, a good registration of unaccompanied minors and separated children is lacking in many countries, including European ones. Due to the underdeveloped and fragmentary evidence-based information, UNICEF, UNHCR, IOM, Eurostat and the Organisation for Economic Co-operation and Development (OECD) have launched a call for action to encourage member states to prioritize their actions to address the evidence gaps and include child-specific considerations within the context of the efforts for Global Compact for Safe, Orderly and Regular Migration and the Global Compact on Refugees (UNICEF, 2018).

We endorse this call as a better registration of unaccompanied minors and separated children will not only allow for better protection of children and assessment of their needs, but also lead to more larger-scaled research with more generalizability and international comparability.

References

Eurostat (2017). *Newsrelease.* 80/2017 - 11 May 2017.

Eurostat (2018). *Newsrelease.* 84/2018 - 16 May 2018.

Hopkins, P.E. and Hill, M. (2008). "Pre-flight experiences and migration stories: The accounts of unaccompanied asylum-seeking children". *Children's Geographies,* 6(3): 257-268.)

Keles, S., Friborg, O., Idsøe, T., Sirin, S. & Oppedal, B. (2018). "Resilience and acculturation among unaccompanied refugee minors". *International Journal of Behavioural Development,* 42(1): 52-63.

IOM/UNICEF (2015). *Migration of Children to Europe.* Data brief, 30 November 2015. Geneva/Berlin.

Sirkeci, I. (2009). Transnational mobility and conflict. *Migration Letters,* 6(1), 3-14.

Sirkeci, I., K. O. Unutulmaz, and D. E. Utku (2017). "Syrian Communities in Turkey: Conflict Induced Diaspora". In: I. Sirkeci, K. Onur Unutulmaz, and Deniz E. Utku, eds., *Turkey's Syrians. Today and Tomorrow,* London, Transnational Press London, pp. 1-22.

Thommessen, S.A., Corcoran, P. & Todd, B. (2015). "Experiences of Arriving to Sweden as an Unaccompanied Asylum-seeking Minor from Afghanistan: An Interpretative Phenomenological Analysis". *Psychology of Violence,* 5(4): 374-383. doi: 10.1037/a0038842

UN General Assembly (1989). Convention on the Rights of the Child. 20 November 1989, United Nations, Treaty Series, vol. 1577: 3- 178.

UNHCR (2018). *Global Trends. Forced Displacement 2017.* Geneva, UNHCR.

UNICEF (2017). *A child is a child. Protecting children on the move from violence, abuse and exploitation.* New York, UNICEF.

UNICEF (2018). *A call to action. Protecting children on the move starts with better data.* February 2018.

CHAPTER 1

SYRIAN UNACCOMPANIED MINORS JOURNEYS TO GERMANY AND INITIAL EXPERIENCES UPON ARRIVAL

Raphael Kamp and Katie Kuschminder

Introduction

A differentiating element of the so-called European migration crisis in 2015 has been a significant increase in the number of children migrating to Europe, many of whom are unaccompanied. Approximately 89,000 unaccompanied minors (UAMs) applied for asylum in the European Union (EU) in 2015, which is the highest recorded number since the beginning of data collection on UAMs in 2006 (UNHCR, 2016: 3). In 2016, Germany received the highest number of asylum claims by UAMs with 35,900 out of 63,300 in the EU. The other two most important destination countries were Italy (6,000 applications) and Austria (3,900 applications) (Eurostat, 2017: 2). Most UAMs in the EU came from Afghanistan (38%), Syria (19%) and Iraq (7%) (Eurostat, 2017: 3).

UAMs form a distinct category of migrants that require special attention within the literature due to their vulnerabilities of being children migrating through adverse journeys on their own. Research has demonstrated that UAMs are more exposed to threats of human trafficking and sexual abuse (Hopkins & Hill, 2008: 264). It has also been shown that UAMs report poorer mental health outcomes than accompanied children due to 'the interplay between traumatic experiences, lack of parental and social support, and multiple losses' (Derluyn et al., 2009). Frequently UAMs travel alone, only making temporary networks in transit that are considered short term and transient (Nardone and Correa-Velez, 2015). Due to the irregularity of their journey, they seek invisibility en route (Nardone and Correa-Velez, 2015). This suggests that UAMs may have less information and access to resources in their migration journeys than older migrants. Finally, UAMs may also bear the burden of having to secure refugee status in a desired European country to achieve family reunification for the rest of the family left behind.

These children are thus not only subject to arduous journeys, but also to the additional stress of being the primary hope for their families' future and survival.

Little research has been conducted on Syrian UAMs and how their decision-making processes influence their integration outcomes. This chapter examines the migration journeys of Syrian UAMs in their journeys to Germany and their initial experiences in Germany upon arrival. The chapter addresses the following research questions:

1. How do Syrian unaccompanied minors make the decision to come to Europe?

2. How do they experience the journey? And how do they make decisions en route?

3. How do these decisions influence their initial short-term integration in Germany?

To answer these questions, qualitative interviews were conducted with seventeen Syrian UAMs in Germany in the spring of 2016. At that time, Germany had officially adopted an open-door policy towards migrants, in particular, Syrian refugees. This policy has since been challenged by rising anti-refugee sentiments in Germany. Germany is an integral case study as it is the main target destination of Syrian asylum seekers globally and it is also a country of divided views on migration and integration facing significant challenges. Public opinion and policy on migration and refugees have shifted significantly from an open-minded to an isolationist approach.

The significant rise in UAMs' arrivals in Europe in 2015 has led to several concerns regarding their wellbeing both in their migration journeys and upon arrival. By having clearer understandings of the experiences of UAMs' journeys, policies can be developed to prevent separations of families and to assist UAMs in transit, at reception and in the integration process. This chapter contributes to this research area by providing insights into Syrian UAMs' migration journeys, decision-making factors and integration experiences. The chapter highlights the role and degree of autonomy that Syrian UAMs have in their migration journeys and making their destination choices. Understanding their agency and motives prior to and during their journeys helps address their needs to achieve successful integration in the host society.

This chapter is organised into the following four sections. The next section provides an overview of the literature on UAMs' journeys and decision-making. This is followed by an explanation of the study methodology and then the results section. The results section first examines respondents' agency in the migration decision. Second, their experiences of the migration journey are presented. Third, their access to information and destination choices, and finally their experiences upon arrival and integration in Germany are examined. The final section of the chapter offers a discussion and conclusion.

Irregular Migration Journeys of Unaccompanied Minors and Decision-Making Processes

Increasing research has demonstrated the significance in understanding how clandestine migrants' and refugees' journeys impact them in the long-term. Mainwaring and Brigden (2016) highlight how journeys are not clear, they often have an ambiguous start and end and are characterised by "violent and unprecedented ruptures in the lives of migrants" (p. 246). Kaytaz (2016) argues that the journeys themselves can be transformational for migrants with specific experiences encountered in the journey changing their life course. For example, a failed onwards migration attempt may result in the decision to stay in a previously intended transit migration country. For UAMs these journeys are often even more stressful as minors have left behind their nuclear family and are in a new situation of the unknown and insecurity (Nardone and Correa-Velez, 2015). Therefore, it is important to better understand UAMs journeys and how these journeys may impact their integration outcomes.

UAMs face several dangers during their journeys, including exploitation or sexual abuse. Traumas of war or separation from the nuclear family are further psychological burdens (Keles et al., 2018). Keles et al. (2016) also find that daily hassles due to the migrant status experienced upon arrival are a risk factor for depression. UAM wellbeing is thus influenced by pre-migration traumas, experience and trauma during the journey, and their situation and integration opportunities upon arrival.

Two key elements of the clandestine migration journey are first, making the decision to go and second, deciding on the destination. Research on UAMs has demonstrated that the decision to migrate for UAMs is often made for them by parents or other family members, and in other cases is made entirely by the migrant (Hopkins and Hill, 2010; Nardone and Correa-Velez, 2015). These variations can depend on the migration culture within the sending area. For example, in high-sending areas in Afghanistan, it is most often a family decision as the family members' knowledge of the journey's dangers tends to be higher. They are also able to arrange the migration (Echavez et al., 2014). Buil and Siegel (2014) also show that UAMs from Afghanistan are hardly involved in the decision-making processes. This differs from situations in low-sending areas in Afghanistan wherein the minors themselves tend to make the decision to migrate on their own (Echavez et al., 2014).

It has also been found that during the migration journey knowledge is very mixed amongst UAM (Hopkins and Hill, 2010; Nardone and Correa-

Velez, 2015; Echavez et al., 2014: 17, 18). Parents and smugglers tend to underplay the dangers of the migration journeys meaning that the minors are ill informed of the realities they will face. In some cases, family members also influence the decision making during the journey itself by giving minors instructions. This is common if those members finance the journey. By making decisions, they decrease minors' autonomy and ability to react quickly to difficulties met on the journey (Mougne, 2010: 16).

Destination choices may be made by the parents or minors before the beginning of the journey, determined by smugglers, or decided within the course of the journey. Previous research is inconclusive for determining the reasons why minors choose to come to Germany specifically. Müller (2014) assumes that they come for similar reasons to Germany as the rest of the refugee population. These reasons include personal safety, Germany's economic situation, a generous medical system, chances of receiving a resident status or just luck. Family and the diaspora generally attract migrants as well. This is highly possible, as Germany has become an attractive destination, in particular for Syrian refugees. At the same time, the unique position of UAMs suggests that they may have different motivations and drivers for choosing Germany.

Methodology

This chapter is based on 17 semi-structured interviews conducted with Syrian UAMs between April and July 2016. This chapter uses the German legal definition of a UAM. As such, a minor is defined by the Directive 2011/95/EU of the European Parliament and the Council of 13 December 2011 as:

> "a minor who arrives on the territory of the Member States unaccompanied by an adult responsible for him or her whether by law or by the practice of the Member State concerned, and for as long as he or she is not effectively taken into the care of such a person; it includes a minor who is left unaccompanied after he or she has entered the territory of the Member States" (chapter 1, article 2 (l)).

The interview guide used a lifecycle approach and focused on the minors' situation in Syria both prior to the war and upon leaving, why they left Syria, their migration routes and reasons why they migrated to Germany. Minors had to fulfil the following criteria to be eligible for the study: (i) they lived in Syria prior to the beginning of the conflict and they emigrated after the outbreak of the civil war in March 2011; (ii) respondents were male as the majority of UAMs in Germany are male (Espenhorst & Kemper, 2015: 131); and (iii) respondents had to have been registered as a UAM in Germany at the age of 17 or younger. This means that some respondents were older than 17 at the time of interview.

The interviews were conducted within the field site of Städteregion Aachen, which is a mid-sized city in Germany situated near both the borders of Belgium and the Netherlands. Since autumn 2015, UAMs have been re-distributed within Germany after their arrival. Before this time, the city where they were registered was responsible for sheltering them as well. As the border police monitor illegal entries and register UAMs if caught, border regions had higher numbers of UAMs with a longer duration of stay at the time of the interviews. This applies especially to Städteregion Aachen due to its size (550,000 inhabitants), as well as being an established transit area with two motorways to Maastricht and Eindhoven in the Netherlands and Liege in Belgium, and train connections from nearby Cologne to Amsterdam, Brussels and Paris.

Further, it is mostly an urban region and the attitude towards refugees was comparable to big centres such as Munich and Western Germany in general. The attitude in Eastern Germany can be described as more reserved, as anti-refugee parties gain comparatively higher political support. The field site is special for its long-term integration approach. The city of Eschweiler, which is part of Städteregion Aachen, won the National German Sustainability Award in 2018 for the integration of UAMs. Therefore, integration outcomes can be expected to be more positive as compared to the national average.

Access to the minors for the interviews was achieved through a staged process. First, the researcher met with the responsible managers from the childcare facilities (wherein the majority of UAMs reside in Germany) to explain the study and gain their permission to interview the UAMs. Permissions to interview the UAMs were also received from the minors' legal guardians and, if deemed necessary, from the childcare facility caseworkers at the municipality's office for youth welfare. Pseudonyms are used throughout this chapter to ensure the respondents' anonymity.

To create a relationship of trust with the UAMs, the researcher met the minors prior to the interviews and engaged with them in leisure activities. The interviews were conducted in the language preferred by the minors. If requested, the participants were allowed to bring a person of trust to the interview. The interviews lasted between 30 and 90 minutes. All interviews were recorded except for one because the minor did not want to be recorded. In that case, the researcher took notes during the interview. Informed consent was obtained before all interviews. In six cases, a follow-up post-discussion interview was held. These post-discussions allowed the researcher to verify the information and ask some follow-up questions. Due to the staged interview approach to establish trust it was not deemed necessary to conduct a second interview in all cases. If the respondents' language levels were sufficient for the interviews, the researcher interviewed them directly. If the language skills were not sufficient, a translator for Arabic or Kurdish

(Kurmanji) was used.

The respondents came from a variety of backgrounds in Syria. Seven respondents were Kurdish and came from the urban and rural areas of Aleppo and Al-Hasakah in northern Syria. Seven respondents were Arabic and came from Idlib (north-east Syria) and rural and urban Damascus. Three respondents were ethnic Palestinians and lived in rural Damascus and Jarmak, a district in Damascus with a considerable Palestinian population. Except for one respondent who lost his father, none of the respondents was orphans. Most respondents came from Syria's (upper) middle class. Thirteen respondents said their family had a medium income or described their situation as normal. Four said their family had an above average income before the civil war. The number of completed school years varied among the respondents between six to twelve years. On average, the participants have attended school for nine years and two months. The respondents were between 14 and 18 years old at the time of the interview. However, the majority were 17 or 18 years old. At the time of the interviews, 15 respondents were living in children's homes, one was living alone, and one was living together with a relative. The respondents arrived in Germany between September 2014 and January 2016. The average length of residence in Germany was 12.5 months.

Starting the Journey: Unaccompanied Minors' Agency in Making the Decision to Migrate to Europe

Most respondents in this study came from middle-class backgrounds. It is likely that minors from poorer backgrounds cannot afford the journey and that wealthier families tend to migrate together. Reasons for migration differ; however, the most important ones are forced military recruitment (10), lacking education in Syria (8), direct war experiences (7), poverty (5), no possibility to work (3), child abductions (2) and lacking freedoms (2).

The respondents had a certain degree of autonomy in their decision-making to migrate. The decision to leave Syria was generally made together by the minors and their parents. The majority of respondents left Syria directly to start their migration journeys (13) and four respondents left from a transit country, namely Turkey (3) and Lebanon (1). The participants departing directly from Syria did so between 2012 and 2015. In most cases, respondents made the decision to migrate with both of their parents and in two cases only with their fathers.

In some cases, other relatives also took part in the decision, such as uncles, cousins and grandparents. Other relatives became involved in the decision-making process for three primary reasons. First, they can act as advisors or facilitate the journey by accompanying the minors. Second, they replaced the father in the decision-making in his absence. Third, grandparents can have the intra-family power to make decisions on behalf of

14

the parents, because they are seen as the heads of the family. Without the consent of their relatives, the journey would have been impossible for most minors, because the family at least co-financed the journey in all cases. Only one respondent migrated to Europe without the parents' consent.

Most respondents had the desire to migrate themselves, and several respondents stated that they were the ones who proposed the journey. Two respondents had mixed feelings about the journey, as they were concerned about being separated from their families. Only in one case the respondent did not want to leave and was forced to by his mother and uncle. He was sent to Germany to bring his family via family re-unification because of the family's worsening financial situation. This form of forced migration may be connected to the respondent's age because he was the youngest respondent (14 years old).

Minors who have been living and working in the first country of refuge have a significantly higher degree of autonomy. Both, Turkey and Lebanon, were intended as countries of refuge for the family, but low living conditions in these countries created the impetus for onwards migration. The respondents worked and earned money and were able to finance their journeys, at least partly, on their own. This enabled them to migrate further without the need to ask for their parents' consent. The average stay of those minors in the first country of refuge was three years and one month.

Respondents made most of the decisions about the route and transit migration on their own, but a range of other actors influenced their routes as well. Respondents' journeys tended to be highly fragmented, as discussed in the background section of this chapter. Therefore, different actors influenced different phases of their journeys. Seven respondents went through the whole journey or at least some parts of it alone. Other family members, friends or smugglers joined them on their way. Smugglers were not reported to play a role in the decision-making; although 16 respondents used a smuggler at some point of the journey, they only facilitated the respondents' wishes.

Unaccompanied Minors' Experiences in their Migration Journeys

Broadly speaking, the respondents' journeys can be characterised in three stages; 1) leaving Syria and entering a first non-EU country, 2) crossing into the EU and 3) moving from the EU border country to Germany. The first phase of the journey, leaving Syria, was mainly organised by or with the respondents' families (10). Seven respondents were accompanied by family members who were not their parents throughout the whole journey. Three respondents said the way was obvious to them (no organisation needed) and four decided on the way on their own. One respondent's journey was planned by his family without his involvement. However, only those crossing the border to Turkey irregularly did it without their family's support. The participants' ethnicity does not seem to influence the decision-making on this first leg.

The second phase, from the first transit country to the first EU country, is rarely organised by the family. Instead, most respondents organised it on their own; people met on the journey showed the way or the respondents hired smugglers to arrange their travel. Four respondents said this part of the journey was known/obvious and another four decided on the journey themselves.

Table 1: Migration Routes and Their Users, Prices and Duration				
Route Taken	Ethnicity of Users	Average Price	Price Range	Average Duration[1]
Eastern Mediterranean Route and Balkan Route	Arabs, Kurds and Palestinians	1,400€	0 – 4,000€	Approx. 1.5 months
Balkan Route via Bulgaria	Arabs, Kurds and Palestinians, mainly before the opening of the Balkan Route	5,750€	2,000 – 9,500€	5.5 months
Transit Lebanon	Arabs	n.a.[2]	n.a.	> 48 hours
Transit Syria	Palestinians	800€[2]	n.a.	Between 10 days and 1 month
Central Mediterranean Route via Sudan and Libya	Palestinians	5,050€	3,900 – 6,200€	27 days

Within this second phase, the minors' ethnicity is important for their routes, the journey's duration and prices paid (see table 1) illustrating that Syrian UAMs cannot be identified as a homogeneous group. The main reasons for the differences are the minors' location in Syria as well as their legal status. Kurds enter Turkey via land and mainly irregularly because Syria's Kurdish areas lie in the border region and many do not possess valid travel documents. From Turkey onwards, they either take the Balkan Route via Bulgaria or the Eastern Mediterranean Route to Greece from where they continue on the Balkan Route. Most Palestinians in Syria do not live in this

---

[1] Excluding stays in transit to earn money

[2] This part of the journey was regular. Only flight tickets needed to be paid

[2] Some participants have been robbed by smugglers. The stolen property is not included in the price.

border region. The Palestinian participants either travelled by land to the Turkish border from where their journeys were similar to the ones taken by Kurds. The journey inside Syria is especially dangerous, because of shifting battlefronts which make smugglers indispensable. Alternatively, they made use of the Central Mediterranean Route. Two participants flew to Khartoum, Sudan, and passed through the Sahara. From Libya, they crossed the Mediterranean Sea to Italy. At the time of the interviews, Syrians had no visa restrictions to enter Turkey. Syrian Arabs mainly possess valid travel documents. Therefore, they were able to travel to Lebanon and then to fly from Beirut to Turkey. From Turkey onwards they took the same routes as Kurds. However, Turkey introduced visa restrictions in 2016. Consequently, it is likely that Arabs have had to take the same routes as Palestinians since then.

Unaccompanied minors are subject to a wide range of dangers on their journeys. Border crossings are the journeys' most dangerous events. Many Palestinians in Syria have refugee status. Generally, they and their descendants do not have passports. Therefore, they can exit Syria only irregularly. Their journeys are the most dangerous, most expensive and longest ones. As many Arabic minors entered Turkey legally via Lebanon, their journeys tended to be safer. Migrants are exposed to maltreatment by the border police in case they are caught. One respondent experienced such violence crossing the border from Syria to Turkey. He recounted his experiences as:

> "(My uncle) got shot and wounded and we were beaten up. Then the [police] chief came. They took us to the police station. They have beaten us up with wood, really my right hand, it became so big […] I could not breathe that well anymore, and they also left us in the sun for 1 or 2 hours, no maybe 15 minutes or half an hour. It was very hot and about 45°C between Syria and Turkey."

Mohammed, Age: 17

The violence experienced during the journey is a psychological burden for the respondents. Although Mohammed is able to talk about his experiences, going through them puts him under immense pressure. Re-experiencing upsetting events makes it difficult for many UAMs to recall their journeys. Mohammed was a unique case as he had the resilience to cope with his experiences and was now able to speak openly about them. This was not the case for many of the respondents who instead downplayed their experiences or skipped them completely during the interviews. The researcher did not insist on the respondents to speak further about their experiences, particularly if it was evident that the respondent was becoming distressed. As a result, the general impression is that the respondents wanted to focus on their future in Germany instead of looking back and dealing with the traumatic events they have experienced. However, symptoms of post-traumatic stress disorder make this focus more difficult. As the level of danger is higher for Kurds and especially Palestinians in contrast to Arabic minors, it is possible that they suffer from more severe symptoms which makes their integration to German society more difficult.

To avoid being caught by the police, several respondents reported crossing borders at night, when the landscape becomes more difficult to pass. One respondent described his experiences of crossing the Serbian-Hungarian border at night as follows:

"We were 40 people in a row, and we went behind each other. Everybody took each other's hands. If you open your eyes, then you see red eyes everywhere. [...] They were scared, the animals. But you only see the red eyes. If you let go the hands, most probably, you are dead."

Ali, Age: 18

This quote reflects the fear felt while crossing the border and Ali's understanding of the risks involved - that holding on and staying in the line was a matter of life or death. The experiences of Ali and Mohammed in crossing borders at the beginning stages of the journey highlight the fear and uncertainty that the respondents experienced.

The level of knowledge about the journeys' dangers prior to migration seems to vary among respondents. Many are aware of the journey's dangers, but this does not determine their decision-making. It seems that positive incentives, such as being re-united with family members, overweigh risks. In one case, a minor living with his family in Turkey decided to visit his grandparents in Syria one last time before going to Europe. Although knowing the risks of the journey from Syria to Turkey, including potential recruitment of the Kurdish army, he still decided to go:

Respondent:

"It was hard, the way was really hard [...]. We took a work permit from the Kurdish army because there was a girlwho had health problems. Otherwise, we would not have passed, because they need soldiers."

Researcher:

"Did you know about these problems when you were in Turkey?"

Respondent:

"Yes, I did."

Hasan, Age: 17

Crossing the Mediterranean requires facing another life-threatening danger. UAMs are highly aware and knowledgeable of these risks:

"We stayed for about 5 hours in the inflatable boat. Then the Turkish coast guard came and took the fuel from our boat, and they prevented us from continuing, but we did not give up. The children were crying as well. To prevent to us from going to Greece, they took some people out of the boat, and they told us to give up, but we did not [...]. The children and the women were so afraid and started shouting and crying. Then we were paddling the boat in the water for 400 meters. Then a ship which belonged to the Greek coast guard rescued us from death."

Recep, Age: 17

Respondents were often aware that this stage was the most dangerous part of the journey. Mustafar said: "I called my father upon reaching Greece since it is the most dangerous step of the whole trip [...]. He felt relaxed after my call. I explained to him how dangerous the way is and I do not want them to go through this" (Mustafar, Age: 17). Several of the respondents are the first family members to experience the journey. As shown in this quote, UAMs feel further pressured to protect their families from the risks and traumas of this experience. This is most likely an additional contributing factor to the immense burden the respondents feel for receiving family re-unification for their families. Knowing and experiencing the challenges of living in Syria, the low quality of life in the countries of near refuge (i.e., Lebanon and Turkey) and the risks of the irregular migration journey, they feel the responsibility to achieve a safe transit to Germany for their families' protection.

The third phase of the journey can be characterised as from the first EU country of entry to Germany. This leg was often organised in the transit countries (7). In 2015, transit countries in the Balkans wanted refugees to pass through their territories as fast as possible. Therefore, national police or NGOs planned and organised transportation, sometimes without the migrants' knowledge about their exact location. However, this was only the case for the Balkan Route at the time it was open. Other decision-makers were people on the road (4), smugglers (2), family members (2), the respondent himself (1) and one said the destination was obvious to him. The next section examines further the experiences of the respondents in their migration journeys across these three phases of the journey.

Unaccompanied minors' access to information and destination choices

The intended destination is most often decided in Syria, generally by the UAM himself. However, some UAMs also mentioned that parents or grandparents decided on the country. In three cases, the parents decided the destination country against the UAM's wish. Those UAMs either wanted to go to the UK or did not want to move at all. Other respondents had been staying in Turkey or Lebanon for several years due to a lack of resources to continue their journey or because they moved there with their families. These UAMs picked Germany as a destination while in these countries.

The knowledge acquired about Germany before migration was generally very limited. The sources of information that UAMs have about Germany before their journeys are diverse. Respondents used three major sources to gather information about Germany. The most frequently mentioned source was family in Germany (13). Family in Germany included close or distant relatives that have been in Germany for varying amounts of time and can offer firsthand accounts of the situation in Germany. As many minors have not had close relations with their family, they often did not receive information directly from them. Instead, the information was channelled, usually via the parents. Some participants doubted this source because they did not know the relatives or did not have good relations with them.

> "They do not really give the correct information about how Germany is like. Where they are and where they go to school. [...] I did not want to go to them. Things like that. I just wanted to go to Germany to learn. They did not give me the correct pieces of information about it."
>
> *Ferhat, Age: 17*

The second most commonly used information source was friends in Germany. Respondents had different definitions of "friends", ranging from people from the village community over family friends to best friends and classmates. Many respondents (10) have had friends living in Germany before leaving Syria. The information provided by friends currently living in Germany was questioned by several respondents.

On the one hand, many friends were not as active as family members in their willingness to help. They did not respond regularly or did not offer support, both during the journey or on arrival in Germany. Some doubted their information because it was seen as too positive.

Further, it was often superficial information such as, that life or the education system is good. Family and friends were not a well-trusted source of information about Germany. However, they were decisive factors because of their promise of support once the minor has arrived in Germany. As Hasan (Age: 17) said: "I came here because I knew they would help, as they help a lot of people with a lot of things."

The third most commonly used information source was the internet (9), which was viewed as the most informative and direct source. For example,

Yavuz (Age: 18) stated how he used the internet to decide to come to Germany:

> "[I received information] from no one. I used to see and read on the internet about Germany. I read on how I can study and how I can work, and what kind of life I will have there. Yeah, they wrote that you could work, for example, you have to know the language so that you can work, and you can't work without it. And it was clear about everything but in details."

Information found on the internet was perceived as highly factual because it was the only direct source of information. Information provided by family or friends was perceived as subjective. Although the internet was also used as a tool to collect information about the country of destination, many respondents used it to inform themselves about the journey and the possibility to enter Germany as well. Consequently, UAMs have a high level of trust in the internet as a source of information.

Many respondents also used social media, mainly Facebook, but also Instagram and others, as a source of information (9). Yavuz (18) described how he used Facebook to gather information about Germany and the route:

> "I started with Facebook. Syrians started to make Facebook pages announcing that there is a good and honest trafficker who does not lie to people. I searched and found it. I found a page called "Syrians in Germany". I started to think whether there is a page called "Syrians want to go to Germany". I posted on the page that I want to go to Germany. And I also posted "whoever can help me, chat with me privately". Seven people entered the private chat. We started to talk about how to reach Germany. Then they sent me phone numbers of the traffickers. They started to talk about one of the traffickers - that he is honest and doesn't cheat."

Yavuz's experience illustrates the new ways in which social media can provide platforms to connect refugees with information. Although he did not know any of the people in the private chat, their advice and network support were vital in his decision-making and journey to Germany.

The reasons UAMs decide to come to Germany are multiple. Family relations are the most important reason for them to come to Germany (7). Receiving support from family in Germany, but especially actually having a family network itself in the destination country was the major criterion. Frequently, respondents are not actually able to join or get in touch with family members upon arrival in Germany. However this connection is still a central reason for them choosing Germany. Other reasons are employment

(5) and education opportunities. Respondents had a strong perception that both employment and education opportunities were good in Germany.

Furthermore, the generally good treatment of refugees and foreigners (3) and governmental assistance for their education or starting a business (2) were mentioned. Finally, two respondents came because of the high level of protection and safety in Germany, and two ones also mentioned personal freedoms. One respondent decided Germany because of the modern lifestyle and another one was stuck in Germany, because he could not finance his remaining journey to the UK. Two UAMs chose Germany to achieve family re-unification.

Experiences in Germany: Identities and Uncertainties

Unaccompanied minors are dissatisfied by their refugee status in Germany. Many felt inequalities between Germans and refugees in the education sector and in their everyday life. The respondents also appeared to be highly aware of the political developments and conflict in Germany. One respondent stated that he was scared about the conflict in Germany between political parties stating: "The Germans – there are some parties which do not want refugees. We were a bit scared because of that…" (Mohammed, Age: 17). This quote demonstrates the impact of these right-wing, anti-migrant sentiments on the respondents. Considering the challenges and arduous journeys they faced the feeling of being unwanted and unwelcome adds another layer for them to overcome in Germany. This was also reflected by Ferhat (Age:17):

> "Foreigners… I hate that word […]. They (Germans) look at foreigners and think that foreigners are not good. [I wish] that foreigners and Germans become more similar and that Germans do not think like that about us. For example, if one of us is a terrorist in Syria, this does not mean that all the others are terrorists as well".

In addition to feeling unwanted, Ferhat's statement reflects the further awareness of the respondents as being labelled terrorists only because they are Syrian. Respondents reported feeling resentment from locals and reflected heavily on these concerns in the interviews. It was clear that the political situation created an added stress for them in their daily lives. This unwelcoming dynamic also leads to a notion of rootlessness in their new environment in Germany. Having lost their homes in Syria and being separated from their families, the respondents expressed the common need amongst migrants and refugees to have a place to belong: "I actually do not want to be a refugee. So, I did not want that. I actually hate it – being a refugee. I also do not want to be German. I want to have a home[3] that Germans have" (Mohammed, Age: 17).

Many minors are dissatisfied because they came with unrealistic expectations to Germany that could not be met. Especially those who want to bring their family members via family re-unification were disappointed by the system and felt frustrated or guilty for not being able to bring their family (5). Kadir (Age: 14) said:

"I want my family to come here. They also do not have that much money. Coming here is very difficult, and my siblings are very small. It is difficult [...]. Some friends of mine are also in Germany, and they brought their family here. I did not [...]. But before, it was possible. I do not understand why this is not possible for me. I am very sad without my family."

However, the separation from the family also creates integration problems. First, the minor is pressured to send remittances to the family, as the family usually provided the financial means for the journey. Some respondents were even accused of enjoying the Western lifestyle by their relatives and not supporting them while the rest of the family is still living in transit states or Syria. This contributes to the second challenge of the separation threatening the psychological well-being of minors because they live alone without familial support.

Family reunification is therefore of high importance to the wellbeing of UAMs. Family re-unification is only granted under strict conditions, which makes it de-facto impossible for the vast majority:

"My family, they are right now in... they are in Greece. Normally, I would be allowed to bring my family to Germany. And I want to bring them. I have been waiting for one year, and I also applied for family re-unification to Germany. But that did not work out. That was unfair. Unfair. They were in Lebanon when I was 18. I applied when I was 17, and they were somewhere else. And my result... My family went 4 or 5 times to Lebanon. That was also very expensive. At that time, you could go from Greece to Germany. They could come illegally. That was the same way. They said they would be coming by plane legally. Legally to Germany. But that did not work out."

Ali, Age: 18

---

[3] The respondent does not mean it in the sense of a house or shelter. He means a place of belonging.

The inability to bring their family to Germany creates an immense strain on the minors, as illustrated in the above quote by Ali.

All respondents wanted to have a "normal" life in Germany. This means they generally want to start a family, have a job and want to live in security. While some have concrete plans of what they want to achieve, others feel lost without guidance: "Right now, all I'm thinking about is to study the language, then to finish my high school, then to enrol into college" (Abdelhadi, Age 18). However, some also felt lost in German society and did not have plans for the future: "How would I know; we might die tomorrow, nobody knows the future." (Hasan, Age 17). Those who have already worked sometimes do not see benefits in going to school and want to start working immediately. They want to support their family members who are not in Germany or want to live independently (2). All participants except for one do not want to go back to Syria, even if the situation has improved. They either do not expect a peace process in the near future or do not see benefits for themselves in moving back. Some minors see Germany as their new home. Those minors identify themselves as part of German society and do not have strong links to Syria anymore.

Conclusion: Unaccompanied Syrian minor's journeys to Germany and initial experiences upon arrival

This chapter has explored Syrian UAMs' decision-making processes, their knowledge of information about Germany before and during their journeys and their integration challenges in the short time since their arrival. The findings demonstrate that although based on a small sample, UAMs form a heterogeneous group with different degrees of autonomy in their decision-making processes, which is similar to the finding of Kulu et al. in this volume.

The journeys differ among Syrian UAMs in terms of their duration, danger and price. Especially ethnic Palestinians' journeys tend to be more difficult. As various studies (e.g. Nardone and Correa-Velez (2015), Huemer et al. (2009), Keles et al. (2018), Keles et al. (2016)) have shown, UAMs are more vulnerable towards psychological problems resulting from their journeys and separation from their family than other refugees. Further research should evaluate if the ethnicities' differences result in different health and integration outcomes.

Syrian UAMs take part in the decision-making processes. They are often the ones to suggest migration to their family. The decision to migrate is most often taken together with the parents or other relatives, who have a veto-right. The familial decision-making strategy reflects a difference to Afghan UAMs who have limited influence on the decision (Hopkins and Hill, 2010; Nardone and Correa-Velez, 2015). The destination country is often chosen in Syria. Unaccompanied minors tend to have weak knowledge about destinations and relatives dominate destination choices. Migration choice processes are different for those UAMs who have been living in first countries of refuge and have been earning money. They can afford the journey on their own and are seen as more independent by their family. Therefore, they are more autonomous in their decision-making and can even migrate without their parents' consent.

In contrast to findings on Afghan UAMs journeys by Echavez (2014) wherein respondents were poorly informed about the dangers of the journeys, the respondents in this study stated that they were often well informed of the risks. Despite the risks, the respondents felt that the journeys were necessary, and they persevered. All respondents reflected on difficulties in the journey and for most these were difficult to discuss. This corroborates findings from Nardone and Correa-Velez (2015) regarding the difficulties and stress of the journey for minors. It is well known that journeys are highly dangerous and stressful for minors, which has prompted further debate at the international level by UN agencies on how to protect minors within their migration journeys.

Most minors had been seeking information on Germany in preparation of their arrival. Most respondents had family members or a friend already in Germany who provided information about the country. Social networks are a decisive factor in the decision for Germany as a destination country. Very often these were familial networks, such as uncles. The promise of support after arrival is an additional factor for the destination choice. However, that support after arrival seems to be limited because, with the exception of one minor, all participants lived in children's homes. From the minors' perspective, the internet and social media were viewed as a more reliable source of information because it was independent and not channelled via other family members. The importance of social networks has been stressed in the literature on destination choices and was a key factor in this case.

Yet, arrival and the initial integration also proved challenging. Although minors selected Germany due to networks, they were not living with their family connections at the time of interview. Furthermore, at the time of this fieldwork in 2016 debates were prevalent in German media regarding anti-migration sentiments towards Syrian refugees. These sentiments impacted the respondents by making them feel unwelcome. This is especially remarkable because of the so-called "Willkommenskultur" (culture of welcoming refugees), which spread over Germany at the beginning of the refugee situation in 2015. The most famous example was the cheering of Germans at Munich central station upon arrival of refugees from Hungary.

This chapter contributes to an emerging body of literature on understanding the migration journeys, experiences and decision-making of migrants in their travels to Europe. In this chapter, we focus specifically on Syrian UAMs that travelled to Germany during the height of the migration flows in 2015. The results illustrate that Syrian UAMs have varying degrees of autonomy from their family members in their decision-making, difficult journey experiences, and at the time of interview in 2016 continued to face uncertainty and challenges in their integration. The results provide further evidence for the need for assistance to minors during their journeys, support upon arrival, and the need to prioritise family re-unification for UAMs. Although it has not always been a reason to migrate, family re-unification is an important element for UAMs' integration to German society. The core family can support the minor with their social networks in Germany and reunification can relieve the minor of the burden of being obliged to support their family. It is therefore recommended that family re-unification should be prioritised for UAMs arriving in Germany.

References

Buil, C. & Siegel, M. (2014). "Destination Europe: Afghan Unaccompanied Minors Crossing Borders". In: S. Spyrou, & M. Christou (eds.) Children and Borders: Studies in Childhood and Youth. (pp. 99 -113). London: Palgrave Macmillan.

Derluyn, I., Mels, C. and Broekaert, E. (2009). "Mental Health Problems in Separated Refugee Adolescents". Journal of Adolescent Health 44(3): 291–297.

Echavez, C. R., Bagaporo, J. L. L., Pilongo, L. W. R. & Azadmanech, S. (2014). "Why do children undertake the unaccompanied journey? Motivations for departure to Europe and other industrialised countries from the perspective of children, families and residents of sending communities in Afghanistan". Retrieved March 31, 2016, from http://www.unhcr.org/548ea0f09.pdf

Espenhorst, N. & Kemper, T. (2015). "Gekommen, um zu bleiben? Auswertung der Inobhutnahmen nach unbegleiteter Einreise aus dem Ausland im Jahr 2013". Jugendhilfe, 53 (2): 128 – 134

Eurostat. (2017). "63,300 unaccompanied minors among asylum seekers registered in the EU in 2016". Retrieved February 23, 2019 from https://ec.europa.eu/eurostat/documents/2995521/8016696/3-11052017-AP-EN.pdf/30ca2206-0db9-4076-a681-e069a4bc5290

Hopkins, P. E. & Hill, M. (2008). "Pre-flight experiences and migration stories: the accounts of unaccompanied asylum-seeking children". Children's Geographies, 6: 257-268

Hopkins, P. E & Hill, M. (2010). "The needs and strengths of unaccompanied asylum-seeking children and young people in Scotland". Child and Family Social Work, 15 (4): 399-408

Huemer, J., Karnik, N. S., Voelkl-Kernstock, S., Granditsch, E., Dervic, K., Friedrich, M. H. & Steiner, H. (2009). "Mental health issues in unaccompanied refugee minors". Child and adolescent psychiatry and mental health, 3: 13

Kaytaz, E. S. (2016). "Afghan journeys to Turkey: narratives of immobility, travel and transformation". Geopolitics, 21 (2): 284–302

Keles, S., Friborg, O., Idsøe, T., Sirin, S., & Oppedal, B. (2016). "Depression among unaccompanied minor refugees: the relative contribution of general and acculturation-specific daily hassles". Ethnicity & Health, 21 (3): 300-317. doi: 10.1080/13557858.2015.1065310

Keles, S., Friborg, O., Idsøe, T., Sirin, S., & Oppedal, B. (2018). "Resilience and acculturation among unaccompanied refugee minors". International Journal of Behavioral Development, 42 (1): 52-63. doi: 10.1177/0165025416658136

Kulu- Glasgow, I., S. Noyon, M. Smit (2019). I just wanted to be safe: unaccompanied minors in the Netherlands – see this book

Mainwaring, C. & Brigden, N. (2016). "Beyond the border: clandestine migration journeys". Geopolitics, 21 (2): 243–262

Mougne, C. (2010). "Trees only Move in the Wind. A Study of Unaccompanied Afghan Children in Europe". Retrieved March 31, 2016, from http://www.unhcr.org/4c1229669.html

Müller, A. (2014). "Unbegleitete Minderjährige in Deutschland". Retrieved March 31, 2016, from https://www.bamf.de/SharedDocs/Anlagen/DE/Publikationen/EMN/ Studien /wp60-emn-minderjaehrige-in-deutschland.pdf?__blob=publicationFile

Nardone, M. & Correa-Velez, I. (2015). "Unpredictability, invisibility and vulnerability: Unaccompanied asylum-seeking minors' journeys to Australia". Journal of Refugee Studies, 29 (3): 295 - 314

UNHCR. (2016). "Global Trends. Forced Displacement in 2015". Retrieved February 23, 2019 from https://www.unhcr.org/statistics/unhcrstats/576408cd7/unhcr-global-trends-2015.html

CHAPTER 2

'I JUST WANTED TO BE SAFE': AGENCY AND DECISION-MAKING AMONG UNACCOMPANIED MINOR ASYLUM SEEKERS

Işık Kulu-Glasgow, Sanne Noyon, Monika Smit

Introduction

The year 2015 was characterised by a peak in the number of asylum seekers arriving in the European Union, with over 1.2 million first time asylum seekers applying for protection.[1] Among them were over 96,000 minors who arrived without parents or other adult relatives. Sweden received the highest number of these so-called unaccompanied minor asylum seekers (UMAs), followed by Germany, Hungary, and Austria. The Netherlands, ranked seventh among the destination countries with 3,859 UMAs, representing almost a fourfold increase compared to the year before.[2] An overwhelming majority (85%) of the 'Dutch' UMAs came from Syria, Eritrea and Afghanistan (IND, 2015).

How do UMAs end up in specific countries and what is their agency in the decision to leave and in the choice of their destination? Over the last decade, several studies sought answers to these questions. Findings imply that the extent of agency minors have regarding migration decision and destination choice varies: some are active agents, while others are dependent on family and/or other actors. According to a study on minors who arrived unaccompanied in Italy in 2016 from a variety of countries from the Horn of and West Africa, 75% of them made the decision to migrate themselves, mostly due to some form of violence, but lack of livelihoods or limited public services were also mentioned as reasons. The majority of these minors had a specifically intended destination at departure. This was not necessarily always

---

[1] http://ec.europa.eu/eurostat/documents/2995521/7203832/3-04032016-AP-EN.pdf

[2] In 2014 less than a thousand UMAs had arrived in the Netherlands. In 2016, compared to 2015, the number of applications by UMAs more than halved, with Eritrea, Syria and Afghanistan again in the top three countries of origin (IND, 2016).

Italy but in some cases a country in the region of their country of origin, where they originally intended to stay (UNICEF/REACH, 2017). Several studies on Eritrean UMAs report similar results as above regarding the agency on migration decision making: they decide and flee Eritrea without telling their parents (Amnesty International, 2015; Røsberg & Tronvoll, 2017). Avoiding compulsory, long lasting National Service (Amnesty International, 2015), and/or improving the standard of living were the main drivers of migration (Røsberg & Tronvoll, 2017).

Other studies show that the migration and the destination are decided by a family member or a smuggler, without the UMA being aware of the destination (e.g. Hopkins & Hill, 2008; Crawley, 2010; Staring & Aarts, 2010; UNHCR, 2010; Kuschminder et al., 2015; Vervliet et al., 2015). Some minors even learn about the destination only once they arrive there (e.g. Crawley, 2010; Staring & Aarts, 2010; Kuschminder et al., 2015). In their study among Afghan minors in the Netherlands, Buil and Siegel (2014) report that, although the decision to leave was predominantly taken by the family, the minors had agreed with this decision. The decision was taken due to violence in the country - because of the Taliban or other criminal groups, or relational disputes (see also Kuschminder & Siegel, 2016) -, as well as the desire to build a better future (Buil, 2011). In only a few of these cases, the intended destination at the departure was the Netherlands. Donini et al. (2016) report that Afghan UMAs are sometimes sent to Europe as 'scouts' by their families to allow other family members to come later.

The question of agency is relevant not only regarding decisions at departure but also during the journey - when ultimately the decision was to end up needs to be made. Then information and networks become essential. In their study on adult Eritrean asylum seekers, Brekke and Aarset (2009) report that once in transit, family members were contacted, even when the decision to leave Eritrea was made independently by the UMA. Koser and Kuschminder (2016) show that while the decision to leave the country of origin is often made under stress and rather hastily, in transit countries, migrants have more time to build up networks and find out about potential destination countries. The - mainly adult - respondents in Gilbert and Koser's study (2006) had received false or misleading information from their smugglers about their destination at some point in their journey. This is not a unique example of agents providing false information. Some adult Eritrean refugees for example, who had recently arrived in the Netherlands, were told by their smugglers that Amsterdam was the capital of Sweden (Sterckx & Fessehazion, 2018). There is little knowledge about how minors make the decision regarding their final destination during the journey and where the agency lies in this process. There are studies which indicate that this decision is not always deliberate and some minors arrive in the country of destination by chance, as a result of border control (Staring & Aarts, 2010; Buil, 2011).

The studies mentioned above show that there are different factors at play in the migration process of unaccompanied minors, which also influence their agency therein. The systems theory of migration (originally by Mabogunje, 1970)[3] considers migration as a dynamic process of consecutive events that take place through time and identifies three levels on which such factors operate. At the macro level economic, social, cultural, and political conditions in different places create the context of migration (e.g. wars, norms and values of a society, political repression, migration policies); at the micro level perceptions, expectations and motives of potential migrants, but also those of members of their household, as well as social networks operate. Such networks create feedback mechanisms and provide information (Mabogunje, 1970), and play a facilitating role in the aspiration of others to migrate to the same place or region (De Haas, 2014). At the meso level, other actors such as those working in the 'migratory industry' (e.g. human smugglers) provide information and other services (Castles & Miller 2009). In this framework, migrants are considered active agents who apply deliberate strategies. The purpose of the present chapter is to contribute to the existing literature on the migration processes of unaccompanied minor asylum seekers within this framework, while not aspiring to test the model. It focuses on the extent to which unaccompanied minor asylum seekers act as active agents during the migration process, with a particular focus on the decision to migrate and the choice of destination, in a context determined by factors operating at different levels. These are the political, social and cultural context at the macro level, the role of information, and aspirations of the minors as well as their parents' at the micro level, and the role of human smugglers and other agents at the meso level. The chapter draws upon a recent study by Kulu-Glasgow et al. (2018) on the cohort of UMAs who arrived in the Netherlands in 2015 and sought answers to the following questions: what were the driving forces behind their migration, how were the decisions regarding migration and destination made, was there an intended destination at onset? If not, how did the decision-making process regarding the destination develop during the journey? These questions have hardly been answered in other European countries that had received a good share of the UMA cohort in the peak year 2015.

Our results show that the agency regarding decision making throughout the migration process of unaccompanied minors does not necessarily lie with the same person. We can speak of a continuum in this agency, which differs between and within nationalities. While some minors are active agents throughout the whole migration process, others might be drifting toys of fate with little or no agency.

---

[3] Mabogunje (1970) developed the systems approach for rural-urban migration. Since then, it has been applied to international migration by many scholars (e.g. Fawcett & Arnold, 1987; Boyd, 1989; Fawcett, 1989; Zlotnik, 1992, De Haas, 2014).

Method

The data used in this chapter originates from a study conducted by the Dutch Research and Documentation Centre (WODC) among the top three nationalities of the 2015 cohort of unaccompanied minor asylum seekers in the Netherlands: Syrian, Eritrean and Afghan UMAs. Between August 2017 and March 2018, a total of 45 minors (16 Afghan, 15 Syrian, and 14 Eritrean) from the top three nationalities in the 2015 UMA cohort were interviewed.

The target population of respondents consisted of Syrian, Eritrean, and Afghan minors in the 2015 UMA cohort who were aged between 14 and 17 at the time of arrival in the Netherlands.[4] The respondent group was selected to reflect the age and sex distribution of the respective cohort populations and the acceptance rates for these three nationalities. The majority of the respondents were males[5] aged 16 or older at arrival. Except for three, all interviews were conducted face-to-face across the country.

In line with the acceptance rates for the Afghan male UMAs, about five respondents had their asylum application accepted, while the applications of the rest were rejected. The asylum applications of all the Syrian and Eritrean respondents were accepted.[6] We obtained permission from the UMAs' legal guardians and their mentors before approaching them for interviews. In this regard, the question of whether they were mentally capable of being interviewed played an important role. Out of the minors whom the legal guardians considered 'suitable' for our interviews in this respect, a random selection of respondents was made. The minors were mostly approached and interviewed in their native language and were informed that the anonymity and confidentiality of their responses would be ensured. During the interviews, utmost attention was given to guarantee the psychological wellbeing of the minors. Topics that might distress them were avoided, and they were repeatedly informed that they could skip questions, or end the interview at any time.[7]

In addition to the interviews with the minors, six focus groups were held with 30 experts, mainly legal guardians of unaccompanied minors. The main purpose of the focus groups was triangulation, collecting additional data (for example on younger UMAs whom we had not interviewed), as well as

---

[4] We decided not to interview younger age groups because of the sensitivity of the research topics. In addition, we assumed that for the younger UMAs it would be difficult to comprehend the difference between an interview for our research and those of the immigration authorities.

[5] In the 2015 cohort population of UMAs, 91% of the Syrian UMAs, 97% of the Afghan UMAs and 70% of Eritrean UMAs were boys. In line with this distribution, all of our Afghan respondents, almost all of the Syrian respondents (we have interviewed one Syrian girl) and 8 of the 14 Eritrean respondents were boys.

[6] The acceptance rates for asylum applications in the 2015 UMA cohort were as follows: 96% for Syrian minors, 98% for Eritrean minors, and 32% for Afghan boys and 77% for Afghan girls (reference date August 2017; Kulu-Glasgow et al., 2018).

[7] None of our respondents quit the interview; occasionally some topics were cut short.

comparison of the three groups under study. In this chapter, we concentrate on materials from the interviews with the minors, while occasionally, we refer to findings from the focus groups.

Results

Drivers of migration

The reasons why our respondents left their countries of origin, were mostly related to macro factors. Insecurity was the common denominator for all minors for leaving their countries of origin.

Among key sources of unsafety were the ongoing war in the country (Syrian UMAs), ethnic violence, as well as a family feud and consequent death of a family member (Afghan UMAs), and lack of intellectual and physical freedom (Eritrean UMAs). According to the experts in the focus groups, many Syrian and Afghan minors were also under the risk of being recruited by armed groups, respectively by Islamic State or the Taliban. Eritrean respondents named mandatory 'national service' - which consists of military enrolment that is officially 18 months, but practically can last ten years or longer (Van Reisen, 2016) -, and lack or poor quality of education also as reasons for leaving the country. For some, a 'culture of migration' (Massey et al., 1993)[8] played a role as well:

I saw my neighbours and many others in my village leaving for Europe. I thought 'how is that possible? I want to do that too.' I heard that some of my fellow villagers were in Germany, others were in Sweden, and some were in 'Holland'. It was not important which country I ended up in. I thought that all these countries were 'Europe'. They are all in Europe, aren't they?' I thought. I was just curious about 'Europe'.

Finally, some Afghan minors named factors related to personal issues such as conflicts with parents due to partner choice or sexual preferences as reasons for leaving Afghanistan.

The narratives of our respondents showed that about half of the Syrian and Eritrean minors first lived in a third country in the region before they moved to Europe: Syrian respondents in Turkey, Egypt, Lebanon, Yemen or Iraq, and Eritrean respondents in Ethiopia or Sudan. Some respondents lived in more than one third country. The period spent in the third country ranged from six months to five years; most of the respondents (or their families)

---

[8] A situation in which increasing migration within a community leads to changes in values and cultural perceptions, so that the prospect of migration becomes a 'norm'. Belloni (2016) also refers to a 'culture of migration' among young Eritreans.

initially had the intention to make a living in these countries.[9] For these minors, the reasons to leave the third country in the region and head for Europe were feeling unsafe as a result of hostile attitudes towards refugees or asylum seekers, and resulting negative experiences, lack of future prospects regarding work and education[10], cultural differences, example of others leaving for Europe, and/or an intention of family reunification.

None of the Afghan minors we interviewed lived in a third country before migrating to Europe. Four respondents were born in Iran or had migrated there with their family when they were very young. Lack of future prospects or other problems as a result of being undocumented were the main reasons to leave Iran.

Agency in decision making regarding migration and destination

In this section, we focus on agency of the UMAs in our research group. We present the results per nationality, emphasizing the role of the minors themselves regarding the migration decision and the choice of the destination, the influence of the family and possible other third parties.

Afghan UMAs

Typical in the narratives of our Afghan respondents was the limited agency they had regarding the decision to flee. An overwhelming majority of the minors left suddenly, after an unexpected or escalated conflict or an immediate threat of violence. The decision that the minor should leave was predominantly taken by the family – the mother, the father but also an uncle or a grandfather, with the minor barely having any say in the matter:

> *In Afghanistan, it is the elderly who take the final decisions. The youngster of the household has no say in whatever decisions are being taken for them.*

The role of the family also included arranging and financing these UMAs' journeys. Typically, this meant arranging practical stuff (e.g. papers, clothing, food, medicines), and finding a smuggler. A respondent's father travelled with him to hand him over to the smuggler at the border. It seems that parents sometimes chose the smugglers carefully, as some entrusted money to them to be handed over to the respondent once they were on safer grounds. Only in exceptional cases did the agency regarding the decision to leave lie with the minors; in those cases mostly personal matters were at play. For example, one of our Afghan respondents who was born in Iran decided

---

[9] In cases where the minors stayed in a third country for less than six months, or did not intend to make a living there, we considered this stay as a part of the journey from the country of origin to the Netherlands (that is, transit stay).

[10] According to Belloni (2016) lack of socio-economic opportunities in neighboring countries (Ethiopia and Sudan) pushes young Eritreans who fled their country, to move further to look for a better life, in order to be able to take care of themselves and their families.

to leave after he refused to marry a partner that his parents had arranged for him:

I escaped Iran, from my family from their mentality and from the Iranian people. I didn't want to become like them, close-minded. They don't respect your wishes, they don't respect your choices. They don't allow you to be you.

His elder brother who respected his choice helped him to flee and arranged a smuggler. In some cases, the minors left in the company of adult family members, but regularly the companions lost each other during the journey, and the minors continued on their own, often in the company of other asylum seekers or peers:

Coming to Europe is not easy, you have to change routes and buses here and there, and because there are continuous changes in your routes, you will easily lose each other. I still don't know where my brother is.

Considering the hasty nature of their departure, it is not surprising that the Netherlands was an intended destination for none of our Afghan respondents (see Figure 2.1)[11]. They either left for Europe with no specific country in mind, or with no destination at all – basically because they 'just wanted to be safe' no matter where that would be. A few minors originally wanted to end up in either Sweden or Finland. We have indications that for some respondents the destination was decided by the parents and the smuggler without the minor knowing where he was heading.

Hardly any Afghan minors in our study had social networks in the Netherlands, and a minority had some vague knowledge about the Netherlands, often limited to bits of information such as: 'the Dutch football team', 'bicycles', 'cows', and 'milk'. Information about possible destinations in Europe was almost always acquired after arrival in Europe. As some respondents stated, the journey to Europe was very dangerous, and there was hardly any opportunity to seek information about possible destinations. Information about the Netherlands and other European countries usually came from 'weak ties' (cf. Granovetter, 1973; Brown & Kondrad, 2001),[12] other peers met during the journey, and sometimes (also) from other parties. The information concerned, for example, the reputation of the Netherlands being a 'favourable' country regarding procedures (mostly concerning asylum and family reunification), possibilities regarding work and education, as well

---

[11] The figure shows a schematic overview of the intended destination of our respondents at departure and the changes therein along the journey. Different styles of the lines refer to different destinations as shown in the legend, while the thickness of the lines shows the relative frequency in a certain trajectory.

[12] Weak ties exist between lesser-known people, such as those whom we met by coincidence through others, while strong ties are connections with whom one interacts frequently on a social basis (e.g. family and friends) (Granovetter, 1973; Brown & Konrad, 2001). According to Granovetter, weak rather than strong ties provide us with new, valuable information.

as it being a safe and free country.

Figure 2.1: (Changes in) *intended destination*, Afghan respondents

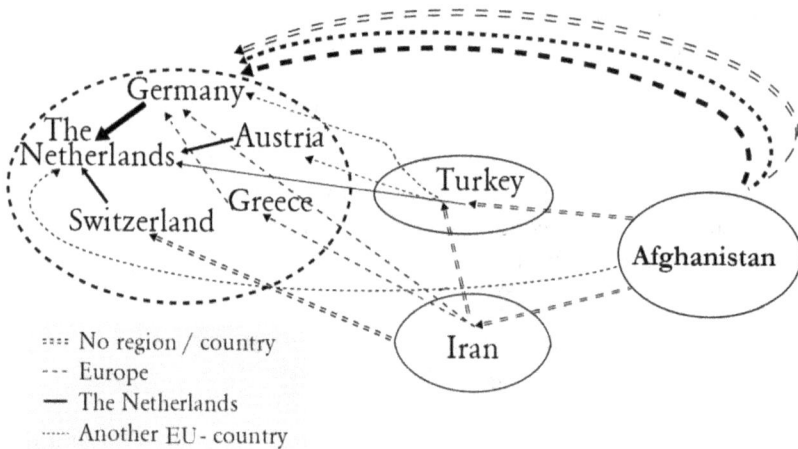

As can be seen in Figure 2.1, the destination change in favour of the Netherlands mostly took place in Germany (as shown by the solid line from Germany to the Netherlands), and occasionally in other countries. It looks like Germany was an important 'transit hub' – a juncture, where these minors re-evaluated their situation and decided on a destination. While some minors made a deliberate choice to come to the Netherlands on the basis of this information or occasionally simply due to the presence of a family member, this was not the case for others: almost half of our Afghan respondents ended up in the Netherlands as a result of coincidence. For example, one of our respondents who left Afghanistan with the intention of going to Europe, without a specific country in mind, made a decision in Germany to follow his peers to the Netherlands (one of the cases shown by the dashed line from Afghanistan to Germany and the solid line from Germany to the Netherlands in Figure 2.1):

> *When we arrived in Germany, we were met with open arms; there were other Afghans and Afghan girls who took care of us and offered us food. They advised us to settle in Germany. They told us that Germany was a good country, that they respected refugees and provided the refugees everything [...]. But my Iranian friends told me to join them to go to Holland. Because we became very good friends during our journey, I didn't want to lose them and therefore I joined them to travel to Holland.*

Thus, although this minor who was 'drifting' with peers had no agency over his destination, the agency to follow these peers was his.

In another case, a minor and his friend met an Afghan man, a 'grey agent'[13] in a shopping centre in Germany, simply followed him, and ended up in the Netherlands:

> *He was apparently a refugee staying at the same camp as us. He asked us whether we wished to go to a better place. We agreed to follow him. When someone older tells you something good, you believe him, and you follow him. We went to the train station where he bought us and himself train tickets. He told us: 'wherever I go, just follow me. Don't ask me what or where […].' At the end we arrived in the Netherlands. But we did not know where to go or what to do. He bought himself another ticket. I asked him, 'can you at least tell me your name, where are you going, where am I? What can you tell me about this country? He said: 'I can not give you any sort of information. If I do that, maybe while exchanging information with a stranger, you will tell the stranger that you met me and that I helped you and that stranger will think I am a human smuggler. I am no one. I just offered you my help, bought you a ticket. Now take care. I am just from the same country as you.'*

In such examples, the minors made a 'conscious' choice to follow others, but the agency regarding the choice of the destination lied with third parties. Among minors who ended up in the Netherlands, there were also those who actually were on their way to another European country but could not travel any further, as a result of taking a wrong train and/or due to border control. They were 'passive victims' (cf. Crawley, 2010) regarding the 'choice' of destination, especially considering that in some cases it was family members who made the decision that the minor should head for that - other - European country in the first place.

Syrian UMAs

As mentioned before the migration trajectories of our Syrian respondents to Europe did not always consist of a 'single journey'. Some initially lived in a third country in the region such as Turkey, Egypt or Lebanon. In these cases, the decision to move was often made by the parents. This is not surprising considering the young age of our respondents at the time of travel. However, in the process of migration to the European continent, either from the third country or directly from Syria, a 'joint agency' appears as a common aspect in the migration narratives of the Syrian minors. In almost all cases, the minors and their parents took a joint decision regarding the decision to migrate, and where to migrate. The family's desire to reunite in Europe seems to be an explanation for this shared decision-making. There are, however, variations in the development of the decision-making process and in how the agency shifted between minors and their parents. Mostly, the decision to

---

[13] We named people who had determined the destination of our respondents but whose function is not clear to us, 'grey agents'. They might be smugglers, working in the black market or simply be serving for the good of their fellow countrymen.

leave was initiated by the UMA, and then discussed with the family. The minors did not leave before their parents approved their decision.

> *My role was to whine that I wanted to leave Syria... I wanted to continue with my study, but schools were closed; we had no life anymore... At the end my parents decided that I should leave.*

In a few cases the migration decision was initiated by the parents:

> *My father asked me whether I wanted to go to Europe. First, I didn't want to leave, I wanted to stay with my family. But later I agreed; I did want to go to Europe and study, I wanted to build a new future for us. My father and I took the final decision together.*

While in the above examples the migration decisions seem to have been taken unanimously regardless of who initiated the decision, in others, more negotiations between the parties and 'give-and-take' were necessary. For example, two brothers who desperately wanted to leave for Europe, were confronted with the strong objection of their father who first tried to convince them to stay in Syria. However, when the father realised that he could not stop his children, he tried to persuade them to move to a neighbouring country instead of undertaking the dangerous journey to Europe. Consequently, the brothers agreed to cater to their father's wish and gave it a try to live in that country, but after a while decided to head for Europe anyway. They started their journeys to Europe at different points in time, as the father feared to lose both sons during the journey. This example shows how the agency shifted between the parties during the process.

It is not surprising that the parents of our Syrian respondents were also almost universally involved in the planning of and preparations for the journey. Similar to the case of our Afghan respondents, parents arranged simple, practical things, as well as financing the trip, arranging a smuggler and (adult) travel companions – in this case, a mother travelled with her son until the border. However, some minors had to leave Syria suddenly, as a result of the situation becoming more threatening or smugglers or other travel companions leaving unexpectedly. In an exceptional case, a Syrian minor worked and saved money to finance the journey himself. In the example mentioned above of the two brothers, they were the ones who had arranged the smuggler, but the father paid him.

Figure 2.2 shows that, in contrast to the Afghan minors, for the majority of our Syrian respondents the intended destination at departure from Syria or the third country in the region, was the Netherlands (indicated by the solid lines). A striking aspect of the narratives of these minors is that they all made a carefully considered, deliberate decision regarding their final destination.

Figure 2.2: (Changes in) *intended destination*, Syrian respondents

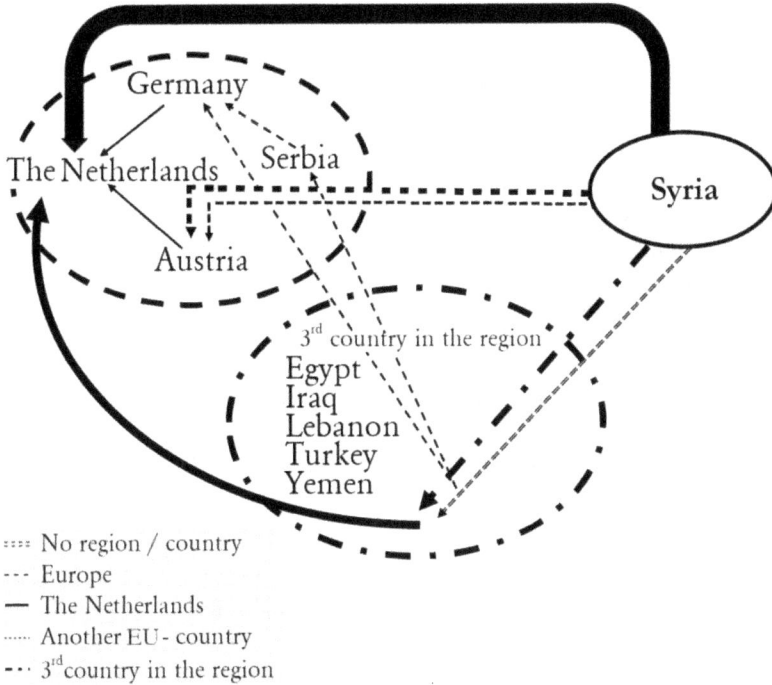

---- No region / country
--- Europe
— The Netherlands
····· Another EU - country
-··- 3rd country in the region

Similar to the decision to migrate, regarding the decision where to migrate, the minors were mostly involved as active agents, together with their parents, by collecting information on different destinations. 'Strong ties' (i.e. family members and friends) in the Netherlands and/or other European countries were important sources of information as well as the Internet:

> *I just wanted to go to a safe country. I wanted to study; I was 15 years old. My friend in the Netherlands told me on the phone: 'the Netherlands is a beautiful and quiet country, people are not racist. Discrimination does not exist in the Netherlands'.*

> *My cousin is living in Denmark. She always talks to my father; she advised him to send me to Denmark. But my other cousin, who has friends in the Netherlands, got in touch with them. He told my father that for refugees the Netherlands is a better country; that getting a residence permit and family reunification procedure is much quicker than in Denmark. That's why my father decided to send me to the Netherlands [...]. All European countries are safe. But the Netherlands is better for the future of our family. I want to study and want that my little sister will also study.*

Even in the few cases where our Syrian respondents did not consider the

Netherlands as the intended destination at departure (shown by the dashed and dotted lines in Figure 2.2), the minors made a deliberate choice to come to the Netherlands once they were in Europe. During the journey, they remained in touch with their families, and sometimes negotiations were made regarding the destination: one of our respondents left with destination 'Europe' with no specific country in mind, although his father strongly encouraged him to go to Germany, because of the good education system there. However, during his journey, our respondent heard from other asylum seekers that procedures regarding asylum and family reunification were much easier and quicker in the Netherlands than in Germany, while the education system was just as good. On the basis of this information he decided to head to the Netherlands instead:

> *In Austria, I had to choose where I wanted to go; they were sorting people and bringing them to different buses; there were buses which went to Germany, others went to the Netherlands, or other countries. I called my parents and told them my decision. It was not easy to convince them that the Netherlands was better. But in the end, they accepted my decision.*

Another respondent who headed to Germany met a taxi driver by chance, received similar information about the Netherlands, and solely based on that information decided to change his destination. It is clear from these examples that the agency regarding the destination lied with the minors themselves and their decision was influenced by outsiders.

Eritrean UMAs

Typical to the migration trajectory of the Eritrean UMAs in our study was the nature of their decision to migrate: several of these minors described how this decision was made independently and spontaneously. Even those who had had a vague notion of leaving the country at some point, often departed abruptly, as illustrated by the following account:

> *I wasn't actually planning on leaving Eritrea, I wanted to stay with my family. But my three friends and I all received a letter from the municipality saying that we had to become armed protectors of the village where we lived and that we had to come and collect our guns, like the militia. Neither of us wanted to do this job so we decided it was best to leave the country. Five days later, I was watching my aunt's cattle when my friends came to see me and told me they had decided to leave. I decided to join them then and there and left the cattle just like that.*

Without exception, our Eritrean respondents described how their decision to migrate was made without discussing it with their parents. In this respect, the difference between the Eritrean minors and the Syrian and Afghan UMAs is striking. Whereas the latter two groups involved their families in the migration decision, none of the Eritrean UMAs did so. Our

Eritrean respondents explained that, had they done so, their parents would not have let them leave because of the dangers of the journey. Some of the legal guardians in the focus groups were under the impression that some Eritrean minors did discuss their departure with their parents, but kept it secret from everyone, as in Eritrea emigration is politically sensitive and dangerous for those involved. An explanation regarding the strong agency of Eritrean minors regarding their migration decision may lie in the fact that parents may be less available as they are conscripted in the practically unlimited National Service or fathers work abroad (cf. Sterckx & Fessehazion, 2018). This hints at an interaction of macro and micro level factors in determining the context of migration of Eritrean UMAs.

The strong agency of the Eritrean minors regarding the migration decision does not imply, however, that there was necessarily a plan. While some of the UMAs we talked to, had arranged a smuggler to get them out of the country, for others the 'plan' was limited to buying food and water for the road. More often, the minors simply left and planning only became a priority once they had successfully crossed the border.

It was a sudden decision. I lived in a village close to the border and one afternoon at around four, I left with four friends to go to Ethiopia. Just like that, there was no plan or anything. We walked for a few hours until it got dark and then we were in Ethiopia. Since the goal was to get to Ethiopia we didn't need to make a plan or prepare anything. It was close by.

Just like most of the Eritrean minors in our study did not have a plan, they had no clear destination upon departure either. As shown in Figure 2.3, only a small minority left Eritrea with the intention of coming to the Netherlands. A few of our interviewees had the intention 'to go to Europe', but most simply left without a specific country or even a region in mind.

Once the border was crossed into Sudan or Ethiopia, the situation changed. While some stayed in these countries for longer periods and tried to make a living there, others realized fairly quickly that the Sudanese and Ethiopian realities were not necessarily rosier than the Eritrean one they had left behind. As stated before, for many the lack of future prospects was a reason to continue their journey. This time around, the decision to leave was typically based on information from other asylum seekers, refugees or NGO volunteers, and sometimes also involved family members in diaspora. Whereas the former were important sources of information about potential destinations, the latter were typically contacted to provide support for the journey; parents and sometimes other family members were involved in finding smugglers and/or financing them.

Figure 2.3: (Changes in) *intended destination*, Eritrean respondents

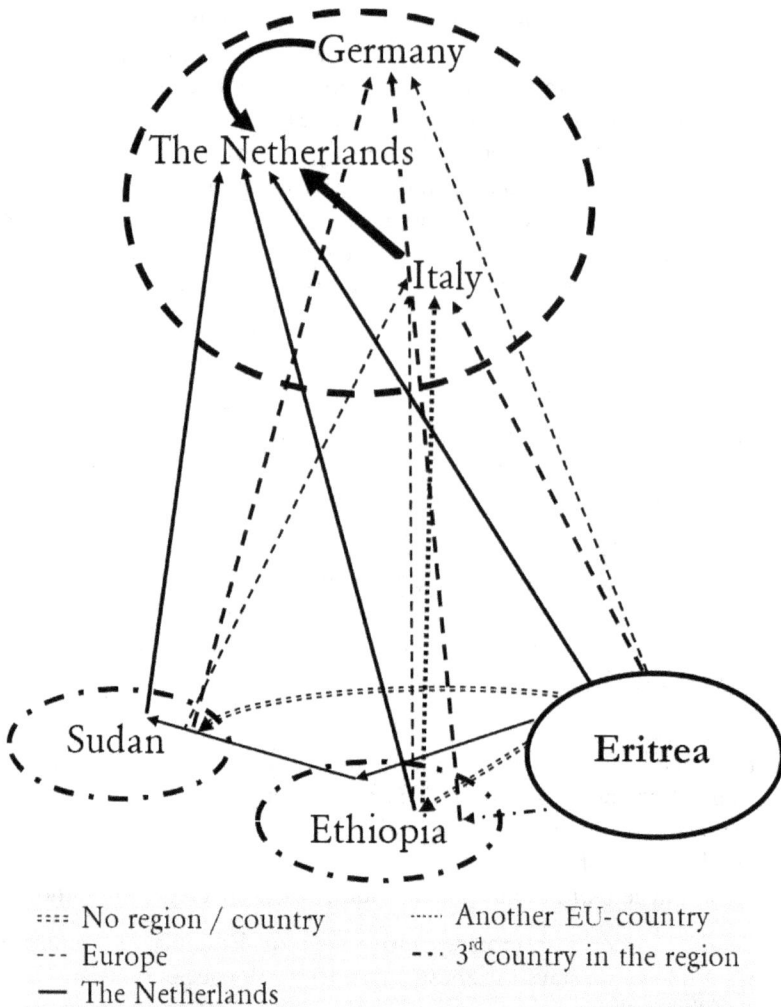

::::: No region / country   ······ Another EU- country
- - - Europe   -··- 3rd country in the region
— The Netherlands

While the involvement of family members in the decision to migrate from Sudan or Ethiopia was in stark contrast with the initial decision to leave the country of origin, the agency in the decision-making process remained mostly with the UMAs themselves. There were cases where the family members in diaspora refused to send money for the journey at first, as they did not consider it to be safe. The minors in question – evidently – ignored their families' precautions and continued their journey anyway. The father of one of our respondents tried to convince her to stay where she was instead of travelling to Europe. However, our respondent told her father that she would leave for Europe anyway, with or without his help. As the father wanted his daughter to be safe, he arranged a trustworthy smuggler for her after all.

In contrast to how they had initially left Eritrea, the UMAs' departure from Sudan and Ethiopia was more planned, as evidenced by the minors' efforts to collect money as well as by the fact that now they all left with a destination in mind. As shown in Figure 2.3, some minors formed the intention to come to the Netherlands in Sudan or Ethiopia, while the majority headed for Europe in general.

It may be clear that the large majority of our Eritrean respondents made their decision to come to the Netherlands at some point during their journey (rather than before departure). The decision was mostly made only after arriving in Europe: in Italy or Germany. As we can see in Figure 2.3, neither of these countries were named as intended destinations at any point in time, but were used as transit hubs, as was the case for our Afghan respondents. For the Eritrean UMAs in our study, Italy was not a viable option, albeit according to them without clear reasons:

Nobody wanted to stay in Italy; everyone just travelled on. I don't know why, maybe they don't want refugees there.

At the European transit hubs, the UMAs made their decisions to travel to the Netherlands for different reasons. For many, fellow refugees were an important source of information, providing knowledge about asylum and family reunification procedures in different countries, which the minors then used to make their decision:

I was also considering to go to England but other refugees in Italy told me that England is very tough and that it's hard to travel there. I don't know why. I haven't seen it myself but that's what they told me.

Similar to the Afghan minors, our Eritrean respondents had only a vague notion of the Netherlands, if any. They all recount similar stories of sharing information. For a few, it seems that information and advice from strong ties, played a crucial role in making the decision to come to the Netherlands: family members who were already in the Netherlands advised them to come. In one case, a combination of strong and weak ties were crucial sources of information: a minor's father living in Israel had gathered information through his own network and then advised his daughter to travel to the Netherlands. She gladly followed her father's advice: 'because he always knows best'. Importantly, the agency in these decisions mostly remained with the UMAs themselves.

In a few other cases, it seems that the minors ended up in the Netherlands by chance. For instance, one respondent recounts how he met another Eritrean boy in Germany at a train station, who was selling tickets to 'newcomers' and sold him a ticket to the Netherlands. The UMA in question had heard some information about the Netherlands during his journey, but had not made a decision regarding his destination yet. While the agency remained with the minor in this case, as he voluntarily bought the ticket and travelled on, the specific destination was influenced by this 'grey agent'.

In situations of arrival by chance, the decision was not so much about the destination as much as it was about the company. As we have seen among the Afghan UMAs, once minors join a group of peers, they sometimes prefer to stick together and let that determine their destination. A female minor who originally intended to go to Switzerland (shown by the dotted line from Ethiopia to Italy in Figure 2.3) is an example:

> *I actually wanted to go to 'Swiss'. I thought the name sounded promising. I travelled along to Amsterdam because I couldn't convince my friends. And I didn't want to stay behind by myself (…). I didn't have a family anymore; I didn't want to lose my friends too. I thought if we travelled to the Netherlands together, we would stay together as a family forever.*

While the destination may have been decided or influenced by others, the choice to value company over destination was the minor's and in that sense the agency remained hers. This observation is crucial and typical to the migration trajectory of the Eritrean UMAs we interviewed. Furthermore, contrary to the Afghan minors, none of our Eritrean respondents ended up in the Netherlands as a 'passive victim'.

Conclusion

This chapter aimed to contribute to the existing literature on the migration processes of unaccompanied minor asylum seekers by providing insights into driving forces behind their migration and their agency in the migration process, with a focus on the migration decision and choice of destination. The results are based on a research conducted by the Dutch Research and Documentation Centre (WODC) among a total of 45 Syrian, Afghan and Eritrean minors (Kulu-Glasgow et al., 2018), who arrived in the Netherlands in 2015, a year which was marked by a high inflow of UMAs in Europe. In that year, the Netherlands was one of the top ten destinations for these minors.

From the perspective of the migration systems theory (originally by Mabogunje, 1970; see also Fawcett & Arnold, 1987; Boyd, 1989; Fawcett, 1989; Zlotnik, 1992, De Haas, 2014), our results suggest that factors operating at different levels determine the context of the migration process of UMAs and their agency, as is the case for any other migrant: the political, social, and cultural context at the macro level, the role of information, and own aspirations (as well as those of family members) at the micro level, and the role of human smugglers and those whom we called 'grey agents' at the meso level. There are also indications that factors at different levels interact with each other to influence the migration process of UMAs.

Firstly, different factors, mostly at macro level, were responsible for the minors fleeing their country: unsafety was a common denominator for all. War (Syrian respondents), compulsory, potentially indefinite national service, lack of possibilities for further study, poor quality of education, lack of physical and intellectual freedom (Eritrean respondents), examples of others leaving the country (Eritrean and Syrian respondents), and risks of being recruited by armed groups (Syrian and Afghan respondents) were often reported reasons. Sometimes micro level factors, embedded in the social, cultural or political context of the society, played a role: family feuds, conflicts within the family due to partner choice or sexual preferences, and personal threats as a result of ethnic violence (especially Afghan respondents) were micro level factors we encountered among our respondents. These findings indicate similarities with the conceptualization of drivers for general patterns of migration. For example, the conflict model of migration argues that conflict at different levels, whether at home, within the community, with or within states is the key driver of migration and that such conflicts (increasingly) drive mobility by leading to a perception of insecurity (Cohen & Sirkeci, 2016; Sirkeci & Cohen, 2016).

Regarding the agency of the minors, the narratives of the minors reveal that agency does not necessarily lie with the same person all the time, but can shift throughout the migration process. In general, there seems to be a continuum in the agency of minors regarding the migration decision across different nationalities - aside from variations within the nationality groups, with striking differences. While the migration decision concerning Afghan UMAs was overwhelmingly made by parents or other family members -a finding cited also in other studies (e.g. UNHCR, 2010; Buil & Siegel, 2014)-, Eritrean UMAs unanimously reported that it was them who took the sole decision to leave Eritrea, without discussing it with their family. Some Dutch legal guardians suspect that sometimes Eritrean minors talk about their departure with their parents, but do not disclose it to others considering the political pressures in the country (see Kulu-Glasgow et al., 2018). However, the independence of Eritrean minors and young adults in the migration decision is also cited in other studies (e.g. Brekke & Aarset, 2009, Amnesty International, 2015, Røsberg & Tronvoll, 2017; Sterckx & Fessehazion, 2018). Although both Afghan and Syrian parents were involved in the preparations for the journey, Syrian parents were involved in the migration decision in a different fashion than Afghan parents: in most cases, regardless of who initiated the migration, the Syrian minors and parents made the migration decision together. Aspirations of the family members and the minors regarding family reunification in Europe seem to be a likely underlying reason for this joint agency, an intention at departure which was hardly referred to by our Afghan and Eritrean respondents. However, we also came across examples where the agency regarding the migration decision lied with the Syrian family. Elsewhere in this book, Kamp and Kuschminder also point to the collective decision-making between Syrian UMAs and their families and to the varying degrees of autonomy among Syrian UMAs regarding the migration decision.

Although we also see a continuum in the agency of the minors regarding the destination choice, this is a rather fuzzy one compared to that in the migration decision: the narratives of our Afghan respondents show that, during the migration process the agency shifted from the family to the minors themselves or to other parties. Furthermore, we see that it is not always simple to point out where the agency lied regarding the choice of destination. Excluding a few exceptions, almost all of our Afghan respondents departed with no destination in mind or just headed for Europe in search of safety and security. Some did not even know where they were heading, but the destination (Europe) had already been decided by the family and/or the smuggler (see also Staring & Aarts, 2010; Vervliet et al., 2015). In spite of the limited agency regarding the migration decision, some of these Afghan minors decided on their destination independently during the journey - mostly while in transit in Germany, which seems to have served as a safe haven and a transit hub where these minors re-evaluated their situation and made a deliberate choice to continue to the Netherlands. The information on which their decisions were based came from third parties, usually peers met during the journey, and sometimes smugglers. This information concerned the reputation of the Netherlands being a 'favourable' country regarding asylum and family reunification procedures, possibilities regarding work and education, as well as it being a safe and free country. But, for almost half of the Afghan minors in our study, ending up in the Netherlands was a matter of coincidence – a situation that we did not encounter among any of our Syrian respondents and only among a few Eritrean minors. In such coincidental instances, minors followed other peers or 'grey agents' who were on their way to the Netherlands. In such situations, the agency in the 'choice' of the final destination lied with third parties, although the decision to follow others to the Netherlands was a 'conscious' choice– an expression of agency. Minors who intended to end up in another European country, but were stuck in the Netherlands due to border control can be considered as 'passive victims'.

The agency during the migration process appears to be more continuous for our Eritrean and Syrian respondents, who are constantly involved as active agents in the migration process. Nearly all the Eritrean minors managed to retain the agency they had regarding the migration decision, also in the decision regarding their destination: they themselves made a deliberate choice for the Netherlands during the journey. Similar to the case of Afghan minors, most Eritrean UMAs based their choice on information from 'weak ties', related to the reputation of the Netherlands regarding easier and quicker procedures, possibilities regarding education and work and the reputation of the Dutch society (e.g. free and democratic). Contrary to their Afghan and Eritrean counterparts, the majority of the Syrian minors had already made a choice for their destination before departure (see also Kamp & Kuschminder in this book). In their case, a joint decision with the family was made in favour of the Netherlands based on similar information from 'strong ties' (i.e. relatives and friends) in the Netherlands, but also in other European countries. In a few situations where the Syrian minors left for another country or simply for Europe, the final destination was the result of a mutual decision even though the agency shifted between the parents and the minor in the process.

Although we have not studied what the household structures looked like around the time when the migration decision was taken, the distinct role of the family in the migration decision of Syrian and Afghan minors implies that UMAs' decision-making processes may fit within the general patterns of migration as well. Cohen and Sirkeci (2011) argue that the household is always present in migration decisions, even though it sometimes overwhelms the migrant or the migrant ignores the household. Even the Eritrean minors in our study, who all made the decision to flee independently, brought the household back into the migration process at a later point in the journey, for instance when the minors contacted their parents or other household members to seek assistance in finding or financing a smuggler, and/or gather information about a potential destination.

Our results prove that it is too simplistic to consider all UMAs either as active agents who always make deliberate choices and decisions, or as 'drifting toys of fate'. Their agency may differ according to nationality as well as the phase of the migration process. Similarities with the general migration patterns provide room for further conceptualisations and study of the migration processes of UMAs.

References

Amnesty International (2015). Just deserters: Why indefinite service in Eritrea created a generation of refugees. London: Amnesty International. https://www.amnesty.org/download/ Documents/ AFR6429302015ENGLISH.PDF

Belloni, M. (2016). Cosmologies of Destinations: Roots and Routes of Eritrean ForcedMigration Towards Europe. PhD thesis, University of Trento.

Boyd, M. (1989). "Family and personal networks in international migration: Recent developments and new agendas". International Migration Review, 23(3): 638-670.

Brekke, J.P. and Aarset, M.F. (2009). Why Norway? Understanding Asylum Destinations. Oslo: Institute for Social Research.https://www.udi.no/globalassets/global/forskning-fou_i/beskyttelse/why-norway.pdf

Brown, D.W. and Konrad, A.M. (2001). Granovetter was right: The importance of weak ties to a contemporary job search. Group & Organization Management, 26(4): 434-462.

Buil, C. (2011). A profile of Afghan unaccompanied minors in the Netherlands. Master's Thesis. Maastricht Graduate School of Governance.

Buil C. and Siegel M. (2014). "Destination Europe: Afghan unaccompanied minors crossing borders". In: S. Spyrou and M. Christou (eds.) Children and borders: Studies in childhood and youth (pp. 99-113). London: Palgrave Macmillan.

Castles, S. and Miller, M.J. (2009). The age of migration: International population movements in the modern world (4th edition). Hampshire: Palgrave Macmillan.

Cohen, J. H. and Sirkeci, I. (2011). Cultures of migration. The global nature of contemporary mobility. Austin: University of Texas Press.

Cohen, J. H. and Sirkeci, I. (2016). "Migration and insecurity: rethinking mobility in the neoliberal age". In: Carrier J.G. (ed.) After the crisis, anthropological thought, neoliberalism, and the aftermath, (pp. 96-113). London, New York: Routledge.

Crawley, H. (2010). Chance or choice: Understanding why asylum seekers come to the UK. London: Swansea University Prifysgol Abertawe/Refugee Council. https://www. refugeecouncil. org.uk/ assets/0001/5702/rcchance.pdf

De Haas, H. (2014). "Euro-Mediterranean migration futures: The cases of Morocco, Egypt and Turkey". In: M. Bommes (†), H.Fassmann and W. Sievers (eds.) Migration systems from Middle East and North Africa to Europe (pp. 29-74). Amsterdam: IMISCOE Research, Amsterdam University.

Donini, A., Monsutti, A. and Scalettaris, G. (2016). Afghans on the move: Seeking refugee and protection in Europe: 'In this journey I died several times; In Afghanistan you only die once'. Geneva: The Graduate Institute Geneva, Global Migration Centre. Global Migration Research Paper, No. 17/2016.https://repository.graduateinstitute.ch /record/293919/files/GMPRS_N17_Donini_Monsutti_Scalettaris_2016.pdf

Fawcett, J.T. and Arnold, F. (1987). "Explaining diversity: Asian and Pacific immigration systems". In: J.T. Fawcett and B.V. Cariño (eds.) Pacific bridges: The new immigration from Asia and the Pacific Islands (pp. 453-473). New York: Centre for Migration Studies.

Fawcett, J.T. (1989). "Networks, linkages and migration systems". International Migration Review, 23(3): 671-680.

Hopkins, P.E. and Hill, M. (2008). "Pre-flight experiences and migration stories: The accounts of unaccompanied asylum-seeking children". Children's Geographies, 6(3): 257-268.

Gilbert, A. and Koser, K. (2006). "Coming to the UK: What do asylum-seekers know about the UK before arrival?". Journal of Ethnic and Migration Studies, 32(7): 1209-1225.

Granovetter, M. (1973). "The strength of weak ties". American Journal of Sociology, 78(6): 1360-1380.https://www.cs.umd.edu/~golbeck/INST633o/granovetterTies.pdf

IND (Immigratie en Naturalisatiedienst) (2015). Asylum trends: Monthly report on Asylum Applications in the Netherlands and Europe. December Rijswijk: IND.https://ind.nl/ en/Documents/ AT_December_2015.pdf

IND (Immigratie en Naturalisatiedienst) (2016). Asylum trends. Monthly Report on Asylum Applications in The Netherlands. December 2016, Rijswijk: IND.https://ind.nl/en/ Documents/AT _December_2016.pdf

Kamp, R. and Kuschminder, K. (2019). "Syrian Unaccompanied Minors Journeys to Germany and initial experiences upon arrival." In: Kulu-Glasgow, I., Smit, M., Sirkeci, I. (eds.) Unaccompanied Minors from Immigration to Integration (pp. 9-27). London: Transnational Press London.

Koser, K. and Kuschminder, K. (2016). Understanding irregular migrants' decision making factors in transit. S.l.: Australian Government, Department of Immigration and Border Protection. Research Programme. Occasional Paper Series, No. 21/2016.

Kulu-Glasgow, I., Noyon, S. and Smit, M., with the contribution of S. Shagiwal (2018). Unaccompanied minor asylum seekers in the Netherlands: choice or chance? The Hague: WODC. https://www.wodc.nl/binaries/Cahier%202018-18_2874_Volledige%20tekst _tcm28-356301.pdf

Kuschminder, K., De Bresser J. and Siegel, M. (2015). Irreguliere migratieroutes naar Europa en de factoren die invloed zijn op de bestemmingskeuze van migranten. Maastricht Graduate School of Governance. Den Haag: WODC.https://www.wodc.nl/ binaries/2553-volledige-tekst_tcm28-73957.pdf

Kuschminder, K. and Siegel, M. (2016). Rejected Afghan asylum seekers in the Netherlands:

Migration experiences, current situations and future aspirations. Working Paper Series, no. 2016/007. Maastricht: Maastricht University/United Nations University.

Mabogunje, A. (1970). "Systems approach to a theory of rural-urban migration". Geographical Analysis, 2(1), 1-18.

Massey, D.S., Arango, J., Hugo, G., Kouaouci, A., Pellegrino, A. and Taylor, J.E. (1993). "Theories of international migration: A review and appraisal". Population and Development Review, 19(3): 431-466.

Røsberg, A.H. and Tronvoll, K. (2017). Migrants or Refugees? The internal and external drivers of migration from Eritrea. Oslo: International Law and Policy Institute. https://www.udi.no/ globalassets/global/forskning-fou_i/asylmottak/migrants-or-refugees-internal-and-external-drivers-of-migration-from-eritrea.pdf

Sirkeci, I. and Cohen, J. H. (2016). "Cultures of migration and conflict in contemporary human mobility in Turkey". European Review, 24(3): 381-396.

Staring, R. and Aarts, J. (2010). Jong en illegaal in Nederland: Een beschrijvende studie naar de komst en het verblijf van onrechtmatig verblijvende (voormalige) alleenstaande minderjarige vreemdelingen en hun visie op de toekomst. Den Haag: Boom Juridische Uitgevers. https://repub.eur.nl/pub/21445/ Jong%20en%20illegaal.pdf

Sterckx, L., Fessehazion, M., m.m.v. Teklemariam, B. (2018). Eritrese statushouders in Nederland. Een kwalitatief onderzoek over de vlucht en hun leven in Nederland. Den Haag: Sociaal Cultureel Planbureau. https://www.scp.nl/Publicaties/Alle_publicaties/ Publicaties_2018/Eritrese_statushouders_in_Nederland

UNHCR (2010). Voices of Afghan children. A study on asylum-seeking children in Sweden. Regional Office for the Baltic and Nordic Countries. https://www.unhcr.org/ protection/ children/ 4c8e24a16/voices-afghan-children-study-asylum-seeking-children-sweden.html

UNICEF/REACH (2017). Children on the move in Italy and Greece. https://www.unicef. org/eca/reports/children-move-italy-and-greece

Van Reisen, M. (2016). The involvement of unaccompanied minors from Eritrea in Human Trafficking. [s.n.] Tilburg University/Universiteit Leiden https://pure.uvt.nl/ws/ portalfiles/portal/ 11742150/Unaccompanied_Minors_Eritrea_Human_Trafficking.pdf

Vervliet, M., Vanobbergen, B., Broekaert, E. and Derluyn, I. (2015). "The aspirations of Afghan unaccompanied refugee minors before departure and on arrival in the host country". Childhood, 22(3), 330-345. http://journals.sagepub.com/doi/ pdf/ 10.1177/0907568214533976

Zlotnik, H. (1992). "Empirical identification of international migration systems". In: M.M. Kritz, L.L. Lim and Zlotnik, H. (eds.) International migration systems: A global approach (pp. 19-40). New York: Oxford University Press.

CHAPTER 3

WAYS INTO AND OUT OF EXPLOITATION UNACCOMPANIED MINORS AND HUMAN TRAFFICKING

Hilde Lidén and Cathrine Holst Salvesen

Introduction

This chapter assesses whether national law, policies and practice in the field of unaccompanied asylum seekers are in compliance with international conventions including the UNHCR guidelines and UN convention of the rights of the child (CRC). We will discuss policy and practices on minors exposed to human trafficking, taking Norway as a case. The Norwegian Immigration Act of 2008 includes provisions and formulations intended to strengthen the legal position and rights of asylum-seeking children as children. The intention was to ensure that national regulations on immigration were in accordance with the CRC and in line with the Norwegian Human Rights Act 1999.[1] The CRC as well as UNHCR guidelines mention human trafficking, including forced labour and sexual exploitation as one main threat to which children may be exposed.[2] The chapter discusses three scenarios which represent distinct forms of how unaccompanied minors are recruited into exploitative relations on their way to or in Europe and how their cases are assessed when applying for asylum in Norway as unaccompanied minors. Ways into and out of exploitation may have decisive implication for how their asylum applications are assessed and for further access to rehabilitation measures.

The political marker for children refers to an inclusive childhood discourse and policy framework based on children's indiscriminate rights. Refugee children are seen as vulnerable when exposed to various dangers in conflicts and wars that affect their lives, survival and development. They may

---

[1] *Lov om menneskerettighetenes stilling i norsk rett*, LOV-1999-05-21-30.

[2] Jf. UNHCR 2009: guidelines on international protection. Child asylum claims. HCR/GIP/09/08. See also CRC Articles 38, and Articles 3 and 4 in the Protocol on the Rights of the Child on the involvement of children in armed conflict under the CRC.

suffer due to child-specific forms of persecution, as well as other forms of persecution as individuals and family members. By contrast, the concept of asylum-seeker activates discourses of border control based on politicized suspicion, welfare restrictions and the expansion of an asylum system.

In Norwegian immigration politics, the UN Convention of the Rights of the Child (CRC) has been a significant part of the political negotiations between a restrictive and a liberal asylum policy. Increasing control measures over the last few years have led to additional ambiguities in both discourses and practices with regard to whether asylum seeking children are defined primarily as children or primarily as asylum seekers. The ambiguities of their status as either children or asylum seekers are revealed also for victims of human trafficking.

Background

Despite the fact that refugees' travel usually involves dramatic events, which is a significant marker in their life, there is surprisingly little research that examines this journey, as an experience and as a phenomenon (BenEzer and Zetter, 2015). Even more infrequent is the systematic knowledge about children and their conditions when recruited into human trafficking. Research on children as victims of trafficking has mainly focused on young girls exploited in the sex industry (Huijsmans and Baker, 2012; Montgomery, 2011; O'Connell Davidson, 2013). Minors are included as informants in empirical studies of women in prostitution, but only in exceptional cases do these studies explicitly discuss the conditions of minors (see e.g. Surtees, Babovic, Bibo, Djordjević, Rusu, Tudorache, 2007; Korsby, 2008; Plambeck, 2014). A few studies include boys, mainly in forced labour or petty crime, where sexual exploitation may also be part of the exploitation (see e.g. Boff, 2013; Mai, 2010). Connelly (2014), in her study, describes how children have moved to a family in the United Kingdom and are exploited as maids and for other forms of forced labour.

Another bulk of studies are evaluations of follow-up programs of identified child victims. The attention is paid to the authorities' organization of social services and measures (Gozdziak, 2010; Pearce, 2011; Pearce, Hynes, Bovarnick, 2013, Hodge, 2014; Franklin and Doyle, 2013; Rigby and White, 2013; UNICEF, 2011). This is also the case in Norway (Vollebæk, 2015; Lidén, Eide, Hidle, Nilsen and Wærdahl, 2013; Sønsterudbråten, 2013; Salvesen, 2014; Tyldum, Lidén, Skilbrei, Dalseng and Kindt, 2015). There are few studies on how human trafficking is made relevant in the asylum case assessments of unaccompanied minors. The knowledge gaps of human trafficking in children linked to transnational migration are still many, including awareness of the young victims' social background, aspirations and survival strategies.

Known cases of child trafficking in Norway are primarily cases of asylum seekers or those who have been included in the asylum process when identified as victims by police or help services. Minors then face overlapping systems of protection and immigration control as they go through the legal system (Staver and Lidén, 2014, see also Menjívar and Perreira, 2017). In accordance with UNHCR guidelines on child asylum claims (2009), trafficking is seen as a child specific form of persecution. The Norwegian immigration legislation has included this claim in the list of persecutions which may give grounds for asylum. A child might be given asylum based on human-rights violations that would not necessarily lead to asylum for adults. The Norwegian Immigration Act articulates the best-interests principle, however this is mentioned in a section that also gives strong consideration to other factors in order to control and/or limit immigration, prevent illegal actions and safeguard society at large (Lidén, Stang and Eide, 2017).

Any person arriving Norway without a legal stay permit is expected to apply for asylum. The person then is directed to the offices of the Police Immigration Service (PU) in Oslo. For unaccompanied minors (UM) a legal guardian, referred to as a representative, supports the minor during the application process.[3] Most asylum seekers lack credible identification when applying for asylum. Difficulties in estimating the age of young unaccompanied asylum seekers without identity documents have long been a problem for immigration authorities. The Police Immigration Service (PU) estimates the age of young unaccompanied asylum seekers. Although the age of not all minors is disputed, unaccompanied asylum seekers whose declared age is 16 to 18 years are frequently referred for age assessment. The decision to conduct an age assessment is taken as part of the initial procedure at the PU. Despite the authorities acknowledge of the uncertain methods to estimate a correct age in this age group, a significant proportion of the minor applicants are assessed to be over 18. The minors may also turn 18 during the asylum assessments, and defined as adult when the decision on residency is taken (Tyldum et al., 2015). An asylum seeker exposed for human trafficking who has been assessed as an adult will seldom obtain a residence permit in Norway; instead they are expected to return to their home country for attending a reintegration program there.

In accordance with The United Nations protocol to prevent, suppress and punish trafficking in persons, the Palermo Protocol elaborates on the nation states' obligations to identify, assist and protect victims of trafficking.[4]

---

[3] The Immigration Act Section 98a states that the provisions regarding guardianship 'apply to persons under 18 years of age (minors) who are applying for protection and who are in the country without parents or other persons with parental responsibility'. Guardianship is a voluntary mandate organised by the local county governor (*fylkesmann*). A mandatory course is needed to become a guardian.

[4] Protocol to Prevent, Suppress and Punish Trafficking in Persons, Especially Women and Children, supplementing the
United Nations Convention against Transnational Organized Crime came into force in 2000.

The use of threats, force or other forms of coercion are not required elements to establish cases of child trafficking. The argument is that children cannot give consent and their consent to an exploitative situation is considered irrelevant. However, this irrelevance of consent remains challenging to apply for law enforcement and the judiciary in cases of child trafficking, especially for young people.

Article 6 of the Palermo Protocol elaborates on states' obligations to assist victims of trafficking. Also when the child is waiting for the asylum application to be proceeded, the authorities have the responsibility to consider implementing measures with the aim of "physical, psychological and social recovery of victims of trafficking in human beings". Measures may include medical, psychological and material assistance, security and opportunities for education, training and employment. Age and gender should be taken into consideration, and they should meet the needs of children for appropriate accommodation, care and education. Thus, the authorities' efforts are met with high expectations. If identified as a victim of human trafficking the Norwegian Child Welfare Services have the main responsibility for re-integration of a child victim, in contrast to follow-up of adult victims, where NGOs are mainly responsible.

Child victims of trafficking in human beings are not easily identified. In most cases it is difficult to confirm the personal details of the victim as they typically do not carry identification documents. Furthermore practitioners often do not recognize that exploitation in forced criminality is child abuse. Children forced to commit crimes are often treated in the first stance as offenders. Victims may also resist cooperation with law enforcement and are at risk of disappearing or being re-trafficked (Europol, 2014).

It is therefore important to raise the question how identification of different forms of recruitment can be relevant for the assessment of the asylum applications of the minors and for their further access to rehabilitation measures. In this chapter we focus firstly on different scenarios of recruitment practices and the travelling routes of minors to and within Europe. This is followed up by a closer look at the distinct forms of exploitation networks described. We then turn to how the Norwegian asylum system deals with different forms and cases of exploitation, before we turn to possible reintegration measures and to some main areas to strengthen policy against trafficking of migrant minors.

Methods and data

The data material was collected when carrying out two applied studies, one commissioned by the Norwegian Ministry of Children and Equality (Tyldum et al., 2015) and one for Save the Children Norway (Lidén and Salvesen, 2016). The studies are based on qualitative research using mixed methods. The aim of the first study was to identify how Norwegian authorities identified and assisted child victims of human trafficking. The study was based on a nationwide survey including the police and child welfare services informing about their involvement in cases of (migrant) child victims. We also interviewed representatives of the immigration authorities, the police and child welfare services in four local communities, the staff in four reception centers and the staff in two shelters for child victims of trafficking. The study also included a review of all court cases in Norway regarding child victims of trafficking in the period 2005-2015 (14 cases)[5] and a review of cases proceeded for the immigration authorities. In addition we reviewed child victim cases handled by the County Child Welfare Board (17 cases). In the survey and the interviews anonymous cases (48 verified cases and 120 supposed cases of child victims) were described. Together with the reviewed court cases and the cases where children had been placed in the foundation for child victims, they constitute the main basis of empirical data for the following analysis. The second study had the aim to go closer to the experiences and voices of the child victims, and eight minors who have been identified as victims of human trafficking and their legal guardians were interviewed. We used a life history approach for the interviews, asking them to tell their stories freely, followed up with supplementary questions about their childhood, journey to Europe, the actual contexts for explorative relations and the way out of these relationships, their situation today and their aspirations for the future. The interviews were tape recorded and transcribed. We have followed the ethical guidelines for research on vulnerable groups.

The three scenarios described below are grounded on the analysis of the broad empirical data set. For each scenario, we have chosen one case, the one of Basir, Zena and Marco[6], to illustrate important aspects. The cases are representative of some main experiences in the three different contexts of explorative relations by transnational organized networks. [7]

Migrant minors exposed for exploration - three scenarios

The three scenarios we will describe below refer to different recruitment forms and ways of organizing trafficking. The first scenario describes unaccompanied asylum seekers exploited on their way to Europe. The second describes how minors may use unexpected opportunities to migrate, which turn out to be under other conditions than they had been told. The

---

[5] See the report from the Office for monitor and combat trafficking in persons (KOM) 2017 for an overview of the court cases.

[6] The names are pseudonyms to ensure the minors' anonymity.

[7] An additional scenario, including children from (Eastern) Europe, was identified when analyzing the cases. In these cases the child welfare service, without addressing the asylum system, followed up the cases, often in collaboration with the welfare authorities in the child's home country. We have not included this scenario into the analysis of trafficking in persons related to the asylum procedures.

third scenario describes exploitations of street-wise migrant minors crossing borders in Europe while searching for a better future. Each scenario is exemplified with an empirical case. The three scenarios expose different contexts for the explorative relations and forms of recruitments as well as how the exploitative networks are organized transnationally.

Scenario 1: Exploiting asylum seekers on their way to and through Europe

Asylum seekers who are migrating towards Europe make use of smugglers for limited legs or for the whole journey. The smugglers' networks consist of many actors and different services. Smugglers are operating both locally and as organized networks across borders to get profit or services from asylum seekers (see e.g. UNODC, 2014; European Commission, 2015). Numerous individuals and networks spot an opportunity for profit by acting as helpers, agents and intermediaries, or by otherwise participating in the chain that secures illegal transport. This includes connections with persons who use ad hoc opportunities for profit as well as well organized criminal networks of human trafficking (Europol, 2015). Although the networks and contacts of smuggling and trafficking overlap, it is also important to emphasize the difference between the two. The smugglers assist with the illegal crossing of international borders and the relationship with the smuggler ends when the travel destination is reached and the journey has been paid for. Trafficking in persons involves profit from a human by way of coercion and control over time.

We will present the story of Basir to inform about the exploitation networks which unaccompanied minors may be exposed to on their way to Europe. Basir is a 16-year-old Afghan boy who seeks asylum in Norway. In his initial interview with the Norwegian Immigration Authorities he described a long itinerary that spans more than a year. He told he had become an orphan and was cared for by some distant relatives. It was an untenable situation and when he eventually got an opportunity, he, like many young people in his situation do, joined someone to Iran, to earn some income.[8] He learned that the situation for young Afghans was very demanding, and after a while he continued to the West. He only managed to finance shorter legs of the journey and constantly had to make contact with new smugglers to negotiate services for the next leg when he had acquired sufficient funds for this. This system to get assistance from smugglers clearly provides a basis for commercial exploitation of migration. He has performed undeclared work in several places to pay for the journey. He hawked lighters and torches on the street and has been a shoe shiner. His earnings were used to pay another smuggler for the next part of the journey, forged paperwork and transport. In Istanbul, he first worked as a construction worker and then in a pizza

---

[8] See Monsutti 2005 on frequent migration from Afghanistan to Iran.

restaurant. He got the contacts through the smuggler. At first he received payment but after a while the employer refused to pay him. The smuggler and the restaurant owner said that his debts had increased because he had been there so long. They said he owed them €4,000 for food, clothing and travel. He decided to escape to Greece with the funds that he had hidden. After a few days in Athens, he learned from other refugees whom he met in a park that someone was looking for him. They had been shown a picture of him and asked whether they knew him. Basir felt unsafe and quickly headed for Germany.

During the journey he joined other young people and migrants in parks, in reception centers and in houses provided by employers. He was also offered a place to sleep by men he met in mosques, cafes and outdoor public areas. Several have demanded sex as payment for food and bed. In Germany he was offered to sell drugs, and for a short time he made a living from this, but he did not want to be part of the drug dealing and refused to continue. He experienced aggravated violence and threats from the drug dealers, but eventually managed to escape. He then came to Norway and applied for asylum there.

Basir's story relates to other stories of unaccompanied minors who were exploited on their way to Norway. However, uncovering exploitation during the young migrants' journey and in crowded migrant hubs is not the main focus during the asylum application process. When still feeling controlled and threatened by traffickers after arriving in Norway, the minors may ask for help from the staff in reception centers or the police. Most cases however are terminated because of their low priority or limited police resources to invest in the cases, and the minors' low credibility in the asylum proceedings (Tyldum et al., 2015). In Basir's case his age test claimed he was 18+, he then received a rejection on his application for asylum. After being refused help and after an investigation into his case at the local police station he thought his only option was to go to another European country to seek asylum there.

Scenario 2: Transported and controlled by transcontinental criminal networks

Some networks of exploitation depend on a far-reaching and well-coordinated organization. Human traffickers who operate as organized groups across continents will have the capacity to coordinate liaison and different functions in different countries. Such a well-organized organization can exploit many victims, and may secure significant profits, especially if they send people to operate in rich Western countries. Such networks can also survive as organizations over time by being flexible and adaptable to new places, to new forms of exploitation and to new conditions. They can, for example, change the route if stricter control is imposed at a stopover or the destination. Networks like this are known, for example, to exploit children as forced labour. In the UK, it is known that Chinese and Vietnamese children have been recruited to work in restaurants, horse farms, in the production of cannabis and as maids (Pearce et al., 2009; Boff, 2014; Connolly, 2014). In Norway too it has been revealed that young people from Asia were recruited as forced labour (Tyldum et al., 2015). Yet the best known are the organized networks for prostitution and sexual exploitation that span continents (Carling, 2005; Plambeck, 2014; Paaske, Plambeck and Skilbrei, 2016). A common factor in such organized networks is that they recruit young people with the promise of a good job in a western country. But when they arrive in Europe, it turns out that they are given completely different types of tasks and conditions than promised.

The opportunity to travel to Europe can be felt as overwhelming. When promised work and assistance with travel, they perceive it as an unprecedented opportunity that they have to seize. Some are aware that they may end up in prostitution while others are unprepared for this. One girl explains: '*I did not know it was like that in Europe. I thought everything was perfect.*' For a closer look at the conditions prior to recruitment and travel, Zana's story is illuminating. On arrival in Norway, Zana is 16 years old. She is from a war-torn African country and has lost both parents before the age of five. She grew up with an 'aunt' who took care of her. For a few years, she went to a primary school and she worked to help support them both. The situation in her home country was difficult and her relation with her aunt was ambivalent. On the one hand she perceived her aunt as a loving caregiver, on the other hand the aunt clearly expressed that the girl made her life difficult. At the age of 13 she was raped by a man who knew her aunt. Once when visiting friends of her aunt, she met a woman who told her that she can help her get a better life in Europe. She offered to get her a job in Europe, as well as organizing the journey. '*I did not know the job I would do, but she said that it would go very well, that it is a job that I would love.*' The woman played on Zana's own desire for a better future with the possibility of employment and education. At the same time Zana thought that underneath the encouragement there was also pressure: '*They said 'you have to'. First I met her and another man and then they said 'you have to, you must travel with us'. Then I was a little bit like… there was some pressure. Finally, I thought that, yes, I can just leave.*' Shortly after their first meeting they left. The woman traveled with her to Norway by plane. She obtained all necessary travel documents and passports. Zana was instructed to say that she was her daughter if questioned. The woman said that she herself was orphaned and had had a hard time earlier in life and in this way she created a relationship of trust and optimism for the journey ahead and for the future. Zana describes the woman she traveled to Norway with, as both kind and cruel. '*She said that she too had been alone and without parents, so she tried to understand me and to say things that made me trust her… She said 'you are very pretty, it is going to be fine'.*'

Similar situations appear in other stories that girls have told in cases that

58

have been investigated in Norway. The adults that Zana and other girls in the same situation meet, appear trustworthy by paying for the journey and identity papers, and later help them with shelter and new clothing. They gradually introduce the girls to new people in the criminal network and the girls grow uncertain about how coincidental the meetings and events are. In Zana's interview she appears as capable of taking action when she explains her reflections about what happened to her and her intentions about a better future. Similar to stories told by others, she perceived that the leaders could help her escape from home and thereby realise the dreams she had had since she was very young. She soon became responsible for her own life, which fostered survival strategies that turned her migration into a deliberate journey.

Zana's journey ended in Norway after a stopover in another European country. On arrival she was entrusted with an unknown white man who spoke English to her. He locked her up in an apartment, and she was exploited by customers who paid him. '*I was beaten and did things that I did not want to do.*' After a long period of being locked up, she managed to escape the apartment, received help from a woman she encountered in the street while exhausted and wearing thin clothing. The woman took her to the local police station, and Zana was eventually identified as a victim of human trafficking. She was placed in a foundation for child victims and granted asylum.

From Zana's story we learn that different people do the recruiting, the transporting and put the victims to 'work', and contact between them may pass through intermediaries. One would assume that the risk of being identified would be substantial when crossing several borders and passing through several points of control, but few transcontinental organized networks dealing in sexual exploitation have been identified. The ringleaders and exploiters in Norway have also not been tracked down. For example, in Zana's case, the specific location she was taken to or the people who exploited her have not been identified until now.

Scenario 3: 'On tour': The street as survival strategy

In young migrants' descriptions the third type of exploitation relationship we will discuss appears more complex and involves more ambivalence. This applies to both how these young migrants describe their contact with and the dependence on the people they encounter. The category consists of boys mainly from North Africa and the Middle East. Many were very young or they had lived 'on tour' for many years with an aspiration to earn money in Europe. They say that they come in contact with various 'helpers' through acquaintances and people they meet by chance. The helpers offered to provide places to stay, things they could sell, food, clothing or help to travel onwards. Common to these helpers and fixers was that their offer tended to have a flip side.

The stories of how they entered into an existence characterized by street life and bonds to 'helpers' who exploit their wandering life are numerous. A representative of a boy, Marco, who sought asylum in Norway, describes how after crossing the Mediterranean by boat to join his father in Spain, Marco was met ashore by criminal leaders who demanded that he paid for the journey: '*His father had no money, and he had no money, so they forced him to sell drugs for them. The network followed him all the way through Europe.*' Another representative explains how the boy he represented by chance had become part of a drug network in another Nordic country:

> He came in contact with a drug lord there. He had nowhere to go, so he joined this man at a large party they were having. There he was drugged and abused, raped and tied up when he tried to get away. Eventually he was sent as a courier in the streets, and he had to take drugs to other countries. He was equipped with a forged passport and raped several times by this huge guy who travelled around. Then he came to Norway and sought protection.

These two quotations show how the boys 'stumble' into drug networks as they try to make a living in Europe. Because of high unemployment in southern Europe in recent years the journey has often continued north in search of papers, work, status and money. They may have a residence permit in southern Europe, like Marco who was supposed to be reunited with his father, but most have no documents. They may have applied for asylum in a country without completing the process, or they may have received a refusal. The limited chance of residence in a European country affects the willingness to talk to authorities they encounter, for that reason they will be more and more dependent on ringleaders and therefore adjust their demands and conditions. This in contrast to the exploitative relationships described in the first scenario. When neither residence permit nor return is seen as a real solution or opportunity in the future, it greatly affects young people's space for maneuvering in both the present and the future.

The street life does not necessarily entail a life on the street. The boys form groups in part based on their country or region of origin. They often call each other 'brothers' or 'cousins' while the 'helpers' are called 'uncles'. They use networks to get in touch with various subcultures that exist in big cities. They can stay with acquaintances, friends or family. Others live in illegal camps, dilapidated buildings or whatever alternative they can find. Many learned at home how to survive on the street. Being streetwise is social capital to be used actively; they know how to obtain food and water, locate safe places for sleeping, and how to make themselves safe.[9]

As migrants without official papers the youngsters are easy to recruit for various types of illegal work. It remains unclear to the authorities how well

---

[9] See Sandberg & Pedersen (2006) for further definition and discussion of the notion 'street wise'.

the networks are organized and how coincidental contact is. The control mechanisms of executives, 'brothers' and ringleaders are part of the boys' understanding of their own room for maneuvering, and has become an integral part of their everyday life and self-understanding. They face multiple forms of exploitation and it stretches over a long period (CEOP et al., 2011; Pearce et al., 2013). Exploitation in the form of human trafficking can thus remain hidden. It is instead viewed as young hoodlums, a threat and public order problem.[10]

A further issue for the authorities is that their identities are perceived as 'blurred'. Many who disappear often reappear but registered under a new name, a different age or a new country of origin (Mikkelsen and Wagner, 2013). These identities are intended to prevent a return to their homeland and prevent information being sent back to the authorities. In addition, they are intended to ensure that the boys are not punished for crimes they have committed in other countries.

Implications of the scenarios

In what follows we will present a discussion along two lines – what the scenarios presented above add to our understanding of distinct recruitment forms and on criminal networks exploiting migrant children. The second theme is the recognition and assessment of exploitation in the asylum procedure.

Adaptable networks for exploitation

If we summarize the commonalities across the recruitment forms presented in the three scenarios we see, firstly, that the life situation before departure is characterized by a lack of close and protective family relations and an early assumption of responsibility for oneself. Life under such conditions makes children vulnerable. Vulnerability is therefore less of a characteristic of the children than the conditions under which they live, which can be characterized as risk-promoting. Migration is one of the few opportunities for action they see to get out of a difficult and vulnerable situation. Another common feature is that most accept what they consider to be an acceptable job offer, given the situation they are in, but that conditions change, that the 'helper' has another agenda, that new reciprocal favors are required, and that they are subjected to pressure, coercion and violence. Without knowledge of the language or a social network in the country they have arrived in, they see few alternatives other than accepting or fleeing.

---

[10] The boys often cross the borders between Denmark, Sweden and Norway. Swedish media have frequently published news and articles on the conditions for boys on the move (Mikkelsen and Wagner 2013).

We also see that recruitment in their home country and transportation is done by people with the same background, and often starting through acquaintances and overlapping communities. This was also documented by international reports on trafficking in person (UNODC, 2016, Europol, 2016). These can be the local contacts of a major international network that is controlled from elsewhere. Exploitation networks rely on local actors who take care of transit, bribery and document forgery. One of the hallmarks is therefore overlap between smuggling networks and human trafficking. Even within smaller regions we may find well-organized mafia-like operations that conduct their business over a long time and are similar to the transcontinental criminal networks described above. Even if the activity takes place within a region, it requires organizing, coordination and local knowledge to recruit local contacts and employees, as in described cases from Sudan, Egypt, Niger, Libya[11] (see e.g. Gatti, 2007; Human Rights Watch, 2014; Amnesty, 2013, 2017). The political management of transnational migration in Europe and beyond has turned trafficking in human beings into a high-profit crime with relatively limited risks (Europol, 2015).

The degree of transnational organization of crime is linked to the scale and persistence of the trade. We find that the greater the costs and the risks are, the greater the need to control is and the reciprocity required. Well-organized networks that span countries and continents also have the capacity to expose family members in their home country or elsewhere to threats and demands if the debt is not repaid. Just the knowledge that this could happen further enhances the burden and the control of the children.

When travelling in Europe, unaccompanied minor asylum seekers, like Basir, may face overlapping networks and experiences with the minors "on tours". Re-migrating after rejection of their application for citizenship increases the marginalization of vulnerable minors. Although the exploitation is well-known by practitioners and NGOs, there is still limited knowledge about exploitation networks in the countries the minors are transported to or passing through Europe. What we do know is that it can be people with the same country background as the victims, with another migrant background, or it may be local residents and well-integrated individuals and networks (UNODC, 2016; Europol, 2016). In addition, the global development of the internet has equipped human traffickers with a new tool yet this has only recently been given attention (European Commission, 2015). Another common feature in stories like Basir's and minors 'on tour' in Europe is that many minors are exposed to several types of exploitation, and that the terms of exploitation may change over time.

---

[11] Special cases are when smugglers work closely with traffickers as, for example, when they sell migrants to groups engaged in blackmail. Kidnapping of refugees with subsequent blackmailing of the family for ransom money is known particularly from the eastern Sahara track to Europe (Human Rights Watch, 2014; Amnesty, 2013).

Young boys in particular are used for several forms of theft, drug dealing and prostitution, but girls too may experience several forms of exploitation.

The three scenarios we have described above refer to different starting points and ways of organizing trafficking. There are, however, no clear dividing lines between them. They can be understood more as different capacities and forms of organization, and a characteristic is that the criminal networks constantly adapt to new conditions and opportunities. Organization and capacity may thus change over time, both by expansion, targeting new forms of exploitation, or when smaller players associate themselves with more professional criminal networks.

Insufficient examinations in the asylum procedure

Because trafficking implies movement, in our cases moving across borders, their migration status makes reintegration conditional. For most minors migration to Europe was the main cause for interacting with exploiters. When assessing the child's asylum application telling about experiences of exploitative relations, the credibility is at core. In Norway the Immigration authorities, police and child welfare services are dependent on each other to identify and confirm exploitative relations and to ensure reintegration. In our study we found that the minors do not necessary disclose sufficient details about the forms and contexts of exploitations in the initial asylum process. Their relationships to exploiters may have been ambivalent, because they are terrified, afraid of reprisals against family and simply because of their positions as minors. The case workers are not necessarily aware of new and complex forms of exploitation which may lead to insufficient examinations and interpretations of the information they get in the asylum interview. The age test which most minors undergo in the asylum process may also be another obstacle.

The Immigration Authorities and Child Welfare Services expect reunion with the family as the best option for children. However, in most cases, as we have seen, this is not an option, because they have no family or have escaped from dysfunctional family ties.

One difference between various recruitment methods concerns the options they have for obtaining legal residence status, and what they see as their way out of exploitation. For the young people, like Basir, who have travelled to Europe to seek asylum, their hopes of reintegration depend on their asylum application being granted. Meeting distrust and being scared of being traced, which was the reality that Basir met, gave him few options for a better future. Like many others he experienced this position as a difficult starting point for recovering from being a child victim (Crawley, 2007; Pearce et al., 2009; Tyldum et al., 2015). This may also have been the situation for Zana and those in her situation. However, Zana who reported her case directly at the local police station after escaping from the flat where she was sexually exploited, got higher credibility and was granted residence. Others who have been exploited through prostitution by similar trans-continental criminal networks have been returned to their home countries. Other girls wanted to return home (Paasche et al., 2016).

For the last scenario including the young boys 'on tour', the starting point for assessing the options for reintegration is that they are usually not granted residency, and for many the motivation to enter into a reintegration process is largely absent. This situation makes them more exposed to continued exploitation as they have little hope of a better future in a new country. The boys fear having to go back home and the shame that this entails. Return implies a loss of status; they have not succeeded with a new life in Europe (Madsen, Kjems and Jeppesen, 2014). The immigration authorities have also learned that it is difficult to return them to their home countries because they lack documents.[12] Although some ask for help, most minors on the move do not want to adjust to the conditions that Child Welfare Services offer. For many, the only option is to disappear from the authorities' control and systems. They consider this as a way to take control of their own future, hoping to make money as irregular migrants in Europe. They also dream of obtaining legal status and normalizing their life.

Those minors who received a residence permit have great expectations for their new life. However the process of reintegration may be challenging. Zana says her aspirations are high but this requires much effort:

"I've been working so hard! I went to a Norwegian course and then I went to elementary school and then I started high school. I plan to go on to college. I will have to see about that."

Another girl explains her worries after settling down like this:

Some days are very difficult because I am thinking about what had happened. Then I want to be alone, to cry and I feel a lot of pain. And I have a lot of questions in my head: Why did this happen to me, why are they doing things like that. I don't understand. I never get an answer. And there are so many questions that only I can find the answer to.

They need to obtain new skills and competence, and maneuver new landscapes without support from familiar networks and resources

Conclusion

In recent years, unaccompanied minors have represented a substantial proportion of migrants entering Europe. The three stories described above show how irregular migration creates conditions in which children are

---

[12] Swedish authorities have negotiated with Moroccan authorities to get a return agreement, but this has turned out to be difficult because the boys also lack Moroccan identity (Barnrättsbyrån, 2016).

particularly vulnerable to exploitation. The various forms of recruitment, exploitation and networks revealed, indicate how the organization of human trafficking intersects smugglers' networks and facilitation of illegal immigration, including document fraud. When trafficking of children intersects illegal transcontinental migration, state authorities face additional challenges in identifying the crime and meeting their obligations to reintegrate child victims. The complex conditions for trafficking increase the effort required by state actors in establishing whether the children's stories are credible and in identifying and investigating cases. Moreover, current policy and political interest in immigration control and security, in Norway, as in other European countries, lead to weakening of the principles and standards of the international human rights law. This contradict making the best interests of the child the decisive principle when assessing asylum cases and the child's need for support and reintegration.

The three scenarios described above stress the importance of awareness of young victims' perspective, their social background, aspirations and survival strategies. Insight into each child's life conditions pre-migration reveals how their former demanding terms of life and dysfunctional families make them vulnerable to exploitation in the first place. The cases also reveal how minors often become involved in multiple forms of exploitation. In previous studies on child trafficking the main focus has been on young girls exploited in the sex industry. However, the picture is more complex, including both boys and girls who have been exposed to a combination of exploitation including petty crime, drug dealing and sexual exploitation. The three cases also describe the limited conditions for returning minors to "their family", which usually does not exist or might even be involved in the trafficking.

Vulnerability applies not only during the journey to and through Europe, but also during re-migration within Europe. Living without documents, make the minors further vulnerable to exploitation. The challenge for immigration authorities and child welfare services is to find sustainable solutions for the child victims. Their unresolved residence status, which is the outcome for many minors, is one of the main challenges that creates uncertainty and limits how authorities can meet their obligations in international human rights instruments.

We have identified three main areas to strengthen policy against trafficking of migrant minors. Firstly, authorities need to gain more insight in the different conditions for recruitment and exploitation. They also need to make clear what is the child's own aspiration and expectations of reintegration. When assessing all the files of verified or possible victims of exploitation we find gender differences, as young girls in sexual exploitation are seen as more credible than boys describing more complex forms of exploitation. Too simplistic understanding of trafficking limits sufficient efforts to follow up victims. Improving the knowledge of the practitioners at the Immigrant Authorities, child welfare services, the police, legal guardians and NGOs is significant to ensure that the victims develop a trustworthy relationship with the authorities. On a political level it is important that nation states collaborate against this kind of exploitations (Gozdziak, 2010; Tyldum et al., 2015). A more child-sensitive, child-rights and migration-orientated approach is needed (Pearce, 2011; Bhabha, 2014). When including the migrant journey as a research field in migration studies, organized crime across national borders will be more evident. As several studies stress, efforts against human trafficking need to take transnational migration policy into consideration (see e.g. Gozdziak, 2010; Bhabha, 2014; O'Connell-Davidson, 2013; Connolly, 2014).

A second effort is to combat the intercontinental human trafficking both on the national state's migration policy level and on the regional (EU) and international levels. It is necessary to put enough resources into investigating the local links of international criminal networks operating in European countries which minors are transported to, like the one Zana was brought into and abused in. Further international collaboration is needed for the tangled problem of young undocumented migrants who are forced into organized crime across European borders (Vollebæk, 2015; Mai, 2010, see also European Commission, 2017). This includes multiple forms of exploitation of young undocumented migrants in Europe, like Basir and the minors "on tour" describe. This asks for increased international cooperation in policing, and, on a political level, increased cooperation between EU law enforcement agencies and sufficient interest and resources for addressing child trafficking.

The third effort indicates that both on national and international levels, legal instruments already in place have to be implemented. Meeting the requirements of the CRC may run counter to the political and public demand for restrictive immigration policies. Taking Norway as case, in recent years, immigration control has been tightened by setting aside key provisions of the CRC. Due to a political commitment to stricter immigration policy, the Norwegian Immigration Act was amended in 2015 and 2016 to include new regulations. One of the new regulations removed the reasonability assessment from the Section on granting asylum of the Immigration Act, making forced return to the country of origin more likely, also when the applicant will be facing internal displacement upon returning (Vevstad, 2017; Lidén, 2018). This has implications also in relation to another clause on the granting of temporary residence permission to unaccompanied minors aged 16 to 18 years. The removal of the reasonability assessment is assessed by experts on children's rights to be in conflict with the CRC.

CRC states that an administrative examination must include an overall assessment of the child's best interests. An asylum request cannot be refused simply on the grounds that the return is justifiable; rather, refusal must be based on relevant and sufficient weighty considerations (Sandberg, 2017). Instead the new regulations in the Norwegian Immigration Act have made the intention to ensure child-sensitive practices more ambiguous and less certain.

References

Amnesty (2013) *Egypt Sudan kidnap and trafficking refugees and asylum seekers must be stop.* https://www.amnesty.org/en/press-releases/2013/04/egypt-sudan-kidnap-and-trafficking-refugees-and-asylum-seekers-must-be-stop/

Barnrättsbyrån (2016). *De oönskade.* Rapport. Stockholm: Barnrättsbyrån

BenEzer, G. and Zetter, R. (2015). Searching for directions: Conceptual and methodological challenges in researching refugee journeys. *Journal of Refugee Studies.* Vol 28(3): 297–318.

Bhabha, J. (2014). *Child Migration and Human Rights in a Global Age.* Princeton: Princeton University Press

Boff, A. (2013). Shadow City. Exposing Human Trafficking in Everyday London. http://glaconservatives.co.uk/wp-content/uploads/2013/10/Shadow-City.pdf

Carling, J. (2005). *Fra Nigeria til Europa – Innvandring, menneskesmugling og menneskehandel.* Oslo: PRIO.

CEOP, Child Exploitation and Online Protection (2011). *'Hidden Children' the trafficking and exploitation of children within the home.* http://ceop.police.uk/Documents/ceopdocs/CEOP_Hidden_Children_report_2011.pdf

Connolly, H. (2014). "For a while out of orbit": listening to what unaccompanied asylum-seeking/refugee children in the UK say about their rights and experiences in private foster care. *Adoption and forstering.* Vol 38 (4):331-345

Crawley, H. (2007). *When is a child not a child? Asylum, age disputes and the process of age assessment.* London: ILPA Immigration Law Practitioners' Association

European Commission (2017). *The protection of children in Migration,* http://eur-lex.europa.eu/legal-content/EN/TXT/PDF/?uri=CELEX:52017DC0211&from=DE

European Commission, DG Migration and Home Affairs (2015). *A study on smuggling of migrants. Characteristics, responses and cooperation with third countries.* Final report. http://www.emn.lv/wp-content/uploads/study_on_smuggling_of_migrants_final_report_master_091115_final_pdf.pdf

Europol (2014), *Child trafficking for exploitation in forced criminal activities and forced begging,* Intelligence Notification, 16/2014. https://www.europol.europa.eu/publications-documents/child-trafficking-for-exploitation-in-forced-criminal-activities-and-forced-begging

Europol (2015). *The trafficking in human beings financial business model.* https://www.europol.europa.eu/publications-documents/trafficking-in-human-beings-financial-business-model

Europol (2016). *Trafficking in human beings in the EU. Situation report.* https://www.europol.europa.eu/publications-documents/trafficking-in-human-beings-in-eu

Franklin, A and Doyle L. (2013). *Still at risk. A review of support for trafficked children.* London: The Children's society. http://www.childrenssociety.org.uk/sites/default/files/tcs/still_at_risk_-_briefing_on_a_review_of_support_for_trafficked_children_2013.pdf

Frontex (2010). *Unaccompanied Minors in the Migrant Process.* http://frontex.europa.eu/assets/Attachments_News/unaccompanied_minors_public_5_dec.pdf

Gatti, F. (2007) Bilal. Viaggiare, lavorare, morire da clandestini. Roma: Rizzioli.

Gozdziak, E.M. (2010). In the best interest of the child: Perceptions, responses, and challenges in providing assistance to trafficked children in the United States. I M.O. Ensor og E.M Gozdziak (red.): Children and migration. At the crossroads of resilience and vulnerability.

Basingstoke: Palgrave Macmillan.

Hodge, D. (2014). Assisting Victims of Human Trafficking: Strategies fo Fascilitate Identification, Exit from Trafficking, and Restoring Wellness. Social Work. Vol 59 (2):111-118. http://www.childtrafficking.com/Docs/listening_to_victims_1007.pdf

Huijsmans R. and Baker, B. (2012). Child Trafficking: Worst Form of Child Labour, or Worst Approach to Young Migrants? Development and Change.43 (4):919-946.

Human Rights Watch (2014). Time for Egypt and Sudan to Rein in Traffickers. www.hrw.org/print/252751

Johnson-Hanks, J. (2002). On the limits of life stages in ethnography: Toward a theory of vital conjunctures. *American Anthropologist,* 104(3): 865–880.

KOM Koordiation unit for victims of human trafficking (2018). Report for the year 2017. https://www.politiet.no/globalassets/03-rad-og-forebygging/menneskehandel/kom-tilstandsrapport-2017.pdf

Korsby, T. M. (2008). *Maneuvering towards subjectivity. An anthropological analysis of young victims of human trafficking in Italy.* Master thesis I Antropologi. København: Universitetet I København

Lidén, H. Eide, K., Hidle, K. Nilsen, A., Wærdahl, R. (2013). *Levekår på mottak for enslige mindreårige asylsøkere.* ISF rapport 02:13. Oslo: ISF

Lidén, H. og C. Salvesen (2016). *«De sa du måtte.» Mindreåriges erfaringer med menneskehandel.* ISF-rapport. Oslo: Institutt for samfunnsforskning.

Lidén, H., Stang, E. G., Eide, K. (2017). The gap between legal protection, good intentions and political restrictions. Unaccompanied minors in Norway. In Special issue: Unaccompanied Minors in Europe – Part I. *Social work and society.* Vol.15:1 http://www.socwork.net/sws/article/view/497

Madsen, C., Kjems, H., Jeppesen O. (2014).*Uledsagede mindreårige asylsøkende med gadeorienteret adfærd.* Syv oplæg fra Røde Kors-konferencen, juni 2014 Frederiksberg: Røde Kors

Mai, N. (2010). Marginalized young (male) migrants in the European Union: caught between the desire for autonomy and the priorities of social protection. In Kanics, J., Senovilla Hernández D., Touzenis, K. (red.) *Migrating Alone:Unaccompanied and Separated Children's Migration to Europe.* UNESCO Publishing

Menjívar C. and Perreira, K.M. (2017). Undocumented and unaccompanied: children of migration in the European Union and the United States, *Journal of Ethnic and Migration Studies,* DOI: 10.1080/1369183X.2017.1404255

Mikkelsen, J. and Wagner, K. (2013). *De förlorade barnen. Ett reportage.* Stockholm: Natur och Kultur.

Monsutti, A. (2005). *War and migration. Social networks and economic strategies of the Hazaras of Afghanistan.* New York: Routledge.

Montgomery, H. (2011). Defining Child Trafficking and Child Prostitution: The case of Thailand. *Seattle Journal for Social Justice.* Vol 9. (2):775-810

O'Connell-Davidson, J. (2013). Telling tales: Child migrant and child trafficking. The Complicated story of children's migration. *Child abuse and neglect* vol. 11; 37-49.

Paasche, E, Plambech, S., Skilbrei, M-L. (2016). *Når migranter sendes hjem. Rapport om migranter fra Nigeria rummer elleve anbefalinger til myndighederne.* Rapport. Oslo: Universitetet i Oslo

Pearce, J. (2011).Working with Trafficked Children and Young People: Complexities in Practice. *British Journal of Social Work* (2011) 41:1424-1441

Pearce, J., Hynes, P., Bovarnick S. (2009). *Breaking the wall of silence: Practicitioners' Responses to Trafficked Children and Young People.* London, NSPCC

Pearce, J., P. Hynes, S. Bovarnick (2013). *Trafficked young people. Breaking the wall of silence.* Routledge. London and New York.

Plambech, S. (2014). Between "Victims" and Criminals": Rescue, Deprotation, and Everyday Violence Among Nigerian Migrants. *Social Politics* Vol. 21 (3):382-402

Rigby, P. & White B. (2015). Children's Narrative within a Multi-Centred, Dynamic Ecological Framework of Assessment and Planning of Child Trafficking. *British Journal of Social Work* 45: 34-51

Salvesen, C.H. (2014). *You don't see it until you believe it. Identification of children as victims of trafficking.*

A qualitative study of Norwegian public agency's effort to identify unaccompanied minors as victims of trafficking. Master thesis, Comparative Politics. Bergen: University of Bergen.

Sandberg, K. (2017). *Barnets beste i lovgivningen. Betenkning til barnevoldsutvalget.* [The best interests of the child in Norwegian legislation. Legal considerations for the Commission on Child abuse and violence]. https://www.regjeringen.no/contentassets/a44ef6e251cd 443396588483e97402ab/NO/SVED/3.pdf

Sandberg, S. and Pedersen W. (2006). *Gatekapital.* Oslo: Universitetsforlaget

SOCTA (2017). European Union (EU) Serious and Organised Crime Threat Assessment 2017 https://www.europol.europa.eu/activities-services/main-reports/european-union-serious-and-organised-crime-threat-assessment-2017

Sønsterudbråten, S. (2013). *Bistand og beskyttelse til ofre for menneskehandel. Tverretatlig samarbeid i Oslo og Bergen.* Oslo, Fafo.

Staver A. and Lidén, H. (2014). *Unaccompanied Minors in Norway: Policies, Practices and Data in 2014* ISF Rapport 2014:014. Oslo: Institutt for samfunnsforskning.

Surtees, R., Babovic, M., Bibo, G., Djordjević, M, Rusu, V., Tudorache, D. (2007). *Listening to Victims. Experiences of identification, return and assistance in South-Eastern Europe.* International Centre for Migration Policy Development

Tyldum, G., Lidén, H., Skilbrei, M-L., Dalseng, C.F. Kindt, K.T. (2015). *Ikke våre barn. Identifisering og oppfølging av ofre for menneskehandel i Norge.* FAFO-rapport 2015:45. Oslo: FAFO

UN United Nations (2000). Protocol to Prevent, Suppress and Punish Trafficking in Persons, Especially Women and Children, supplementing the United Nations Convention against Transnational Organized Crime. https://www.unodc.org/documents/middleeastand northafrica/organised-crime/united_nations_convention_against_ transnational_ organized_crime_and_the_protocols_thereto.pdf

UNHCR (2009). *Guidelines on international protection. Child asylum claims.*HCR/GIP/09/08

UNICEF (2017). *The Protection of Children in Migration.* 10th European Forum on the Right of the Child. 29 March 2017, p. 3.

UNICEF and Save the Children (2014). *National Study on children in street situation in Albania.* www.unicef.org/albania/NationalStudy-childen_in_street_situation-June2014.pdf

UNICEF Innocenti Research Center (2008). Child trafficking in Europa. A broad vision to put children first. Firenze: UNICEF Innocenti Research Center

UNODC United Nations Office on Drug and Crime (2014). *The socio-economic impact of human trafficking and migrant smuggling in Pakistan.* https://www.unodc.org/documents/ pakistan/ The_Socio-economic_impact_of_human_trafficking_and_migrant_smuggling _in_Pakistan_19_Feb_2015.pdf

UNODC United Nations Office on Drug and Crime (2016). Global Report on Trafficking in Persons, United Nations publication

Vacchiano, F. (2010). Bash n'ataq l-walidin ('to save my parents'): personal and social challenges of Moroccan unaccompanied children in Italy. In Kanics, J., D. Senovilla Hernández and K. Touzenis (eds.) *Migrating Alone: Unaccompanied and Separated Children's Migration to Europe.* UNESCO Publishing

Vevstad, V. (2017). *Hva er en flyktning* [What is a refugee?]. Oslo: Universitetsforlaget.

Vollebæk, L. R. (2015). Knuste drømmer. Mindreårige nordafrikanske migranter og gatelivets realiteter. In *Sommerfugl, fly! En artikkelsamling av barnevernspedagogor 2015.* pp. 107-115.

CHAPTER 4

BEST INTERESTS OF THE CHILD ASSESSMENTS TO FACILITATE DECISION-MAKING IN ASYLUM PROCEDURES

Carla van Os and Elianne Zijlstra[*]

Introduction

The Convention on the Rights of the Child (CRC) gives asylum-seeking children the right to an asylum decision that gives due weight to their best interests (UN 1989). This right follows from article 3, section 1, of the CRC:

> "In all actions concerning children, whether undertaken by public or private social welfare institutions, courts of law, administrative authorities or legislative bodies, the best interests of the child shall be a primary consideration."

Before a decision can be taken in a child's asylum procedure, an assessment has to be made of the child's best interests. The UN Committee on the Rights of the Child (UNCRC, 2013) has published guidelines for these assessments in General Comment No. 14 (hereafter: GC 14). These guidelines describe the relevant elements, i.e. the subjects and topics that should be part of the assessment, as well as the procedural safeguards that should be taken into account when determining the best interests of the child (GC 14, para. 46-47).

The concept of the best interests of the child was used in behavioural and legal science before the United Nations (UN) adopted the CRC in 1989. In 1973, for example, Goldstein, Freud and Solnit proposed guidelines for decision-makers regarding the best interests of the child, which could be used in the determination process of a child's placement in a foster family or alternative setting. The best interests of the child are still relevant in today's forensic mental health assessments involving children; assessments which are

---

[*] This chapter is based on Van Os (2018); Van Os et al. (2016, 2018a, 2018b, 2018c). The authors thank co-authors Erik J. Knorth, Wendy Post, and Margrite Kalverboer for their contributions to these studies.

customary within child protection law, family law, and juvenile justice to facilitate legal decision-making (Galatzer-Levy et al., 2009; Hoge, 2012; Koocher, 2006). Forensic mental health professionals formulate recommendations for legal decision-makers to optimally serve the best interests of the child (Bala & Duvall-Antonacopoulos, 2006).

However, within migration law, these forensic assessments of the best interests of the child are rarely carried out (Arnold et al., 2014; Kanics, 2018; Ottosson & Lundberg, 2013). In the international context, there is a growing awareness of the need for stricter implementation of the child's best interests in migration law (Arnold, 2018; Bhabha, 2014; Drywood, 2011; Pobjoy, 2015, 2017).

The same observation can be made in the Dutch context with regard to how the best interests of the child are served in legal procedures in child protection law, family law, and juvenile justice on the one hand, and migration law on the other hand (Van Os et al., 2018b). Within Dutch child protection law, family law and juvenile justice the best interests of the child principle, although to varying degrees, has been incorporated (Blaak et al., 2012). This self-evident positioning of the best interests of the child lacks in migration law (Beltman et al., 2016; Herweijer, 2017; Meijer, 2016; Van Os & Beltman, 2012). In the most recent Concluding Observations concerning the implementation of the CRC in the Netherlands the Committee is concerned (UNCRC, 2015, para. 52) about a:

> "… lack of adequate consideration for the best interests of the child in asylum cases and insufficient training of professionals dealing with asylum requests involving children."

Therefore, the Committee recommends (UNCRC, 2015, para. 53) the Dutch State to:

> "Ensure that best interests of the child is taken as a primary consideration in all asylum cases involving children and provide appropriate training to the professionals dealing with such cases."

This chapter focuses on unaccompanied children. In most cases, these children ask for asylum and therefore can be defined as asylum-seeking children in the legal sense. Legally, these children are called 'refugees' once their asylum claim has been accepted. We use the term 'refugee children' for children who seek protection in another country, whether on the grounds of being a refugee in the sense of the 1951 Refugee Convention or other forms of perceived danger in the home country (UN, 1951; UNHCR, 1994: 70).

Since 2004 professional assessors (hereafter: assessors) from the Study Centre for Children, Migration and Law at the University of Groningen perform behavioural Best Interests of the Child (BIC) assessments, which are used in legal migration procedures (Kalverboer et al., 2017; Kalverboer

& Zijlstra, 2006; Zijlstra, 2012). These BIC assessments provide evidence and child-rights based information to the migration authorities, which could be taken into account when the migration decision regarding a residence permit is made. The BIC assessments consist of various components such as a diagnostic interview and several instruments concerning children's mental health and development. The BIC assessments performed by the professionals of the Study Centre follow the guidelines of the Committee on the Rights of the Child on how to assess children's best interests (Kalverboer, 2014; UNCRC, 2013).

BIC assessments are practised in all stages of migration procedures, for example before a decision is taken or in the appeal phase in a court case in order to provide the decision-maker with information about the child's interests at stake, e.g. the protection needs, access to education and health care, family ties, and vulnerability of the child (Van Os et al., 2018b). The outcomes of the BIC assessment in migration procedures indicate which interests of the child should be considered when a decision about a future rearing environment is made and which decision in the migration procedure would serve best the interests of the child (Zijlstra, 2012). This could be a prolonged stay in the Netherlands, or a return to the country of origin.

The methodology for the BIC assessments has been adapted for the group of *recently arrived refugee children* (Van Os et al., 2018b). Assessing the best interests of an asylum-seeking child who has recently arrived in a host country might be difficult due to the insecure and unstable situation of recently arrived refugee children.

Firstly, refugee children have often experienced a relatively high number of stressful life events, which might cause trauma-related stress for some of them (Abdalla & Elklit, 2001; Fazel et al., 2012; Goldin et al., 2001; Jensen et al., 2013; Van Os et al., 2016; Vervliet et al., 2014b). In general, traumatic memories and stress may hamper a valid and reliable forensic mental health assessment with children (Bruck & Ceci, 2009; Eisen & Goodman, 1998; Klemfuss & Ceci, 2012). This is highly relevant in the context of evaluating the situation of refugee children. During the asylum procedure, refugee children have to provide a valid and reliable account of their (traumatic) memories to facilitate the decision-making process to determine their eligibility for refugee protection (UNHCR, 2014: 146).

Secondly, refugee children might hesitate to share details of their life stories due to previous experiences, a mistrust towards authorities, or a perceived self-interest in increasing their chances of receiving refugee protection (Chase, 2013; Colucci et al., 2015; Kohli, 2011; Ní Raghallaigh, 2014; Van Os et al., 2018a).

The adjustments of the BIC assessments for recently arrived refugee children regard the content and the procedure. Based on knowledge about the situation of refugee children who recently arrived in a host country, special attention is paid to stressful life events and trauma-related stress complaints by adding relevant instruments to the BIC assessment (Van Os et al., 2016). Based on a systematic review of what helps and what hampers refugee children's disclosure of their life stories, more non-verbal techniques are employed, more time is taken to build trust, and the assessors provide the refugee children with as much agency as possible during the BIC assessment (Van Os et al., 2018a).

This chapter aims to provide insight into the theoretical framework, the content and procedure of the BIC assessment (section 2) and illustrates how the BIC assessments are practised with the case study of Elsa, an unaccompanied recently arrived refugee child from Eritrea (section 3).

Theoretical framework, Procedure and Instruments of the BIC assessment

This section describes the theoretical framework, the procedure of the BIC assessment as well as the content, e.g. the instruments that are used for the assessment of the refugee child's best interests.

The theoretical framework of the BIC assessment

The theoretical framework of the BIC assessment is based on a comprehensive international social science literature review compiled in the Best Interests of the Child-Model (BIC-Model) which interprets the best interests of the child as the child's right to live in an environment that ensures his or her holistic development (UNCRC, 2013, GC 14, para. 42; Zijlstra, 2012). The model comprises 14 conditions for the child's development that together represent the child-rearing environment: (1) adequate physical care, (2) safe direct physical environment, (3) affective atmosphere, (4) supportive, flexible child-rearing structure, (5) adequate examples by parents or caretakers, (6) interest, (7) continuity in upbringing conditions, (8) safe wider physical environment, (9) respect, (10) social network, (11) education, (12) contact with peers, (13) adequate examples in society, (14) and stability in life circumstances. The first seven conditions are related to the family context, the last seven to the societal context (Kalverboer & Zijlstra, 2006). The fourteen conditions for the child's development are linked to the CRC and GC 14 (See Table 4.1). The BIC-Model identifies which rearing environment best guarantees the development of the child (Kalverboer & Zijlstra, 2006; Zijlstra, 2012) by taking into account the cumulative and interactive effects of stress factors on the child's development (Zijlstra, 2012).

Table 4.1. *The Best Interests of the Child-Model with references to the related Articles in the Convention on the Rights of the Child (CRC) and to the paragraphs of the General Comment No. 14 (GC 14) of the UN Committee on the Rights of the Child on the best interests of the child assessment and determination.*

Best Interests of the Child-Model	
Current situation	
Family	Society
1. Adequate physical care Adequate physical care refers to the care for the child's health and physical well-being by parents or care-providers. They offer the child a place to live, clothing to wear, enough food to eat and (some) personal belongings. There is a family income to provide for all this. In addition, the parents or care- providers are free of worries about providing for the child's physical well-being. CRC Art. 24, 26, 27. GC 14 para. 70, 71, 77, 78, 84.	*8. Safe wider physical environment* The neighbourhood the child grows up in is safe, as well as the society the child lives in. Criminality, (civil) wars, natural disasters, infectious diseases etc. do not threaten the development of the child. CRC Art. 33, 34, 35, 36, 37. GC 14 para. 70, 71, 73, 74, 77, 78, 84.
2. Safe direct physical environment A safe direct physical environment offers the child physical protection. This implies the absence of physical danger in the house or neighbourhood in which the child lives. There are no toxics or other threats in the house or neighbourhood. The child is not threatened by abuse of any kind. CRC Art. 19, 24. GC 14 para 61, 70, 71, 73, 74, 77, 78, 84.	*9. Respect* The needs, wishes, feelings and desires of the child are taken seriously by the child's environment and the society the child lives in. There is no discrimination because of background, race or religion. CRC Art. 2, 13, 14, 15, 16, 30, 37. GC 14 para. 56, 70, 73, 74, 79, 84.
3. Affective atmosphere An affective atmosphere implies that the parents or care-providers of the child offer the child emotional protection, support and understanding. There are bonds of attachment between the parent(s) or care-giver(s) and the child. There is a relationship of mutual affection. CRC Art. 19. GC 14 para. 70, 71, 72, 84.	*10. Social network* The child and his family have various sources of support in their environment upon which they can depend. CRC Art. 20, 37, 31. GC 14 para. 70, 73, 84.

Table 4.1. Continued.

Best Interests of the Child-Model	
Current situation	
Family	Society
4. Supportive, flexible childrearing structure A supportive, flexible childrearing structure encompasses several aspects like: enough daily routine in the child's life; encouragement, stimulation and instruction to the child and the requirement of realistic demands; rules, limits, instructions and insight into the arguments for these rules; control of the child's behaviour; enough space for the child's own wishes and thoughts, enough freedom to experiment and to negotiate on what is important to the child; no more responsibilities than the child is capable of handling. CRC Art. 13, 14. GC 14 para. 70. 71, 84.	*11. Education* The child receives a suitable education and has the opportunity to develop his personality and talents (e.g. sport or music). CRC Art. 17, 28, 29, 31. GC 14 para. 70, 73, 84.
5. Adequate example by parents The parents or care-providers offer the child the opportunity to incorporate their behaviour, values and cultural norms that are important, now and in the future. CRC Art. 10. GC 14 para. 70, 71, 84.	*12. Contact with peers* The child has opportunities to have contacts with other children in various situations suitable to his perception of the world and developmental age. CRC Art. 31. GC 14 para. 70, 73, 84.
6. Interest in the child The parents or care-providers show interest in the activities and interests of the child and in his perception of the world. CRC Art. 31. GC 14 para. 70, 71, 84.	*13. Adequate examples in society* The child is in contact with children and adults who are examples for current and future behaviour and who mediate the adaptation of important societal values and norms. CRC Art. 2, 8, 13, 14, 15. GC 14 para. 70, 73, 84.

Table 4.1. Continued.

Best Interests of the Child-Model	
Future and past	
Family	Society
7. Continuity in upbringing conditions, future perspective	*14. Stability in life circumstances, future perspective*
The parents or care-providers care for the child and bring the child up in a way that attachment bonds develop. Basic trust is to be continued by the availability of the parents or care-providers to the child. The child experiences a future perspective.	The environment in which the child is brought up does not change suddenly and unexpectedly. There is continuity in life circumstances. Significant changes are prepared for and made comprehendible for the child. Persons with whom the child can identify and sources of support are constantly available to the child, as well as the possibility of developing relationships by means of a common language. Society offers the child opportunities and a future perspective.
CRC Art. 5, 6, 9, 10, 18.	CRC Art. 6, 9, 10, 20.
GC 14 para. 65, 66, 67, 70, 72, 74, 84.	GC 14 para. 65, 70, 74, 84.

Procedure of the BIC assessment for recently arrived refugee children

In general, BIC assessments performed at the Study Centre are requested by lawyers and occasionally also by guardians, social workers, or children themselves. BIC assessments are not initiated by the immigration authorities. A diagnostic interview is held at a place and time chosen by the child or the family to provide them with as much agency as possible in deciding the logistic details of the assessment, like the time and place of the assessments. For the same reason, the unaccompanied children are offered the possibility to bring a person they trust to the interview if they think this will support them. Providing agency is known to be supportive in facilitating refugee children's disclosure of their life stories (Adams, 2009; Chase, 2010; Van Os et al., 2018a). Children and parents are interviewed together as well as separately. The interviews take three to four hours, including breaks. An interpreter is present. If the child or family think it is necessary, a follow-up interview is arranged. The interview is audiotaped if the child or parents give consent. For interviews that are recorded, a transcript is made. If no recording is made, notes are taken during the interview.

The assessors follow the general guidelines for interviewing of vulnerable children (Saywitz et al., 2011) and work on the basis of the best interests of the child principle. First, they try to make contact and build trust with the child as much as possible, adapting the language to the development and age of the child. They are aware of cultural dilemmas and loyalty problems that may hamper the child from speaking freely. Nevertheless, they never put pressure on the child but repeatedly reassure the child that his or her story is 'good', compliment the child and show a positive and respectful attitude (Zijlstra et al., 2013).

The assessors record their observations, analysis and conclusions on the best interests of the child in a diagnostic report of the BIC assessment (Zijlstra et al., 2013). Depending on the phase of the procedure, the lawyer sends the report to the migration authorities or the migration judge (Van Os et al., 2018b).

Content of the BIC assessment for recently arrived refugee children

File information record. Before a BIC assessment is scheduled, the lawyer or the guardian sends the legal file of the child or the family to the assessors of the Study Centre who will perform the BIC assessment. This file contains the reports of the interviews with the Immigration and Naturalization Service (IND) and, if available, medical or educational reports. For the unaccompanied children, the guardians provide a pedagogical journal with their own notes made after meetings with the child and reports from professionals who work with the child, like mentors in a reception centre or teachers. Furthermore, human rights reports about the country of origin from the United Nations, non-governmental organisations, or the Dutch Ministry of Foreign Affairs are extracted for relevant information. The file information is used to prepare the assessors for the diagnostic interview and to collect information needed to complete the Best Interests of the Child-Questionnaire (BIC-Q) on the quality of the child-rearing environment (see BIC-Q).

Diagnostic interview and observation with child and families. Two assessors from the Study Centre conduct a semi-structured interview with the child and with the parents of accompanied children, based on a topic-list of the 14 conditions for the child's development derived from the BIC-Model (Kalverboer & Zijlstra, 2006) (see also BIC-Q). The interview also focuses on the factors that influence the vulnerability and resilience of the child as well as on the child's views regarding the potential consequences of the authorities' decision (Sleijpen et al., 2016; Rutter, 1987; UNCRC, 2013, para. 75-76; 89-90; Zijlstra, 2012, pp. 52-53; Zijlstra et al., 2013). The assessors have no connections with the child and his or her family and lawyer. Observations are made regarding the child's behaviour, non-verbal communication, and interactions with the other people present at the interview. When parents are present, they too, are observed in the same manner, with a particular focus on their interactions with the child (Zijlstra et al., 2013).

Interviews with professionals. After the diagnostic interview, external professionals who work with the refugee children are interviewed about their observations regarding the child's development and well-being (UNCRC, 2013, para. 92; Van Os et al., 2018b; Zijlstra et al., 2013). These professionals are usually, mental health care professionals, teachers and, in the case of the unaccompanied children, mentors who work with the children at a reception centre and guardians. The information gathered during these interviews is used to complete the BIC-Q and to assess the vulnerability and resilience of the child.

Best Interests of the Child-Questionnaire (BIC-Q). The BIC-Q evaluates the child-rearing environment. It is based on the BIC-Model (Kalverboer & Zijlstra, 2006; Zijlstra, 2012). The BIC-Q includes 24 questions on those 14 conditions for development. For example, to evaluate condition 1 'adequate physical care,' the following question is included: Are the child's necessities of life provided for?[1] To qualify the fourteen conditions, the following answer categories are used: unsatisfactory (0), moderate (1), satisfactory (2), and good (3). The minimum total score on the BIC-Q is 0 (14 x 0), and the maximum total score is 42 (14 x 3) for each situation that has to be assessed. For recently arrived refugee children the quality of the rearing environment is assessed in the situation before departure and the expected situation after return. The assessors give a score of 'unknown' if insufficient information is available regarding the extent to which a condition for development is fulfilled. The assessors complete the BIC-Q after studying the written file information and the interviews with the child, parents and external professionals. The psychometric properties of the BIC-Q, the construct validity (i.e. the internal scale structure) of the BIC-Q proved to be good (Zevulun, 2017; Zijlstra, 2012; Zijlstra et al., 2013). There is a significant correlation between internalizing problems and the conditions for development in the BIC-Model (Zijlstra, 2012: 76-77). The inter- and intra-rater reliability of the BIC-Q is fair to good (kappa = .65 and .75, respectively) (Zijlstra et al., 2012). The BIC-Q has been evaluated as a culturally sensitive measure (Zevulun, 2017: 55; Zevulun et al., 2015).

Strengths and Difficulties Questionnaire (SDQ). The SDQ is a behavioural screening questionnaire with 25 questions that provides an indication of the child's strengths and problems. The SDQ is divided into the following scales: total problems, emotional problems, conduct problems, hyperactivity, peer problems and prosocial behaviour. The answer categories of the questions are: 'not true' (0), 'somewhat true' (1), and 'certainly true' (2). The maximum total score is 40, the sum of the four problem subscales. The outcomes of the SDQ scales are presented in four categories: 'average', 'slightly raised', 'high', and 'very high', with cut-off points based on research with UK

---

[1] See for a full text version of the BIC-Q for example: Zijlstra (2012, pp. 191-196): https://www.rug.nl/research/portal/files/2448739/Proefschrift_Elianne_Zijlstra_2012.pdf

children (Mullick & Goodman, 2001). The reliability and validity of the SDQ is satisfactory (Achenbach et al., 2008; Goodman, 1997; Goodman et al., 2003). The SDQ was used in research with refugee children in various cultural settings (Cartwright et al., 2015; Dalgaard et al., 2016; Zwi et al., 2017). The self-report version of the SDQ for 12- to 17-year-old children is used. Parents of accompanied children and guardians of unaccompanied children complete the parent version of the SDQ for children between 4 and 12 years old. The SDQ is available in over 80 languages, including most of the languages the children in the sample speak.

Stressful Life Events (SLE). The SLE is a checklist of 12 dichotomous (yes/no) questions about whether the refugee has experienced certain stressful life events, e.g., separations and losses within the family, experiencing or witnessing violence, and experiencing war or natural disasters and one open option for stressful life events that are not mentioned in the list. The maximum score is 13, summing the events that the child has experienced. The average number of stressful life events unaccompanied refugee children report is 6.5 (Bean et al., 2004a).

Reactions of Adolescent on Traumatic Stress (RATS). The RATS is a self-report questionnaire that includes 22 items on a 4-point scale ranging from 'not at all' (1) to 'very much' (4). The items are arranged along a total scale and three sub scales that reflect criteria for Post-Traumatic Stress Disorder (PTSD): intrusion, avoiding and hyper-arousal. The minimum RATS total score is 22; the maximum is 88 (Bean et al., 2004b).

The SLE and RATS are short self-report instruments for children above the age of 12 with good validity and reliability (Bean et al., 2004a, 2004b). For accompanied children below the age of 12, the assessors fill in the SLE based on the diagnostic interview with the parents. The instruments are culturally sensitive and available in the main languages of refugees. Together, the SLE and RATS give an indication of the level of traumatic stress refugee children have experienced (Bean, 2006: 110).

The best interests of Elsa

In this section, the case of Elsa[2] illustrates how the adjusted BIC assessment for recently arrived refugee children is performed.[3] We describe the process of the BIC assessment as well as the content; the results on various instruments: the BIC-Q, SDQ, SLE and RATS. We focus the description of the diagnostic interview with Elsa on the procedural methods the assessors practised to support Elsa in sharing important details about what happened to her. In the final part, we show how the results of the BIC

---

[2] To protect the privacy of the child, Elsa is not her real name. Personally identifiable details in her life story are not included.

[3] This case study has previous been published in Van Os et al. (2018b).

assessment were described in the assessment report.

Procedure of the BIC assessment for Elsa

Elsa is an unaccompanied Eritrean asylum seeker who came to the Netherlands at the age of 16. She failed to tell the reason for her leaving Eritrea in a coherent and consistent way. Therefore, the migration authorities did not believe she came from Eritrea and took a draft rejecting decision upon her asylum request. On behalf of Elsa, her lawyer had to present her views on the draft decision. At that moment, Elsa's guardian asked the Study Centre to conduct a diagnostic assessment to find out what happened to her, and why she was not able to tell about her life in Eritrea. The report could be sent to the IND as a professional analysis of the best interests of Elsa to sustain the views of the lawyer on the draft rejecting decision. The lawyer asked the IND to delay their final decision and wait for the diagnostic research report, to which they agreed. The assessors obtained the transcripts of the asylum hearings and the draft rejecting the decision of the IND and written information from the guardian about Elsa, which will be summarised below.

Like all refugees, Elsa was checked by a health professional to determine whether she was able to join the IND hearings. The health professional declared that Elsa could join the hearings with the IND, but she would need a break every 20 to 30 minutes due to her concentration problems. The first interview about her identity and travel route took from 9 a.m. till 4 p.m. After a few hours, it became obvious Elsa started to get nervous about the detailed questions about the landscape and school buildings in Eritrea, which she had difficulties in answering. She complained about a headache and told the interviewer from the IND she was confused and did not feel well.

During the second interview with the IND, which concerns the motivation for an asylum claim, again, most of the questioning was spent on discerning details about her neighbourhood, and school buildings. The part of the hearing questioning her reasons for fleeing Eritrea is relatively short. In summary, Elsa tells the interviewer that she fled Eritrea because she had a difficult life and she feared to be forced to join the army. During a first attempt to leave the country, she was arrested and brought to a prison where she was severely physically abused.

In the draft rejecting decision, the IND wrote that Elsa could not prove her identity and Eritrean nationality. Because she did not provide any documents that could prove her identity, the IND had to rely on the details given by Elsa about her home country in order to find out whether she was telling the truth about her Eritrean nationality. With satellite photos, the IND showed that Elsa was not accurate in her description of the school buildings and the landscape. Since the IND did not believe Elsa has the Eritrean nationality, they did not consider the motivations for asylum. About the stress complaints, the IND stated that Elsa only received headache painkillers and was not referred for medical treatment. Consequently, according to the IND, there is no reason to suggest that she is traumatised in a degree that could explain the incorrect details she provided in the hearings.

The guardian wrote in her reports that she feels very worried about Elsa, noting that Elsa was sad, had sleeping problems, cried a lot and generally gave the impression that she was stressed. The guardian believed that Elsa might have had more traumatic experiences than she had talked about. Elsa told the guardian that was difficult for her to remember things that happened before she fled.

After reading the file, one of the assessors called the guardian to guide her in preparing Elsa for the diagnostic interview. Considering the concentration problems and the difficulties Elsa faces in talking about her past, it was decided in advance to divide the interview over two meetings of maximum of two hours each. The assessor asked the guardian to speak with Elsa about how the interview setting could be as comfortable as possible, what was the best time for her to speak, what location she preferred and whether she thought it would be supportive for her to take someone she trusts with her to the interview. Elsa chose to come to the Study Centre at the University and bring her best friend with her because she was the only person 'who knows everything'. The friend accompanied her during a part of the migration journey. Elsa was very precise in indicating what she expected from the guardian during the interview. She asked her to travel together to and from the University, to be around, not to be present at the interview, 'just being available'. It was decided that during the interview, the guardian would wait in the diagnostician's workspace, located in the same building.

The assessors spend the first session almost completely on building trust with Elsa. By way of introducing themselves, the assessors made drawings of their houses and the people who live there. During the first meeting, the assessors concentrated on the current situation of Elsa and the happy period in her life – before the age of twelve. Elsa told the assessors about the people who lived in her neighbourhood, the games she played with her friends, the tradition of storytelling within the family, and the bonds she felt with her family members. Elsa seemed to leave the first session quite relaxed. Afterwards, the guardian confirmed that Elsa on the way back home told her, 'You have brought me to a good place'. The second meeting, one week after the first, Elsa stated at the beginning that she had been thinking a lot about the previous session and that she felt it would be important for her to talk about more difficult things, too. Two traumatic experiences, about which she could not talk before, became the central themes of the session. Both happened during the flight. Elsa could tell the assessors the smallest details about these events.

During the first meeting Elsa had told the assessors she misses her mother a lot. She could reach her mother by phone only occasionally. The interviewers asked Elsa if she thought it was a good idea to try to call her mother during the second meeting. She agreed to this plan. Calling Elsa's mother together seemed a way for Elsa to become closer with the assessors. She shared her fear of having to cry when she would speak with her mother. She refused the offer to provide her privacy during a part of the phone call and wanted the assessors to speak with her mother, too.

As far as necessary to assess her best interests, Elsa could share her life story with the assessors. Being asked why that was not possible for her at the asylum hearings, Elsa said:

> "They only asked me 13 things and I had 27 things to tell them. When I did not remember things well and replied with 'might so' or 'maybe' they said they needed clear answers. They wanted exact dates all the time. Every time I started to tell something I had to stop because they wanted more details. Then I forgot all the things I wanted to say. It was really hard, I could not do anything well."

Elsa explained who the important persons in her life were at various moments: in the receptions centre, in the Netherlands and in Eritrea. This was useful in being able to analyse whether the crucial persons in her life were and are able to guarantee her safety and development. Elsa drew her own house in Eritrea roughly. She took more time to draw the hill beside the house and stated – without being asked for an explanation – that this was an important place for her where she went whenever she had to think about something or felt sad. During the two meetings, the hill remained an important reference point. Whenever difficult topics were touched upon, Elsa went back to the hill in her thoughts, pointed at the hill and could tell what she thought while she was sitting there.

Elsa made schematic drawings of the two scenes that represent the central traumas she experienced during her migration journey. She used the drawings to point out who was standing where at the crucial moments. While talking about these stressful moments in her life, it seemed to help her to look at the drawing and point to the persons involved in the happenings. The assessors drew a lifeline together with Elsa, marking the crucial points in the story she told. They decided whether the crucial moments and periods were 'happy' or 'sad' by adding 'emoticons'. While working on the lifeline, Elsa decided that she needed to talk more about the period she was detained. She gave detailed information about the ill-treatment and the general living circumstances in the prison.

After the two sessions with Elsa, and with her agreement, the assessors held an interview by phone with three professionals working with Elsa. Elsa's guardian described her as being insecure and shy, while sometimes being enthusiastic and amicable. The guardian thinks Elsa has difficulty expressing her feelings. When the guardian tries to speak about emotions, Elsa's thoughts seem to drift away. According to the guardian, Elsa experiences a lot of stress due to the uncertainty about the outcome of the asylum procedure. Elsa looks beautiful and is happy when she gets compliments about her appearance. She is popular within her living group at the receptions centre and gets along with everyone well. The teacher described Elsa as often enthusiastic and alert at school. She has the impression that Elsa wants to look happy but that she hides her true feelings. The teacher expressed a strong feeling that Elsa is affected by traumatic experiences but did not want to speak with her about them. The teacher thinks Elsa is intelligent; her school results are good despite the fact that she faces difficulties with her concentration. Her work tempo is extremely low; sometimes she falls asleep during the lessons or does not attend the lessons at all. The mentor believes Elsa prefers to keep people she does not know at a distance. If she knows someone, Elsa becomes more open. The mentor observed that Elsa seems to feel sad often. She was heavily disturbed when her group mates had to move to another receptions centre. It was difficult for her to say farewell. The mentor is worried about the fact that Elsa withdraws from the group and thinks a lot on her own. She does not want to talk at these moments. However, at other times, she can be social and helpful.

Outcomes of the instruments

Elsa reported having experienced eight stressful life events (SLE). The average stressful life events unaccompanied refugee children report is 6.5. This high number of stressful events and the intensity of the traumatic experiences put Elsa at risk for developing psychological problems. Elsa had a 'very high' score on the RATS total scale, as well as on the three subscales: intrusion, avoiding and hyper-arousal. Elsa has nightmares very often. She feels very upset and sad when she has to think about her traumatic memories. Although she tries to avoid thinking about the experiences, Elsa does not succeed in doing so. She is hyper-aroused and jumps at loud or unexpected noises. She has intensive problems with her concentration. Elsa feels desperate about the future. The outcomes on the SLE and RATS taken together indicate that Elsa might suffer from PTSD.

Elsa filled in the self-report version of the SDQ. She had a 'very high' total score and the subscale on emotional symptoms, a 'slightly higher' score on attention/hyper-activity problems, a 'high score' on social problems and a 'near average' score on conduct problems and pro-social behaviour. The emotional and attention problems highlighted by the SDQ confirm the information found during the interview and other instruments. The social problems give a more ambiguous picture. Elsa feels insecure about what other children think about her despite being well-liked, according to others.

According to the scores on the BIC-Q, it was concluded that due to societal circumstances, Elsa's environment in Eritrea could not ensure her safety and development prior to her departure and the situation is expected to be the same or worse if she would be forced to return to Eritrea. Table 4.2 shows the scores on the BIC-Q.

Table 4.2. *Scores on the Best Interests of the Child-Questionnaire for Elsa*

Quality of the child-rearing environment	Before departure from Eritrea	Expected after return to Eritrea
Family		
1. Adequate physical care	Satisfactory	Satisfactory
2. Safe direct physical environment	Satisfactory	Satisfactory
3. Affective atmosphere	Good	Good
4. Supportive, flexible child-rearing structure	Satisfactory	Satisfactory
5. Adequate example set by parents	Unknown	Unknown
6. Interest	Unknown	Unknown
7. Continuity in the upbringing conditions, future perspective	Unsatisfactory	Unsatisfactory
Society		
8. Safe wider environment	Unsatisfactory	Unsatisfactory
9. Respect	Unsatisfactory	Unsatisfactory
10. Social network	Satisfactory	Unsatisfactory
11. Education	Unsatisfactory	Unsatisfactory
12. Contact with peers	Satisfactory	Moderate
13. Adequate example set in society	Unsatisfactory	Unsatisfactory
14. Stability in life circumstances, future perspective	Unsatisfactory	Unsatisfactory

Diagnostic report

In order to provide an insight into how the BIC assessment was described in Elsa's case, we include below some fragments of the concluding answers to the diagnostic questions as they were formulated in the report.

"Elsa is extremely vulnerable due to a number of factors (UNCRC, 2013, para 75-77). She has experienced a disproportionally high number of stressful life events and has mental health problems that are likely associated with PTSD. Elsa's reactions to the traumatic stress show she is struggling to cope with her experiences. This makes it remarkably difficult for Elsa to think about her flight and time in Eritrea and to tell others her story about this period. It is important that time and energy is spent on winning her confidence before she will be able to share details of her life story."

"Elsa has always been a reserved child, not willing to share her feelings with others. The traumatic experiences reinforced this personality trait and made it even more difficult for her to speak openly. Research with traumatised children confirms it is difficult for them to tell a story coherently, consistently and chronologically (Christianson, 1992). For Elsa, this is especially true. In general, traumatised children are known to be able to tell in detail on key events surrounding the trauma, but all details and events before and after the trauma may be difficult to retrieve or even lost. A focus on details, time and spatial concepts may disturb the child's ability to unlock a story (Saywitz et al., 2011). The assessors observed this confusing effect of talking about details not related to the central traumas with Elsa. Elsa's social behaviour is a factor that promotes her resilience. She has one very good friend who she fully trusts. Children at the reception centre and school like her to join activities. She is quite popular and even admired a bit."

"Elsa's parents offered her an affective atmosphere at home and could fulfil the basic conditions for development. However, her parents could not protect Elsa against the risks in Eritrean society, threatening her development. She experienced fear she would have to join the army. She was ill-treated in prison. Elsa's story about her experiences in prison is supported by various sources. The inhumane treatment of prisoners, the torture during interrogations and the underground prisons are a known phenomenon in Eritrea. The prisons are notorious for the ill-treatment of detainees (UN Human Rights Council, 2015: 11). Elsa had no stability in her life and no prospects in Eritrea. The conditions for development in the society were insufficiently fulfilled (UNCRC 2013, para. 71-73)."

"Elsa fears for her life if she has to return to Eritrea because she has fled the country twice (UNCRC 2013, para. 53-54). This fear is realistic given the current situation in Eritrea. There is a high risk of being detained again and to be forced to enter the military (European Asylum Support Office, 2015: 42). The army in Eritrea is known to be particularly unsafe for women. They are regularly exposed to rape and sexual abuse (UN Human Rights Council, 2015: 13). Political and social conditions in Eritrean society do not guarantee the safety and development of Elsa. Due to these circumstances, Elsa's family is not able to provide security and Elsa will not experience continuity and stability in living circumstances. The conditions for development will be insufficiently fulfilled if she has to return (UNCRC, 2013, para. 74). For Elsa's development, it is important that she is able to envision a future for herself, that she feels safe in her environment, and that she can build a life without life-threatening risks. Given the current situation in Eritrea, the expectation is that she will not be able to experience this in her country of origin (UNCRC, 2013, para. 82)."

Elsa's lawyer sent the report of the BIC assessment together with her views on the draft rejecting decision to the migration authorities. The IND withdrew the draft rejecting decision and took a favourable decision instead. Elsa was offered protection as a refugee in the Netherlands.

Discussion

This chapter aimed to provide an insight in the theoretical framework, content and procedure of BIC assessments for recently arrived refugee children and to illustrate the practice of the BIC assessments in the Netherlands with a case study. This chapter is based on a PhD study on diagnostic conditions that must be fulfilled for a valid and reliable Best Interests of the Child-assessment for recently arrived refugee children (Van Os, 2018). To the best of our knowledge, this systematic way of assessing the best interests of asylum-seeking children, following the guidelines of the UN Committee on the Rights of the Child (UNCRC, 2013), based on a scientific framework, for the purpose of decision-making in asylum procedures is not practised in other countries. The child's best interests are in general not taken into account in migration law, which violates their rights as laid down in the CRC (UNCRC, 2015).

It is important to take the mental health problems recently arrived refugee children face into consideration because they might impede the child's ability to share a valid and reliable account of why they are asking for international protection in a host country (Colucci et al., 2015; Kalverboer et al., 2009; Steel et al., 2004; UNHCR, 2014: 61-62). The knowledge of the refugee children's mental health upon arrival that is gathered with the BIC assessments is also relevant outside the context of migration law, for example for mental health professionals. Since it is known from literature that many refugee children still face mental health problems after spending more time in the host country, it is important that these problems are addressed in an early phase (Bean et al., 2007; Bronstein et al., 2012; Montgomery, 2008, 2011; Oppendal & Idsoe, 2012; Seglem et al, 2011; Vervliet et al., 2014a).

Taking time to listen to the child seems to be a prerequisite for a reliable assessment of the best interests of refugee children. Guardians and mentors of unaccompanied children could provide children with time and support to become again the owners of their life narratives (Van Nijnatten & Van Doorn, 2007). Taking time to reveal the child's life story requires migration authorities to delay asylum hearings until the child, and the professionals have assessed the child's views on his or her needs for protection. By providing the children time to feel safe and build trust, and by providing agency regarding the disclosure of their backgrounds and motives to leave the home country, we think that in the end migration authorities could benefit from more valid and reliable information provided by the children during the asylum procedure. This could lead to a more accurate assessment of the child's needs for protection or for a durable return to the county of origin.

Implications for research and practice

The expected quality of the child-rearing environment in the country of origin should the refugee child return is assessed *prospectively* in the BIC assessments. In line with the research of Zevulun et al. (2015, 2017), assessments in the *actual* return situation of children that participated in this study and whose refugee claim has been rejected would provide information on the accuracy of the initial prospective assessments of the quality of the child-rearing environment. Moreover, in general, further research on the situation of returned children is necessary in order to facilitate durable solutions for these children (Zevulun, 2017: 171-172).

Conducting research on how children's best interests can be assessed in order to facilitate decision-making in migration law is a bit like picking your way through a minefield. The focus of behavioural professionals and the UN Committee on the Rights of the Child on how to promote the healthy development of the child is not self-evident in the world of migration law, which has a focus on regulating migration (Brennan, 2016; Gornik et al., 2018). To support migration authorities in considering the best interests of asylum-seeking children, it seems to be necessary to include the best interests of the child as a legal ground for protection in national aliens acts. This could then be applied to asylum-seeking children who ask for and are in need of international protection but do not fulfil the requirements for being admitted as refugees (Drywood, 2011; McAdam, 2006; Pobjoy, 2015, 2017).

Migration authorities could consider the information provided in the BIC assessments in their decisions on the asylum request of children when these assessments are submitted by the children's lawyers. Moreover, migration authorities could take the initiative in asking behavioural experts to assess the best interests of asylum-seeking children, conform the guidelines of the UN Committee on the Rights of the Child (UNCRC, 2013, para. 94-95) and EU law (EU, 2013a, art 10, sec. 3d). Considering the specific expertise in forensic assessments for children, it would be advisable to examine whether behavioural experts working at child protection services could be involved to perform BIC assessments in migration law (Kalverboer et al., 2017). A joint General Comment of the UN Committee for the Protection of Migrant Workers and Members of their Families and the UN Committee on the Rights of the Child (2017) provides inspiration for this point of view. The Committees encourage giving the authorities responsible for the protection of children's rights, the lead in decisions affecting children in the context of various migration procedures, including asylum:

"The Committees encourage States parties to ensure that the authorities responsible for children's rights have a leading role, with clear decision-making power, on policies, practices and decisions that affect the rights of children in the context of international migration. Comprehensive child protection systems at the national and local levels should mainstream into their programs the situation of all children in the context of international migration, including in countries of origin, transit, destination and return (...)" (para. 14).

Finally, it would be interesting to elaborate this research to include other EU countries in order to find out whether it is feasible to provide the Common European Asylum System (CEAS) with a universal method for implementing the best interests of the child principle in their migration procedures. If so, the BIC assessment could be offered to migration authorities who have the 'possibility to seek advice, whenever necessary, from experts on particular issues, such as medical, cultural, religious, *child-related* or gender issues' based on the EU directive on common procedures for granting and withdrawing international protection (EU, 2013b, Art. 10, section 3, sub d). The call for scientific input to enhance children's rights in migration procedures has grown louder lately (Arnold, 2018; Bhabha, 2014; Drywood, 2011; Pobjoy, 2015, 2017; Yanghee, 2013). The momentum to implement the best interests of refugee children in migration law is mounting.

References

Abdalla, K., & Elklit, A. (2001). "A nationwide screening survey of refugee children from Kosovo". *Torture, 11* (2), 45-49.

Achenbach, M.T., Becker, A., Döpfner, M., Heiervang, E., Roessner, V., Steinhauzen, H.C., & Rothenberger, A. (2008). "Multicultural assessment of child an adolescent psychopathology with ASEBA and SDQ instruments: research findings, applications, and future directions". *Journal of Child Psychology and Psychiatry, 49*, 251-275. doi: 10.1111/j.1469-7610.2007.01867.x

Adams, M. (2009). "Stories of fracture and claim for belonging: young migrants' narratives of arrival in Britain". *Children's Geographies, 7* (2), 159-171. doi:10.1080/14733280902798878

Arnold, A. (2018). *Children's rights and refugee law. Conceptualising children within the Refugee Convention.* Oxon/New York: Routledge.

Arnold, S., Goeman, M., & Fournier, K. (2014). "The role of the guardian in determining the best interest of the separated child seeking asylum in Europe: A comparative analysis of systems of guardianship in Belgium, Ireland and the Netherlands". *European Journal of Migration and Law, 16* (4), 467-504. doi: 10.1163/15718166-12342066

Bala, N., & Duvall-Antonacopoulos, K. (2006). "The controversy over psychological evidence in family law cases." In: B. Brooks-Gordon, & M. Freeman (eds.) *Law and psychology* (Current legal issues, Vol. 9) (pp. 118-241). Oxford, UK: Oxford University Press.

Bhabha, J. (2014). *Child migration & human rights in a global age.* Princeton, New Jersey: Princeton

University Press.

Bean, T.M. (2006) *Assessing the psychological distress and mental health care needs of unaccompanied refugee minors in the Netherlands*. PhD Dissertation, Leiden University.

Bean, T., Eurelings-Bontekoe, E.H.M., Derluyn, I. and Spinhoven, P. (2004a). *Stressful Life Events. User's Manual*, Oegstgeest: Stichting Centrum '45.

Bean, T., Eurelings-Bontekoe, E.H.M., Derluyn, I. and Spinhoven, P. (2004b). *RATS User's Manual*, Oegstgeest: Stichting Centrum '45.

Bean, T. Eurelings-Bontekoe, E., & Spinhoven, P. (2007b). "Course and predictors of mental health of unaccompanied refugee minors in the Netherlands: One year follow-up." *Social Science & Medicine, 64* (6), 1204-1215. doi:10.1016/j.socscimed.2006.11.010

Beltman, D., Kalverboer, M., Zijlstra, E., van Os, C., & Zevulun, D. (2016). "The Legal Effect of Best-Interests-of-the-Child Reports in Judicial Migration Proceedings: A Qualitative Analysis of Five Cases". In: T. Liefaard, & J. Sloth-Nielsen (eds.) *The United Nations Convention on the Rights of the Child: Taking Stock after 25 Years and Looking Ahead* (pp. 655-680). Leiden/Boston: Brill/Nijhoff.

Blaak, M., Bruning, M., Eijgenraam, M. Kaandorp, M., & Meuwese, S. (eds.) (2012). *Handboek internationaal jeugdrecht [Handbook International Youth Law]*. Leiden, the Netherlands: Defence for Children.

Brennan, F. (2016). "Human rights and the national interest: The case study of asylum, migration, and national border protection". *Boston College International & Comparative Law Review, 39* (1), 47-88.

Bronstein, I., Montgomery, P., & Dobrowolski, S. (2012). "PTSD in asylum-seeking male adolescents from Afghanistan". Journal of Traumatic Stress, *25* (5), 551-557. doi:10.1002/jts.21740

Bruck, M., & Ceci, S. J. (2009). "Reliability of child witnesses' reports". In: J.L. Skeem, K.S. Douglas, & S.O. Lilienfeld (eds) *Psychological science in the courtroom. Consensus and controversy* (pp. 149- 262). New York: The Guilford Press.

Cartwright, K., El-Khani, A., Subryan, A., & Calam, R. (2015). "Establishing the feasibility of assessing the mental health of children displaced by the Syrian conflict". *Global Mental Health, 2*. doi:10.1017/gmh.2015.3

Chase, E. (2010). "Agency and Silence: Young people seeking asylum alone in the UK". *British Journal of Social Work, 40* (7), 2050-2068. doi:10.1093/bjsw/bcp103

Chase, E. (2013). "Security and subjective wellbeing: the experiences of unaccompanied young people seeking asylum in the UK". *Sociology of Health & Illness, 35* (6), 858-872.

Christianson, S. (1992). "Emotional stress and eyewitness memory: A critical review". *Psychological Bulletin, 112* (2), 284-309. doi:10.1037/0033-2909.112.2.284

Colucci, E., Minas, H., Szwarc, J., Guerra, C., & Paxton, G. (2015). "In or out? Barriers and facilitators to refugee-background young people accessing mental health services". *Transcultural Psychiatry, 0* (0) 1–25. doi: 10.1177/136346151557162

Dalgaard, N. T., Todd, B. K., Daniel, S. F., & Montgomery, E. (2016). "The transmission of trauma in refugee families: Associations between intra-family trauma communication style, children's attachment security and psychosocial adjustment". *Attachment & Human Development, 18* (1), 69-89. doi:10.1080/14616734.2015.1113305

Drywood, E. (2011). "'Child-proofing' EU law and policy: interrogating the law-making processes behind European asylum and immigration provision". *International Journal of Children's Rights, 19* (3), 405-428. doi:10.1163/157181811X584541

Eisen, M. L., & Goodman, G. S. (1998). "Trauma, memory, and suggestibility in children". *Development and Psychopathology, 10* (4), 717-738. doi:10.1017/S0954579498001837

EU (2013a). *Regulation (EU) No 604/2013 of the European Parliament and of the Council of 26 June 2013 establishing the criteria and mechanisms for determining the Member State responsible for examining an application for international protection lodged in one of the Member States by a third-country national or a stateless person (recast).* Retrieved from: http://eur-lex.europa.eu/legal-content/EN/TXT/HTML/?uri=CELEX:32013R0604&from=EN

EU (2013b). *Directive 2013/32/EU of the European parliament and of the Council of 26 June 2013 on common procedures for granting and withdrawing international protection* (recast). Retrieved from:

http://eur-lex.europa.eu/legal-content/EN/TXT/HTML/?uri=CELEX: 32013L0032&from=nl

European Asylum Support Office (2015). *Eritrea Country Focus*. Retrieved from: https://coi.easo.europa.eu/administration/easo/PLib/EASO-Eritrea-CountryFocus_EN_May2015.pdf

Fazel, M., Reed, R. V., Panter-Brick, C., & Stein, A. (2012). "Mental health of displaced and refugee children resettled in high-income countries: Risk and protective factors". *The Lancet, 379* (9812), 266-282. doi:10.1016/S0140-6736(11)60051-2

Galatzer-Levy, R. M., Gould, J., & Martindale, D. (2009). "From empirical findings to custody evaluations". In: R. M. Galatzer-Levy, L. Kraus, & J. Galatzer-Levy (eds.) *The scientific basis of child custody decisions* (2nd ed.) (pp. 1-47). Hoboken, NJ: Wiley.

Goldin, S., Levin, L., Persson, L.A., & Hägglof, B. (2001). "Stories of pre-war, war and exile: Bosnian refugee children in Sweden". *Medicine, Conflict, and Survival, 17* (1), 25-47.

Goodman, R. (1997). "The Strengths and Difficulties Questionnaire: A research note". *Journal of Child Psychology and Psychiatry*, 38: 581-586.

Goodman, R., Ford, T., Simmons, H., Gatward, R., & Meltzer, H. (2003). "Using the strengths and difficulties questionnaire (SDQ) to screen for child psychiatric disorders in a community sample". *International Review of Psychiatry, 15* (1-2), 166-172. doi:10.1080/0954026021000046128

Goldstein, J., Freud, A., & Solnit, A.J. (1973). *Beyond the best interests of the child*. New York: The Free Press.

Gornik, B., Sedmak, M., & Sauer, B. (2018). "Unaccompanied minor migrants in Europe: Between compassion and repression". In: M. Sedmak, B. Sauer, & B. Gornik, (eds.) *Unaccompanied children in European migration and asylum practices: In whose best interests?* (pp. 1-15). Abingdon, UK: Routledge.

Herweijer, M. (2017). "In de kinderschoenen. Naar een volwassen benadering van het belang van het kind in het vreemdelingenrecht" [At an infant level. Towards a mature approach to the best interests of the child in migration law]. *Asiel- en Migrantenrecht, 8* (8), 341-345.

Hoge, R. D. (2012). "Assessment in juvenile justice systems: An overview". In: E. Grigorenko (ed.) *Handbook of juvenile forensic psychology and psychiatry* (pp. 157-166). New York: Springer.

Jensen, T.K., Fjermestad, K.W., Granly, L., & Wilhelmsen, N.H. (2013). "Stressful life experiences and mental health problems among unaccompanied asylum-seeking children". *Clinical Child Psychology and Psychiatry, 20* (1), 106-116. doi:10.1177/1359104513499356

Kalverboer, M.E. (2014). *The best interests of the child in migration law: significance and implications in terms of child development and child rearing*. Amsterdam: SWP Publishers.

Kalverboer, M., Beltman, D., Van Os, C., & Zijlstra, E. (2017). "The Best Interests of the Child in Cases of Migration: Assessing and Determining the Best Interests of the Child in Migration Procedures". *International Journal of Children's Rights, 25* (1), 114-139. doi:10.1163/15718182-02501005

Kalverboer, M.E., & Zijlstra, A.E. (2006). *Het belang van het kind in het Nederlands recht: Voorwaarden voor ontwikkeling vanuit een pedagogisch perspectief [The interests of the child in Dutch law: Conditions of child development from a pedagogigal perspective]*. Amsterdam: SWP Publishers.

Kalverboer, M.E., Zijlstra, A.E., & Knorth, E.J. (2009). "The developmental consequences for asylum-seeking children living with the prospect for five years or more of enforced return to their home country". *European Journal of Migration and Law, 11* (1), 41-67. doi:10.1163/157181609X410584.

Kanics (2018). "The best interests of unaccompanied and separated children. A normative framework based on the CRC". In: M. Sedmak, B. Sauer, & B. Gornik, (eds.) *Unaccompanied children in European migration and asylum practices: In whose best interests? (*pp. 37-58). Abingdon, UK / New York, US: Routledge).

Klemfuss, J. Z., & Ceci, S. J. (2012). "Legal and psychological perspectives on children's competence to testify in court". *Developmental Review, 32* (3), 268-286.

Kohli, R. (2011). "Working to ensure safety, belonging and success for unaccompanied asylum-seeking children". *Child Abuse Review, 20* (5), 311-323.

Koocher, G. P. (2006). "Ethical issues in forensic health assessment of children and adolescents". In: S. N. Sparta & G. P. Koocher (eds.) *Forensic mental health assessment of children and adolescents* (pp. 46-63). Oxford, UK: Oxford University Press.

McAdam, J. (2006). "Seeking asylum under the Convention on the Rights of the Child: A case for complementary protection". *International Journal of Children's Rights, 14* (3), 251-274. doi:10.1163/157181806778458130

Meijer, M. (2016). "Belang van het kind te vaak genegeerd. Kinderbeschermingsmaatregelen en vreemdelingenrecht" [The best interests of the child too often ignored. Child protection measures and migration law]. *Asiel- en Migrantenrecht, 7* (2), 68-73.

Montgomery, E. (2008). "Long-term effects of organized violence on young Middle Eastern refugees' mental health". *Social Science & Medicine, 67* (10), 1596-1603.

Montgomery, E. (2011). "Trauma, exile and mental health in young refugees". *Acta Psychiatrica Scandinavica, 124,* 1-46.

Montgomery, E., & Foldspang, A. (2001). "Traumatic experience and sleep disturbance in refugee children from the Middle East". *European Journal of Public Health, 11* (1), 18-22.

Mullick, M. I., & Goodman, R. (2001). "Questionnaire screening for mental health problems in Bangladeshi children: a preliminary study". *Social Psychiatry & Psychiatric Epidemiology, 36* (2), 94.

Ní Raghallaigh, M. (2014). "The Causes of mistrust amongst asylum seekers and refugees: Insights from research with unaccompanied asylum-seeking minors living in the Republic of Ireland". *Journal of Refugee Studies, 27* (1), 82-100.

Oppedal, B., & Idsoe, T. (2012). "Conduct Problems and Depression among Unaccompanied Refugees: The Association with Pre-Migration Trauma and Acculturation". *Anales de Psicologi, 28* (3), 683-694.

Ottosson, L., & Lundberg, A. (2013). "'People out of place'? Advocates' negotiations on children's participation in the asylum application process in Sweden". *International Journal of Law, Policy & the Family, 27* (2), 266-287. doi: 10.1093/lawfam/ebt003

Pobjoy, J. M. (2015). "The best interests of the child principle as an independent source of international protection". *International & Comparative Law Quarterly, 64* (2), 327-363. doi:10.1017/S0020589315000044

Pobjoy, J.M. (2017). *The child in International Refugee Law.* Cambridge, UK: Cambridge University Press.

Rutter, M. (1987). "Psychosocial resilience and protective mechanisms." *American Journal of Orthopsychiatry, 57*(3), 316-331. doi:10.1111/j.1939-0025.1987.tb03541.x.

Saywitz, K.J., Lyon, T. D., & Goodman, G.S. (2011). "Interviewing children". In: J.E.B. Myers (ed.) *The APSAC Handbook on Child Maltreatment* (pp. 337-360). Thousand Oaks, CA, US: SAGE Publications.

Seglem, K. B., Oppedal, B., & Raeder, S. (2011). "Predictors of depressive symptoms among resettled unaccompanied refugee minors". *Scandinavian Journal of Psychology, 52* (5), 457-464. doi:10.1111/j.1467-9450.2011.00883.x

Sleijpen, M., Boeije, H. R., Kleber, R. J., & Mooren, T. (2016). "Between power and powerlessness: a meta-ethnography of sources of resilience in young refugees". *Ethnicity & Health, 21* (2), 158-180. doi:10.1080/13557858.2015.1044946

Steel, Z., Frommer, N., & Silove, D. (2004). "Part I- the mental health impacts of migration: the law and its effects failing to understand: refugee determination and the traumatized applicant". *International Journal of Law and Psychiatry, 27* (6), 511-528. doi:10.1016/j.ijlp.2004.08.006

UN (1951). *Convention relating to the Status of Refugees.* Retrieved from http://www.ohchr.org/EN/ProfessionalInterest/Pages/StatusOfRefugees.aspx.

UN (1989). *Convention on the Rights of the Child.* Retrieved from http://www.ohchr.org/en/professionalinterest/pages/crc.aspx.

UN Committee on the protection of the rights of all migrant workers and members of their families and UN Committee on the Rights of the Child (2017). *Joint general comment No. 3 (2017) on the general principles regarding the human rights of children in the context of international migration.* CMW/C/GC/3-CRC/C/GC/22. Retrieved from http://tbinternet.ohchr.org/

Treaties/CMW/Shared%20Documents/1_Global/CMW_C_GC_3-CRC_C_GC_22_8361_E.pdf.

UN Human Rights Council (2015) *Report of detailed findings of the commission of inquiry on human rights in Eritrea.* A/HRC/29/42. Retrieved from https://www.ohchr.org/Documents/HRBodies/HRCouncil/CoIEritrea/A_HRC_29_CRP-1.pdf

UNCRC (2013). *General comment No. 14 (2013) The right of the child to have his or her best interests taken as a primary consideration (art.3, para 1).* CRC/C/GC/14. Retrieved from http://www2.ohchr.org/English/bodies/crc/docs/GC/CRC_C_GC_14_ENG.pdf

UNCRC (2015). *Concluding observations on the fourth periodic report of the Netherlands.* CRC/C/NLD/CO/4. Retrieved from http://tbinternet.ohchr.org/Treaties/CRC/Shared%20Documents/NLD/INT_CRC_COC_NLD_20805_E.pdf.

UNHCR (1994). *Refugee Children: Guidelines on Protection and Care.* Geneva: UNHCR. Retrieved from http://www.unhcr.org/3b84c6c67.html.

UNHCR (2014). *The heart of the matter. Assessing credibility when children apply for asylum in the European Union.* Brussels: United Nations High Commissioner for Refugees. Retrieved from: http://www.refworld.org/docid/55014f434.html.

Van Nijnatten, C., & Van Doorn, F. (2007). "Creating communication. Self-examination as a therapeutic method for children". *Journal of Social Work Practice, 21* (3), 337-346. doi:10.1080/02650530701553641.

Van Os, E.C.C. (2018). *Best Interests of the Child-Assessments for recently arrived refugee children: Behavioural and children's rights perspectives on decision-making in migration law.* University of Groningen, the Netherlands (PhD dissertation).

Van Os, C., & Beltman, D. (2012). "Kinderrechten in het migratierecht" [Children's rights in migration law]. In: M. Blaak, M. Bruning, M. Eijgenraam, M. Kaandorp, & S. Meuwese (eds.) *Handboek internationaal jeugdrecht* [*Handbook on International Youth Law*] (pp. 647-818). Leiden, the Netherlands: Defence for Children.

Van Os, E. C. C., Kalverboer, M. E., Zijlstra, A. E., Post, W. J., & Knorth, E. J. (2016). "Knowledge of the unknown child: A systematic review on the elements of the Best Interests of the Child Assessment for recently arrived refugee children". *Clinical Child and Family Psychology Review.* doi: 10.1007/s10567-016-0209-y

Van Os, E. C. C., Zijlstra, A.E., Knorth, E. J., Post, W.J., & Kalverboer, M.E. (2018a). "Finding keys: A systematic review of barriers and facilitators for refugee children's disclosure of their life stories". *Trauma, Violence & Abuse,* 1524838018757748. doi: 10.1177/1524838018757748

Van Os, C., Zijlstra, E., Knorth, E. J., Post, W. & Kalverboer, M. (2018b). "Methodology for the assessment of the best interests of the child for recently arrived unaccompanied refugee minors". In: M. Sedmak, B. Sauer, & B. Gornik, (eds.) *Unaccompanied children in European migration and asylum practices: In whose best interests? (*pp. 59-85). Abingdon, UK / New York, US: Routledge, Taylor and Francis group, (Routledge research in asylum, migration and refugee law).

Van Os, E. C. C., Zijlstra, A. E., Knorth, E. J., Post, W. J., & Kalverboer, M. E. (2018c). "Recently arrived refugee children: The quality and outcomes of Best Interests of the Child assessments". *International Journal of Law and Psychiatry, 59,* 20–30. doi:10.1016/j.ijlp.2018.05.005

Vervliet, M., Lammertyn, J., Broekaert, E.,& Derluyn, I. (2014a). "Longitudinal follow-up of the mental health of unaccompanied refugee minors". *European Child and Adolescent Psychiatry, 23* (5), 337-346. doi:10.1007/s00787-013-0463-1

Vervliet, M., Meyer Demott, M. A., Jakobsen, M., Broekaert, E., Heir, T., & Derluyn, I. (2014b). "The mental health of unaccompanied refugee minors on arrival in the host country". *Scandinavian Journal of Psychology, 55* (1), 33-37. doi:10.1007/s00787-013-0463-1

Yanghee, L. (2013). "Address: Creating new futures for all children: The promise of international human rights law". *Australian International Law Journal, 20* (1), 3-16.

Zevulun, D. (2017). *Repatriation and the Best Interests of the Child. The rearing environment and wellbeing of migrant children after return to Kosovo and Albania.* University of Groningen, the Netherlands (PhD dissertation).

Zevulun, D., Kalverboer, M. E., Zijlstra, A. E., Post, W. J., & Knorth, E. J. (2015). "Returned Migrant Children in Kosovo and Albania". *Cross-Cultural Research, 49* (5), 489-521. doi:10.1177/1069397115608173

Zevulun, D., Post, W.P., Zijlstra, A.E., Kalverboer, M.E., & Knorth, E.J. (2017). "Migrant and asylum-seeker children returned to Kosovo and Albania: predictive factors for social–emotional wellbeing after return". *Journal of Ethnic and Migration Studies,* doi: 10.1080/1369183X.2017.1391076

Zijlstra, A.E. (2012). *In the best interest of the child? A study into a decision-support tool validating asylum-seeking children's rights from a behavioural scientific perspective.* University of Groningen, the Netherlands (PhD dissertation).

Zijlstra, A.E., Kalverboer, M.E., Post, W.J., Ten Brummelaar, M.D.C. & Knorth, E.J. (2013). "Could the BIC-Q be a decision support tool to predict the development of asylum-seeking children?". *International Journal of Law and Psychiatry, 36,* 129-135. doi:10.1016/j.ijlp.2013.01.005

Zijlstra, A. E., Kalverboer, M. E., Post, W. J., Knorth, E. J., & Brummelaar, M. T. (2012). "The quality of the childrearing environment of refugee or asylum-seeking children and the Best Interest of the Child: Reliability and validity of the BIC-Q". *Behavioral Sciences & The Law, 30* (6), 841-855. doi:10.1002/bsl.1998

Zwi, K., Rungan, S., Woolfenden, S., Woodland, L., Palasanthiran, P., & Williams, K. (2017). "Refugee children and their health, development and well-being over the first year of settlement: A longitudinal study". *Journal of Paediatrics & Child Health, 53* (9), 841-849. doi:10.1111/jpc.13551.

CHAPTER 5

NAVIGATING THE IMMIGRATION PROCESS ALONE: UNACCOMPANIED MINORS EXPERIENCES IN THE UNITED STATES

Jennica Larrison and Mariglynn Edlins

Introduction

Unaccompanied minors (UMs) in the United States first garnered national attention in 2014. In the summer of 2014, an unprecedented number of UMs (68,541) entered the United States from the US-Mexico border. While the number of youth crossing appeared alarming in itself—the rate was a 77% increase over the previous year—a significant shift in origin of UMs also dramatically affected the way in which the Government would respond. The majority of unaccompanied youth previously crossing the border were from Mexico, however by 2014 the majority were from Guatemala, El Salvador, and Honduras (Department of Homeland Security, 2014). Youth continue to cross and in 2018, the United States apprehended 50,036 UMs, with 76% from Guatemala, El Salvador, and Honduras.

The relatively consistent large number of unaccompanied youth entering the US since 2014 raises questions regarding what happens to these UMs once they enter the US. What are the rules, regulations, and practices of the US in addressing UMs entering the United States at its Southern border: What is the process for unaccompanied minors once they enter the United States? What interactions take place between public servants and unaccompanied minors? Where do UMs ultimately reside within the United States?

In seeking answers to these questions, we aim to add to current thinking about how these youth experience the migration process once in the US, and how interactions with public servants implementing public policy affect this experience. This chapter relies on qualitative research with UMs currently residing in the US to better understand how the migration process affects unaccompanied minors once in the United States. The chapter will first examine who these youth are, the policies that guide their treatment, and the process they must navigate. The chapter will then draw upon qualitative data to analyze the experiences of youth in light of their migration process.

Who are Unaccompanied Minors in the United States and Why do they Migrate

According to the United States Government, to qualify as an unaccompanied minor, an individual must meet the following criteria: 1) be under 18 years of age; 2) be a citizen of a country other than the United States; 3) have entered into the US illegally; and 4) come without a parent or guardian. Over the past 10 years, the majority of unaccompanied minors originated from four countries: Mexico, Guatemala, Honduras, and El Salvador. Prior to 2014, the majority of unaccompanied minors were from Mexico. However, as noted above, this shifted dramatically in the years following. By 2018, 92 percent of unaccompanied minors in the United States were from the northern triangle of Central America: El Salvador, Honduras, or Guatemala, with only 3 percent originating from Mexico (Figure 5.1). Similar to other regions in the world, the majority of unaccompanied minors in the US are between the ages of 13 and 17, with boys traveling more frequently than girls, 66 percent: 34 percent in 2014, and 71 percent: 29 percent in 2018 (Office of Refugee Resettlement, 2018).

Figure 5.1. Unaccompanied Children Apprehended at the Southwest Border by Country of Origin, FY2008-FY2018

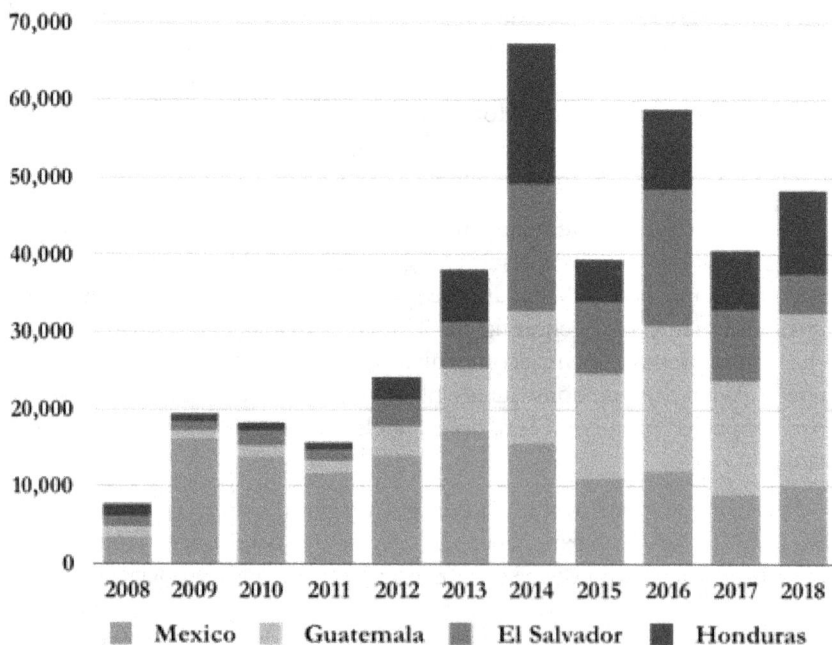

While a variety of factors influence a youth's reason for migrating, in the case of UMs in the US, violence, poverty, and family reunification are the most common factors affecting the decision to leave (Menjívar & Perreira, 2017). Violent civil wars led to destabilization in the northern triangle countries, which has failed to stabilize decades later. Political corruption plays a significant role in keeping individuals in power. Many feel that their government fails to provide and there are no viable prospects.

In the absence of government stability, gangs provide stability for many. Gang violence thrives due to weak institutions, political instability, and distrust of law enforcement/military (Tello, Castellon, Aguilar, & Sawyer, 2017). The majority of UMs cite violence from gangs and in the home as the reason for leaving their countries (Stinchcomb & Hershberg, 2014; Tello et al., 2017). Many children flee out of fear that they will be killed or their families will be endangered. While crime in the region has remained steady, the level of violence is incredibly high, which continues to act as a major push factor in migration (Clemens, 2017). Violence and fear of gang recruitment frequently prevent youth from attending school. Resistance is increasingly dangerous. One study found that over one-third of UMs cited gang violence as their sole reason for leaving (Stinchcomb & Hershberg, 2014). More recently, studies have shown that not only current violence, but also past violence impacts the UM's decision to migrate (Clemens, 2017). Lack of stability externally is often mirrored internally in UMs home life (Stinchcomb & Hershberg, 2014), as nearly one-fifth of UMs reported some type of abuse in the household.

The second factor pushing UMs to migrate is poverty. Over 60 percent of rural residents across the Northern Triangle of Central America live in poverty. More specifically, 50.4 percent, 48.8 percent, and 31 percent of the total populations live in poverty respectively in Honduras, Guatemala, and El Salvador (World Bank, 2018). A scarcity of economic opportunities translates into a high percentage of young people who have no prospects in terms of jobs. These two push factors are interdependent. Threats of violence prevent youth from attending school, which ultimately limits the skills youth can attain and impedes the economy from growing (Stinchcomb & Hershberg, 2014). Pull factors are also often cited as important decision-making points. While most UMs are reunited with a family member in the United States (Kandel, 2017), there is little evidence to support that pull factors greatly affect the decision of UMs in the Northern Triangle to leave (Menjívar & Perreira, 2017).

Acts and Policies that Guide Treatment of Unaccompanied Minors

Once youth reach the United States, they must navigate a complex migration system. The 1997 Flores court settlement, the Homeland Security

Act of 2002 (HSA 2002), and the Wilberforce Trafficking Victims Protection Reauthorization Act of 2008 (TVPRA 2008) guide the treatment of unaccompanied minors in the US. The Flores settlement agreement was a result of a class-action lawsuit against Immigration and Customs Enforcement (ICE) regarding the treatment of unaccompanied youth in the 1980s. The settlement recognized the vulnerability of UMs and created a national policy for detaining, treating, and releasing youth without a guardian. In addition, the settlement provided specific guidelines for supervision and protection, conditions of shelter, and provision of food and water (Seghetti, Siskin, & Wasem, 2014). According to the Flores Settlement, youth should be released without "unnecessary delay" to a parent. If a parent is unavailable youth should be released to another adult relative, and if this is not possible, then to the custody of licensed programs. For UMs for whom placement cannot be located, Flores requires the Government to place youth in the "least restrictive" setting suitable given their age and needs (United States District Court, 1997).

The Homeland Security Act of 2002 established the Department of Homeland Security (DHS), and separated the tasks and responsibilities for UMs between DHS and the Department of Health and Human Services (HHS). Most notably, it separated the tasks of capture and removal from those of care and placement, which were all previously under the former Immigration and Naturalization Service (INS). Specifically, DHS became accountable for "responsibilities of capturing, transferring, and repatriating minors," while HHS became responsible for "coordinating and implementing the care and placement of [UMs] in appropriate custody; reunifying [them] with their parents abroad if appropriate; maintaining and publishing a list of legal services available to [them]; and collecting statistical information on [them], among other things" (Seghetti et al., 2014, p. 3). The Homeland Security Act recognized the innate conflict of interest in having one agency responsible for care *and* deportation. As such, the care for unaccompanied minors moved toward a child welfare based model of care and away from an adult detention model (Administration for Children and Families, 2014).

Although both the Flores Settlement and the Homeland Security Act offered improved guidelines for the treatment of unaccompanied minors, ongoing concerns that the Flores settlement was not being adequately implemented contributed to the William Wilberforce Trafficking Victims Protection Reauthorization Act of 2008 (TVPRA) addressing UMs. TVPRA reauthorized the 2000 Victims of Trafficking and Violence Protection Act, which attempted to reduce trafficking and create additional safeguards for the process. Most notably, TVPRA required federal agencies to outline methods for safely returning a child to their home country and set separate rules for processing children from contiguous countries (Mexico and Canada) versus non-contiguous countries. Under TVPRA, UMs from

Mexico and Canada can be returned to their home country without penalty, while unaccompanied youth from other countries are to be transferred to the Office of Refugee Resettlement within HHS for care and custody during the removal process. TVPRA expanded the role of HHS with regard to UMs. Children from non-contiguous countries have to "be promptly placed in the least restrictive setting that is in the best interest of the child" while awaiting removal proceedings (Administration for Children and Families, 2014). In addition, TVPRA mandated legal orientation presentations, and to the extent possible, access to counsel for removal hearings.

Administrative Process for Unaccompanied Minors in the US

The above acts and policies, which set out to guide treatment of unaccompanied minors, result in a prescribed process once in the United States. However, this prescribed process often deviates when the system has more youth than it is prepared to accommodate (Edlins & Larrison, 2018). This section will broadly describe the prescribed process and notes the points at which the process may falter in times of stress. Figure 5.2, from Edlins & Larrison (2018), provides a comprehensive visual of this process.

Once in the US, UMs either surrender or are apprehended by DHS agencies: Customs and Border Protection (CBP) at the border, or if already within the US, by ICE. Upon apprehension, UMs are transferred to a CBP processing center where they undergo a range of screenings. Within 24 hours, CBP officers are to determine if the youth meet the definition of unaccompanied and their nationality, as well as whether the youth has a credible fear of returning home or claims of persecution, trafficking, and/or fears of trafficking (U.S. Federal Emergency Management Agency, U.S. Customs and Border Patrol, & U.S. Immigration and Customs Enforcement, 2014). However, at times of overcapacity, youth may be temporarily housed in multiple locations before processing, and determinations may take many more days. For example in 2014, three military bases in Texas, Oklahoma, and California acted as emergency shelters (U.S. Federal Emergency Management Agency et al., 2014). Concurrently, UMs are started on removal proceedings that require them to appear at scheduled court hearings regarding whether they will be allowed to remain in the country. All of this—initial screening, determination as "unaccompanied," and the start of the removal process—happens relatively quickly as TVPRA dictates that UMs must be placed in the custody of the HHS Office of Refugee Resettlement (ORR) within 72 hours (United States Citizenship and Immigration Services, 2009). However, in 2014 and in 2018, UMs were frequently held in CBP custody for more than 3 days while officers determined their status.

Figure 5.2. Unaccompanied Migrant Flowchart

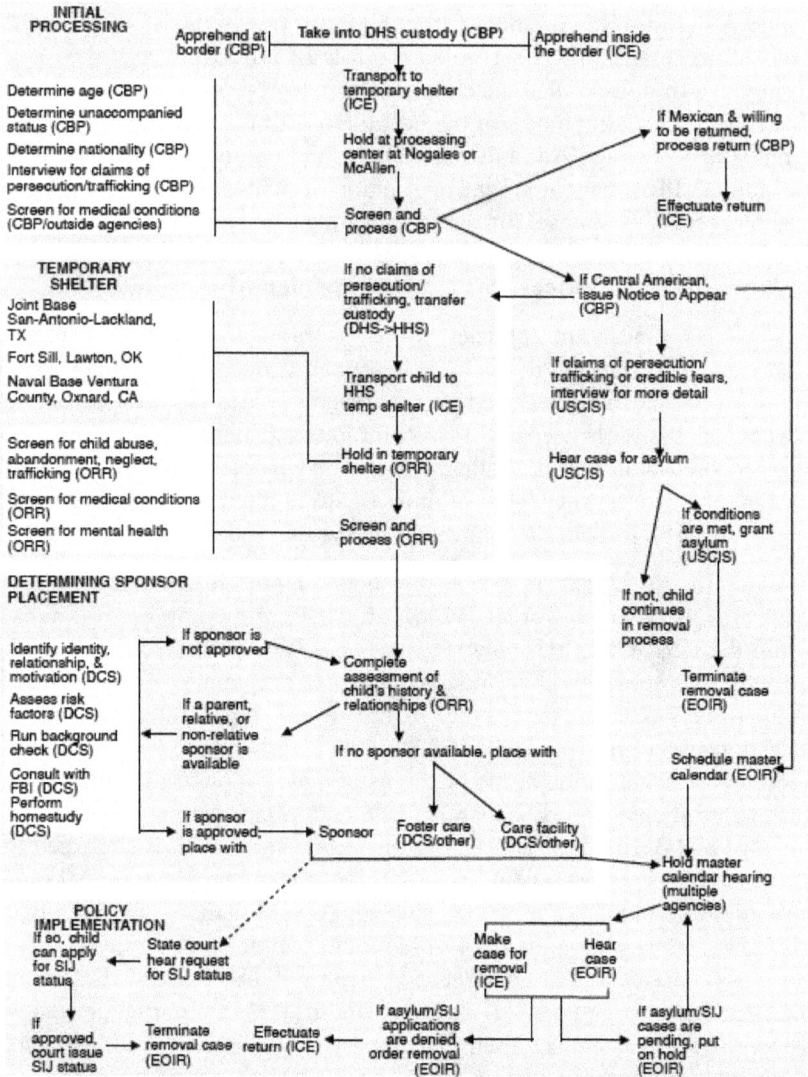

INITIAL PROCESSING

Apprehend at border (CBP) | Take into DHS custody (CBP) | Apprehend inside the border (ICE)

Determine age (CBP)
Determine unaccompanied status (CBP)
Determine nationality (CBP)
Interview for claims of persecution/trafficking (CBP)
Screen for medical conditions (CBP/outside agencies)

Transport to temporary shelter (ICE)
Hold at processing center at Nogales or McAllen
Screen and process (CBP)

If Mexican & willing to be returned, process return (CBP)
Effectuate return (ICE)

TEMPORARY SHELTER

Joint Base San-Antonio-Lackland, TX
Fort Sill, Lawton, OK
Naval Base Ventura County, Oxnard, CA

Screen for child abuse, abandonment, neglect, trafficking (ORR)
Screen for medical conditions (ORR)
Screen for mental health (ORR)

If no claims of persecution/trafficking, transfer custody (DHS->HHS)
Transport child to HHS temp shelter (ICE)
Hold in temporary shelter (ORR)
Screen and process (ORR)

If Central American, issue Notice to Appear (CBP)
If claims of persecution/trafficking or credible fears, interview for more detail (USCIS)
Hear case for asylum (USCIS)
If conditions are met, grant asylum (USCIS)
If not, child continues in removal process

DETERMINING SPONSOR PLACEMENT

Identify identity, relationship, & motivation (DCS)
Assess risk factors (DCS)
Run background check (DCS)
Consult with FBI (DCS)
Perform homestudy (DCS)

If sponsor is not approved
If a parent, relative, or non-relative sponsor is available
If sponsor is approved, place with

Complete assessment of child's history & relationships (ORR)
If no sponsor available, place with
Sponsor   Foster care (DCS/other)   Care facility (DCS/other)

Terminate removal case (EOIR)
Schedule master calendar (EOIR)
Hold master calendar hearing (multiple agencies)

POLICY IMPLEMENTATION

If so, child can apply for SIJ status
State court hear request for SIJ status
If approved, court issue SIJ status
Terminate removal case (EOIR)
Effectuate return (ICE)
If asylum/SIJ applications are denied, order removal (EOIR)
Make case for removal (ICE)
Hear case (EOIR)
If asylum/SIJ cases are pending, put on hold (EOIR)

Once UMs are in ORR custody, ORR is responsible for their care and the coordination of their placement while UMs await their removal proceedings. ORR officials work to place youth in the least restrictive environment conducive for their well being (Administration for Children and Families, 2014). During this period, the majority of UMs are placed in small group homes or larger congregate care settings (LIRS, 2018). In 2014, UMs were in ORR custody for approximately 29 days, after which 95% were released to a parent, relative, or non-relative sponsor (Greenberg, 2014). A small percentage of UMs are transferred to long term foster care and state-approved care facilities, and ORR maintains permanent shelter options when

100

an outside placement is not available (U.S. Department of Health and Human Services, n.d.). By 2018, UMs averaged 60 days in ORR custody (Office of Refugee Resettlement, 2018). Shelters have become increasingly used for longer-term placement. Changes in immigration policies that shared citizenship information of the potential sponsor and the entire household with DHS Immigration and Customs Enforcement (ICE) in 2018 resulted in fewer sponsors claiming custody for their children (Kopan, 2018). Given this, a record 14,000 plus UMs were in ORR custody as of November 2018. UMs legal case continues throughout this process, and they await a verdict of whether they are allowed to legally remain in the country. If their case is unsuccessful, deportation orders will be issued. If successful, UMs will be allowed to remain in the country.

Methodology

This chapter emerges from a larger study on the experiences of unaccompanied minors in the US and their interactions with public servants. For the larger project, we partnered with Lutheran Immigration and Refugee Service (LIRS) to aid in understanding who UMs are, the factors that influence their migration process once in the US, and how public servants play a role.

This chapter relies on qualitative data to explore the experiences of UMs and their governance in the United States. Youth who have a sponsor are relocated to where their sponsor resides. This means that states with a significant immigrant population from the Northern Triangle are likely to have more unaccompanied minors resettled in their state. We examine the experiences of youth who were resettled in the states of Maryland and Virginia between 2015 and 2017. Over these three years, Maryland and Virginia accepted the fifth and sixth most UMs for resettlement, respectively, accepting a total of 16,813 UMs. The research question was how do UMs experience the migration process once they enter the US?

To answer this question, we conducted open-ended focus group discussions with 24 UMs who were resettled with family members. The focus groups took place in three separate locations over the summer of 2017. The project focused on UMs who migrated to the US between 2015 and 2017, were between the ages of 8 and 16 when they arrived in the country, and settled in the states of Maryland and Virginia. The majority of UMs were from Central America: El Salvador (19), Honduras (2), Guatemala (1), and Nicaragua (1), as well as one additional country: Ecuador (1).

Once the data were collected, we employed inductive content analysis to identify themes that emerged in the data. Content analysis is the process of deriving meaning from a large collection of data by bringing "order, structure and interpretation to the mass of collected data" (Marshall & Rossman, 1990, p. 111). This method allowed for the systematic organization and identification of elements within the dataset in order to "to meaningfully interpret and make inferences about the patterns in the content of the overall body" (Bowen & Bowen, 2008, p. 689). This method allowed us to review the data for themes that could help us identify the experiences that UMs have through the process.

Results

The following section outlines themes that arose in response to the above research question. In addressing the UMs' experiences, UMs focused on housing conditions, how they were treated, and the public servants who most affected their experience. Within each category, common experiences emerged from the focus group interviews with UMs, however their treatment varied dramatically depending upon where they were within the process, and who was responsible for their treatment.

Housing Conditions

Housing conditions emerged as a key topic of discussion while in the custody of DHS and HHS. Under DHS, youth were detained in a location referred to as "la hielera", or the "icebox", due to its cold temperature. Youth also may have been detained in a location referred to as "la perrera", or the "dogpound", due to the cages surrounding the area where youth were kept. In these two locations, UMs noted the physical conditions, the lack of privacy, and how these affected their experience.

The "icebox" refers to the custody holding cell at CBP, where youth typically spend 1-3 days. These cells are windowless, and are constructed of concrete with some cells having concrete benches. The temperature is kept uncomfortably cold. Cells contain one toilet with a small privacy wall. Youth are expected to sleep on the floor, and may receive a Mylar blanket to keep warm. Security cameras are visible in all parts of the cell. One youth described the icebox as "a kind of jail, a very cold place. They keep minors there, and also adult people depending on their situation. Older people are deported and minors are not deported and are placed there." The conditions were considered abnormally harsh by many UMs. Maria, 14, explained the impact of the conditions: "I think it was one of the most terrible places. They did not give me a sheet. There weren't any more. You can't sleep. It was full of people in the same situation. I did not sleep because there were too many people. They were kids too." Nelli, 16, felt responsible for her two younger sisters, stating, "I wanted to die. I was with my two little sisters and I felt bad because they were so cold."

Youth described the "dogpound" as cages with mattresses on the floor. Many UMs noted that the surroundings were sterile and unsuitable for kids. In explaining the situation a UM stated, "It's like a gate you put around your house so that no one enters. It looks like a place that's not ideal for kids.

Kids are supposed to play. Yes, you need order, but they go too far."

Youth discussed the housing conditions once they were transferred to the custody of HHS in contrast to their experience with DHS. The majority of UMs are placed in shelters that are either small group homes or larger congregate care settings. These shelters are designed for youth 14 or older without special needs or criminal history. The conditions here were viewed in sharp contrast to the conditions under DHS, as youth stated that the shelters were like summer camp. They also noted that it was "nice", as they received food and clothes.

Treatment

How youth were treated at each location also dramatically affected their experience. Under DHS, youth discussed their treatment in terms of how they were perceived. Youth intimated perception based on direct comments as well as general treatment. Direct comments included being called "disgusting" and making fun of another youth's name. One UM observed that "It was rare that anyone did anything in a nice, loving way...they look at you as if you just came here to cause problems in the country." Another recalled their experience at the icebox as "one of the worst experiences" of their life. Youth discussed how they responded to this treatment, many remembering that they were sad and confused. However, this negative experience was not universal. Some youth explained that DHS officers treated them well, allowing them to stay in the same cell as their friends, providing food, and not using disparaging language.

The experiences largely contrasted once youth were placed with HHS. In the shelter, youth largely regarded their treatment as good, or even "excellent." UMs were particularly mindful of the routine created in the shelter, whereby they were expected to get ready, make their bed, have breakfast, take classes, and participate in a variety of activities. While generally viewed in a positive manner, many youth noted that they felt isolated, not being allowed to go outside the confines of the shelter.

UMs expressed mixed emotions about treatment once they arrived in the community. Youth noted that living with a parent or relative that they had not seen in years was a significant adjustment. Attending school could be great for meeting other people, but many also felt that they were treated unjustly by authority figures.

Overall, UMs described the experience of migrating to the US as "hard", "good", "anxiety-inducing", and "fearful." In particular, youth noted the discrepancy in treatment of themselves versus others. One UM noted that "It's true that people make mistakes here, but that doesn't mean that you have to discriminate against them. Because those people are looked down upon, but we can all change." While another stated, "just because a person has problems doesn't mean that they're crazy or that they want to kill people. Just because you suffer doesn't mean that you have a right to mistreat them."

Public Servants

The final theme that emerged from the data was the public servants that interacted with UMs. How public servants engaged youth affected how youth perceived varying roles. Almost all youth discussed the role CBP officers played in their apprehension and detention. Generally, UMs regarded these officers as being unnecessarily rude or strict. However, the discretion CBP officers maintain was underscored, as some youth had positive interactions with the officers despite the environment.

UMs particularly highlighted the role of nurses and teachers in the shelter. Nurses were one of the first individuals whom youth encountered, as they received 15 vaccinations upon arrival. Youth noted the calm demeanor of nurses despite the anxiety of other UMs receiving so many shots. Through routine and creativity, teachers appear to provide some sense of normalcy in an otherwise abnormal situation. Youth noted how the teacher, "made us forget where we were and we had a lot of fun."

Once placed with their sponsors, youth are expected to integrate into the community. This begins with school enrollment. Some UMs noted how their fellow classmates were helpful, and they enjoyed school. However, in contrast to the teachers in the shelter, who were unanimously praised, many UMs noted teachers within the school system for being unfair and discriminatory. One youth discussed how "Some teachers treat us badly because we're from a different culture. They mistreat us just for that reason. They think we're all the same." Another offered, "I had a teacher who was prejudiced. There were 14 of us and no matter how hard we worked, we always got an F or D." Another added that their teacher was often mean and would call the principal on the students who did not speak English. Overall, UMs seemed to view school skeptically based on their interactions with teachers.

Public servants who stood out to youth for their positive contribution were lawyers and caseworkers. Generally, this positive perception was due to these individuals treating the youth in a thoughtful manner. One commented that she likes to see her lawyer because the lawyer always asks how she is doing. Several youth commented that their social worker has helped them integrate by enrolling in afterschool activities, such as soccer or English classes. The types of public servants with whom youth interact demonstrate the tension expected from these youth: to integrate into society and prepare for departure simultaneously. In general, UMs felt that people should be more patient with them. One explained the need for patience, "Sometimes, people who are almost 18 years old still act like children because we're in a country that we don't know. We don't know how to act." Such concerns demonstrate how language and tone affect the overall experience of migrants.

Discussion and Conclusion

Overall, UMs' experience navigating the immigration process once in the United States varied based on the types of encounters they had. The three themes that emerged from the data—housing conditions, treatment, and public servants—appear to act as significant contributors to the UMs experience. As such, each provides implications for decisions made through policy and how policy decisions impact youth.

With regard to housing conditions, several factors affected how youth viewed their experience. The temperature of the room greatly affected how youth viewed the CBP holding cells. The language used to communicate with youth affected their experience. The type of food that youth received also affected their experience. With this understanding, policies can be implemented to ensure that the experience youth have while in Government custody is as positive as possible.

How UMs perceived their treatment also greatly affects their overall experience navigating the migration process. If public servants spoke in a kind manner or in an authoritative manner affected how youth perceived the experience. If public servants attempted to explain situations or assumed youth should understand affected their opinion. If public servants spoke Spanish, attempted to explain in English, or solely spoke English affected their experience. Understanding their situation and maintaining a routine seemed to be two key factors that influence UMs perception of their treatment. As such, ensuring that public servants who interacted with youth clearly describe the situation and what is to come next can positively affect UMs' experience.

Closely related to treatment are the public servants, themselves. Public servants have a high level of discretion. The results highlighted the power public servants have over youth, affecting their experiences in both positive and negative manners. Youth could easily name the public servants who were thoughtful, engaging, and caring, and could as easily name those who were perceived to negatively affect their understanding of who they are and why they were in the US.

The experiences described by UMs with varying public servants underlines the role of the agencies for which public servants work. UMs seemed to generally view their time under the custody of DHS negatively, their time under the custody of HHS more positively, and their current situation within the community as both positive and negative. While the separation of responsibilities between DHS and HHS was intended to address the tension innate in the responsibilities of the agencies, this tension is still observable in the interactions youth have with DHS in their first days in the United States. DHS appears to be meeting its call of detaining and deporting adults. As such, public servants working for DHS are not consistently trained in interacting with youth, and do not put the well-being of the UM at the forefront. Instead, they are focused on their prescribed role. Meanwhile, the mission of HHS is to consider the best interest of the child. As such, the interactions with public servants working with HHS are perceived by UMs to be more focused on the UMs and what is in their best interest. These interactions appear to have a lasting affect on how youth view their role as kids, as caretakers of younger siblings, and their place in the United States. Overall, the experiences of youth in each location largely reflected the role and responsibility of the agency and public servants working within it.

This project set out to explore how UMs experience the migration process once they enter the United States, given the increased number of youth navigating the immigration system on their own. As they traverse the process, these young people have a range of experiences and encounter a variety of Government representatives. Our analysis demonstrates that the conditions UMs encounter throughout the process and the interactions they have with public servants significantly shape their experience. Conditions and individuals that did not take into account the well-being of UMs led to more negative experiences, while conditions and individuals that were focused on the well-being of the youth led to more positive experiences.

The analysis also highlights how the experiences of UMs are largely aligned with the division of federal government agency whose custody they are in. This again demonstrates the impact of a government agency mission. Rather than one agency to both care *and* deport, those responsibilities are split between two agencies. Yet, as this project highlights, UM's had more positive experiences while in the custody of HHS as compared to experiences in the custody of DHS, which were more negative. As such, this project emphasizes the opportunity and need to increase policies and efforts aimed at "the best interest of the child."

References

Administration for Children and Families. (2014). *Fact sheet: U.S. Department of Human Services, Administration for Children and Families, Office of Refugee Resettlement, Unaccompanied Alien Children Program*. Washington, D.C.: Office of Refugee Resettlement. Retrieved from https://www.acf.hhs.gov/sites/default/files/orr/fact_sheet.pdf

Bowen, C.-C., & Bowen, W. M. (2008). Content analysis. In K. Yang & G. J. Miller (Eds.), *Handbook of Research Methods in Public Administration* (pp. 689–703). Boca Raton, Florida: Taylor & Francis.

Clemens, M. (2017). *Violence, Development, and Migration Waves: Evidence from Central American Child Migrant Apprehension* (CGD Paper No. 459). Washington, DC: Center for Global

Development. Retrieved from https://www.cgdev.org/sites/default/files/violence-development-and-migration-waves-evidence-central-american-child-migrant.pdf

Department of Homeland Security. (2014). Southwest border unaccompanied alien children FY 2014 | U.S. Customs and Border Protection. Retrieved December 3, 2015, from http://www.cbp.gov/newsroom/stats/southwest-border-unaccompanied-children/fy-2014

Edlins, M., & Larrison, J. (2018). Street-level bureaucrats and the governance of unaccompanied migrant children: *Public Policy and Administration.* https://doi.org/10.1177/0952076718811438

Greenberg, M. (2014, July 9). Challenges at the border: Examining the causes, consequences, and responses to the rise in apprehensions at the southern border. Retrieved November 18, 2015, from http://www.hhs.gov/asl/testify/2014/07/t20140709a.html

Kandel, W. A. (2017). *Unaccompanied Alien Children: An Overview* (CRS Report No. R43599) (p. 22). Washington D.C.

Marshall, C., & Rossman, G. (1990). *Designing qualitative research.* Newbury Park: SAGE Publications.

Menjívar, C., & Perreira, K. M. (2017). Undocumented and unaccompanied: children of migration in the European Union and the United States. *Journal of Ethnic and Migration Studies, 0*(0), 1–21. https://doi.org/10.1080/1369183X.2017.1404255

Office of Refugee Resettlement. (2018). Facts and Data. Retrieved October 13, 2018, from https://www.acf.hhs.gov/orr/about/ucs/facts-and-data

Seghetti, L., Siskin, A., & Wasem, R. E. (2014). *Unaccompanied alien children: An overview* (Congressional Research Service Report No. R43599). Washington D.C.: Congressional Research Service.

Stinchcomb, D., & Hershberg, E. (2014). *Unaccompanied Migrant Children from Central America: Context, Causes, and Responses* (SSRN Scholarly Paper No. ID 2524001). Rochester, NY: Social Science Research Network. Retrieved from https://papers.ssrn.com/abstract=2524001

Tello, A., Castellon, N., Aguilar, A., & Sawyer, C. (2017). Unaccompanied Refugee Minors From Central America: Understanding Their Journey and Implications for Counselors. *The Professional Counselor, 7*, 360–374. https://doi.org/10.15241/amt.7.4.360

United States Citizenship and Immigration Services. (2009, September 2). Asylum procedures for minor children, USCIS. Retrieved May 23, 2015, from http://www.uscis.gov/humanitarian/refugees-asylum/asylum/asylum-procedures-minor-children

United States District Court. Flores v. Reno, No. CV 85-4544-RJK(Px) (United States District Court Central District of California 1997).

U.S. Department of Health and Human Services. (n.d.). *Unaccompanied children frequently asked questions.* Administration for Children and Families. Retrieved from http://www.acf.hhs.gov/unaccompanied-children-frequently-asked-questions

U.S. Federal Emergency Management Agency, U.S. Customs and Border Patrol, & U.S. Immigration and Customs Enforcement. Challenges at the border: Examining the causes, consequences, and responses to the rise in apprehensions at the southern border, § Senate Committee on Homeland Security and Governmental Affairs (2014). 342 Dirksen Senate Office Building. Retrieved from http://www.dhs.gov/news/2014/07/09/written-testimony-fema-cbp-and-ice-senate-committee-homeland-security-and

World Bank. (2018). World Bank Open Data | Data. Retrieved December 3, 2018, from https://data.worldbank.org/.

CHAPTER 6

DROPPING OUT OF EDUCATION: REFUGEE YOUTH WHO ARRIVED AS UNACCOMPANIED MINORS AND SEPARATED CHILDREN

Aycan Çelikaksoy and Eskil Wadensjö

Introduction

Unaccompanied minors or separated children (UMs) are children under the age of 18 who are outside their country of origin and came to Sweden unaccompanied by a parent or other legal guardian. Such migration has increased around the world and it is the most fragile type of migration across countries. This population is considered 'vulnerable' due to their young age during the fleeing process combined with the fact that they are unaccompanied by their parents or legal guardians (Derluyn and Broekaert, 2008; Derluyn and Vervliet, 2012; Rodriguez, et al., 2018). These children face heightened vulnerability to exploitation, and violations of their rights by virtue of their age and status. The global movement of unaccompanied and separated children presents challenges for children's rights and wellbeing. Research on unaccompanied minors has often focused on vulnerabilities of this group (Derluyn et al., 2008). However, recent studies have increasingly stressed the strength, resilience, and agency of unaccompanied minors (UMs), despite the traumatic experiences and challenges (see e.g. Luster et al., 2010).

In addition to migration and reception related challenges, what happens to these children after they receive their permits to stay in the destination countries is also an important question. However, there are only a very few large-scale studies focusing on their situation in the educational system and the labor market after they have received their permits to stay. This is partly due to data availability that constrains the possibility of such an analysis, since individual register based yearly data is not available in all countries but also because data on the whole population of UMs is not available in most datasets. We hope that this study will shed light on questions in relation to the situation of this group in the educational system and to the specific mechanisms that are at play in shaping their educational careers in the destination countries.

Education is extremely important for the wellbeing of refugee children, regardless of whether they are unaccompanied or arrive with their families. Education is a protective factor for refugee children especially in the case of unaccompanied minors. Relevant and responsive education offers stability and purpose, opportunities to rebuild social capital, re-establish a routine and continued essential development of skills and knowledge for future generations (Ackerman et al., 2014). Schools are of specific importance for UMs in terms of providing daily routines and a safe environment for their wellbeing (Bhabha, 2004; Seglem et al., 2014). In addition, education is central to their prospects in the labor market and by that has an important influence to their overall wellbeing. It is shown that acculturation in the form of learning the language and culture as well as a self-assessed competence of understanding cultural codes had a positive influence on the risk of depression for UM (Keles, et al., 2018).

There are earlier studies that incorporate both of the strands of literature with regard to vulnerability and resilience and discuss how they coexist in a multifaceted manner even in the same area of life such as the labor market as well as in other areas of life (Çelikaksoy and Wadensjö, 2019, Rousseau, et al., 1998). It is discussed that certain conditions or risk factors bring out the resilience in groups in certain cultural contexts, for example, in the case of UM. Although resilience is mainly discussed as an individual phenomenon, its interactive psychosocial aspects need to be included in the discussions (Rousseau, et al., 1998). In an empirical study, it is shown that this group demonstrates resilience in terms of ability to find work and willingness to work however, this group is potentially vulnerable in terms of career paths pointing out that resilience and vulnerability coexist for UMs in their adjustment process in the destination country. This reflects how the unique circumstances and characteristics of this group are in an interplay shaping and re-shaping their outcomes (Çelikaksoy and Wadensjö, 2017a; 2019). One of the most important factors behind labor market outcomes is educational attainment. Investigating the educational careers of the UMs will also shed light on later outcomes in the labor market. To our knowledge, this is the first study analyzing dropout behavior of this group with a large comprehensive dataset following the whole population of interest for several years. We hope that this study will shed new light on the factors that facilitate or hinder the educational careers of this group and their specific patterns when compared to other groups.

Upper secondary education, which is either in the form of general education or vocational training, is a tuition-free, voluntary form of schooling that young people can choose to attend after completing comprehensive school. Upper secondary education is a very important cornerstone for starting to build a labor market career in Sweden. In this chapter, we investigate the dropout behavior of UM from high school studies. The dropout behavior is analyzed by utilizing register data from Statistics Sweden for the whole population of UMs who were registered during 2003–2005 during the ages of 15-18. In addition, to investigating the specific situation of this group we compare them to other refugee youth who arrived from the same countries of origin at the same ages as well as comparing them to the native population. UMs are a unique group and their challenges and support systems might be different from that of other groups. Our results will increase our understanding of the situation of this group, which in turn will help to facilitate the educational outcomes for UMs.

Our results show that several factors are important in determining the dropout behavior for this group, such as registration age (age getting the permit to stay), gender, family reunification, country of origin as well as area (county) in Sweden lived in. The results also show that this group is more likely to dropout from the educational system before completing high school studies compared to both accompanied minors and natives. We discuss our results in light of the current policies and situation of UMs in Sweden.

Unaccompanied minors in Sweden

Sweden registered the greatest number of asylum claims by UMs within the EU 2010–2015. In Sweden, UMs have been arriving predominantly as asylum seekers instead of through other channels and around 80 percent each year were granted a residence permit during that period. Thus, the majority of the group who crossed the border is included in the register statistics (Çelikaksoy and Wadensjö, 2015a). In 2016 Sweden adopted several restrictions on asylum seekers that has directly affected and harmed UMs, restricting the number of arrivals, the right to permanent residence and family reunification.

Unaccompanied minors have the possibility of family reunification if they are given protection status as a refugee. Their parents then will be able to apply for residence permits for as long as the UM's permit is valid. If they have a protection status as a person eligible for subsidiary protection, then they only have the right to family reunification in exceptional cases. The changes in the family reunification regulations have an important influence on whether UMs can or cannot be reunified with their parents. A number of limitations to the right to family reunification have been introduced through the law on temporary restrictions to obtaining a residence permit in Sweden, which entered into force on 20 July 2016 for a three-year period. Persons who qualify for subsidiary protection, and are granted an initial period of 13 months temporary residence permit, including UMs, have no right to family reunification. In order to be able to reunite with their family, they have to wait until they are granted a permanent residence permit, which can take up to three years. There are several additional practical obstacles to family reunification such as strict ID/passport requirement to prove identity, and long processing times.

The responsibilities for UMs in Sweden shifted on 1 July 2006 from the Migration Board to the local governments, but the Migration Board is still responsible for the asylum investigation and subsidizes local governments for their responsibilities. The National Board of Health and Welfare is responsible for supervising the municipalities and developing guidance, recommendations, and supervision for the care of UMs. When a child enters Sweden, he or she spends some time at an arrival center, after which a municipality takes over the reception (Çelikaksoy and Wadensjö, 2017b). During the asylum-seeking process, all UMs get a temporary guardian. The child gets a permanent guardian if a residence permit is granted. In municipalities, the social services take care of the living situation and the daily care. All children have the right to start school immediately after arrival, regardless of the stage of their asylum claims.

There are three reasons why Sweden is an important case study with regard to this issue. Firstly, UMs came in greater numbers to Sweden to seek asylum than to other countries in Europe in several years (EC, 2012; Eurostat, 2015; Migrationsverket, 2015). Secondly, in Sweden, UMs have been arriving predominantly as asylum seekers instead of through other channels, which means that we in the registers can observe almost all of those who have been entering the country. Thirdly, these facts combined with high-quality data facilities, provide a unique opportunity to analyze data on a wide range of issues for the whole population of this group.

Unaccompanied minors in the educational system in Sweden

Most UM arrive when they are of school age, where the majority is 16 or 17 years old (Çelikaksoy and Wadensjö, 2015a). The majority of them are of an age that for the majority of the other children in the country is in upper-secondary school studies. This is clearly a critical age, which is the starting age for high school studies. The UMs may be at this level, but in many cases, they may also be at lower or much lower levels. Their education has been disrupted in the country of origin but also during the flight and in some cases during a stay in a transit country. This means that they in many cases need to start at a lower level than that corresponding to their age. It is important for the children to be placed at the right level. This often means that they complete a level of education at a higher age than those who were born in the country. In addition, there is an adjustment process going on for these children to a new language and culture.

Clearly, education is one of the most important areas and a gateway into the Swedish society for this group. There is a constant ongoing effort to improve the support and opportunities provided to foreign-born students in the educational system in Sweden. Sweden has been found to have strong and high standards when compared to other EU countries in the areas of 'advice and orientation for new comer pupils', 'additional language courses for migrant pupils', 'additional systematic finances and support for schools', 'teaching of immigrant languages', 'intercultural education and teacher training' (Huddleston and Wolffhardt, 2016). However, those who arrive at a later age and especially UMs might have a different set of needs than natives and other immigrant children. Research shows that there is long list of special needs that need to be a part of the educational system (Huddleston and Wolffhardt, 2016). On the other hand, the literature does not have a consensus or clear guidelines regarding the direction or the methods to be followed in dealing with the complexities. For all newly arrived children but especially for the UMs, education is not only a space for learning new skills but also a secure and safe place for development. Since this group does not have their family as a source of social capital, schools have an even bigger role for accumulation of capital. Accumulation of human capital involves combining previous human capital and experiences with new ones. The Swedish curriculum recognizes the role and need for promoting an international perspective and an understanding of cultural diversity (Skolverket, 2011). A detailed and concrete identification of the level of education of UMs at arrival is crucial for determining their needs, as a basis for a plan for their development. This will ensure that this group has a specific plan that is suitable for their situation and their needs and that they can stay in the educational system until they are ready to start their employment careers and are eligible for the types of jobs they would like to pursue.

Studies that investigate the dropout behavior of students mainly focus on individual and institutional factors. Some of the individual factors are students' early and recent school performance, attitudes towards school, academic engagement, self-esteem, participation in school activities as well as social bonding, which point out the academic and network effects on dropout behavior (Ream and Rumberger, 2008). With regard to social bonding, we expect that there will be no differences in terms of how the native or other students perceive and relate to unaccompanied versus accompanied minors since they are from the same countries of origin and arrived at the same ages. Thus, we expect discrimination towards these students to be similar regardless of whether they have arrived unaccompanied or accompanied. However, their academic engagement might differ depending on their life circumstances such as responsibilities outside the school. Since UMs lack a familial system, they might have a higher degree of responsibility to support themselves. In addition, they might have a higher degree of responsibility to work and send remittances to their families and relatives in the origin or transit countries, which in turn influences their focus on academic achievement. In addition, living conditions and type of living arrangement is also an important factor that influences their overall wellbeing (O'Higgins, et al., 2018). Thus, a continued assessment of their specific life circumstances and needs would be an invaluable support for developing a needs based plan for this group that would facilitate a long-term career.

Education takes place at different levels, varying according to age and education level at arrival. Most UMs who are 16 years old study in secondary school but a quarter are in elementary school. Those who are 17–19 years study in most cases in secondary school. Among the former UMs who are 20–21 years, many remain in secondary school, but it is also common for them to study in municipal education for adults or '*komvux*'. For those who are 22 years of age, *komvux* is the most common form of education, but other forms are also important, like basic university education, folk high school, Swedish for Immigrants (SFI), and labour market education (mainly men).

Education is of great importance for young people's possibilities to establish themselves in the labour market – obtaining a job and, if so, the type of job. Many former unaccompanied minors have primary education as their highest level and quite a few have an education that is shorter than nine years despite being between 20 and 30 years old. Some, but relatively few, have completed upper-secondary education (Çelikaksoy and Wadensjö, 2019).

Up to the age of 19, many unaccompanied minors have not completed any education in Sweden. Among those who are 22 years of age or older, most have compulsory education as their highest school level (Çelikaksoy and Wadensjö, 2015a, 2015b). These results show that UMs have different pathways into continuing their studies after compulsory education. It is therefore of special interest to see whether they have completed their upper secondary school studies.

Some of the UM both study and work during the same year and thus get their first work experience. This can be a way of early entry into the labour market. It is between 10 and 20 per cent in the different year classes. The differences between the three groups (UMs, AMs (accompanied minors) and NY (native youth) are small. However, for men, a slightly higher proportion of UMs are combining studies and work compared to men in other groups (Çelikaksoy and Wadensjö, 2019). This might point out the fact that this group has a higher degree of financial responsibilities when compared to their counterparts. Previous studies show that the employment rate of male UM increases drastically from age 21 (Çelikaksoy and Wadensjö, 2015a). However, the proportion of females in each group who combine work and studies is higher than that of men in each group, especially after age 21, due to that females stay in education longer than males.

Data and methods

To begin with, we investigate the factors that influence the dropout behavior for the refugee youth who arrived as UMs. Dropout behavior is measured by a dichotomous variable that takes the value of one if the individual has not completed a high school study by the end of his/her observation period, which coincides with an average age of 27 and is currently not studying. Although it takes a longer time for UMs to complete their studies, we expect them to have completed high school by late 20s or be under education. We use a probit model to investigate the likelihood of dropout for this group and analyze the factors that influence this behavior, such as the age at registration, gender, internal migration behavior as well as civil status and parental reunification. We expect that the younger they are when they are registered, the more likely it is that they stay in education. It is a well-established result in most migration studies that the duration of stay in the destination country improves outcomes in relation to education and labor market. Furthermore, early age at arrival means that they can learn Swedish at an earlier age as well as starting school at earlier grades. Another factor that can facilitate school success is the family situation. The stability of a family environment can have a positive influence in staying in school. Thus, having parents in Sweden can be a support mechanism for young people and help them to complete their education. In some cases, the UMs have to change the municipality or the county of residence due to administrate challenges. This is not ideal, since it brings disruption and instability to their short and long-term prospects. Thus, changes in ones' area of living could hinder their academic engagement as well as their social bonds with their specific network and environment. In addition, being married can also work as a factor challenging school success since it brings extra responsibilities to one's life such as household chores as well as financial responsibilities. Furthermore, we also investigate the influence of area (county) lived in and country of origin since there might be differences across different regions within Sweden but there might also be different dropout behaviors depending on the country of origin. This might be due to the emphasis different cultures place on education or due to the degree of turbulence and educational disruption in the country that the young refugees are coming from, as well as ethnic network effects.

In addition to investigating the factors that influence dropout behavior for UMs we also investigate whether and how being an UM affects dropout behavior when compared to other groups of youth. We do this by comparing UMs to accompanied minors (AMs), that is, those minors who arrived from the same countries of origin as the UMs and at the same ages but with their parents. We also compare UMs with native youth (NY), that is, those youth who are at similar ages as the UMs but who are born in Sweden and whose parents are born in Sweden. By comparing UMs with their counterparts, we are able to see if their circumstances and challenges are unique in terms of

115

dropout behavior since we are comparing them to other refugee minors who arrived from the same countries and at the same ages.

The data used in the analysis stems from register information at Statistics Sweden (SCB). After receiving a permit to stay, the migrant receives a personal identification number. This high quality register data, where every person has a record, is the by-product of registers held for administrative purposes. The Population Registry, which includes detailed demographic, educational and labor market information, is administered by the Swedish Tax Agency. The personal identification numbers are anonymized when used for research purposes. For our purposes, we use data on the entire population of UMs who were registered during the 2003–2005 aged 15–18. The dataset covers the period 2003–2014. All individuals in the data are observed for at least seven years. Thus, during their last year of observation they are at the age of 22–29. The data is constructed exactly the same way for AMs from a 10 percent random sample of the AMs comparison group. The data on the native youth (NY), 0.01 percent sample, starts from age 19 so we have included those who were at the age of 19 and 20 during the years 2003–2005. Total number of observations for UMs is 4,332, where 37 percent are female. The corresponding figures for AMs and NY are 4,715 and 8,030, where 44 percent and 50 percent are females. The data includes detailed country information for some of the countries where a majority of the UMs are from, however, the rest of the countries are grouped into larger categories for privacy and ethical reasons. Thus, we do not have information specifically on each country of origin.

Results

Sample means are shown in Table 6.1 by arrival status for their last year of observation. It can be seen that a majority of UMs are males; where 37 percent of UMs are females. In the case of AMs and NY, 44 percent and 40 percent are females respectively. The mean age at registration is about the same for UMs and AMs, where UMs were 0.37 years older than AMs on average when they were registered. The dropout rate for UMs is 5.97 and 17.92 percentage points higher on average compared to the dropout rates for AMs and NY. We can see that a higher proportion of UMs have not completed high school and are out of the educational system compared to other groups by the end of their observation period. The table shows that 46 percent of UMs have moved across counties, while this figure is 38 percent for the other two groups. This shows that more UMs have moved across counties when compared to those who arrived with their families as well as native youth. It can also be seen that a lower proportion of UMs are single when compared to the other groups. We can see that 9 percent of the UM have been reunified with their parents. A higher proportion of UMs are from Afghanistan and Somalia compared to AMs. We can also see that a higher proportion of UMs and AMs live in Stockholm compared to NY.

Table 6.1. Sample means for youth who arrived as unaccompanied minors as well as native youth

Demographic characteristics	Unaccompanied	Accompanied	Native
Female	37.27	43.60	49.74
Age at registration	16.86	16.49	-
Dropout rate	24.93	18.96	7.01
Age	27.25	26.69	28.67
Moving across counties	45.93	37.91	38.44
Number of moves	0.78	0.57	0.68
Single	48.56	55.45	77.14
Parental reunification	8.92	-	-
Place of birth			
Afghanistan	13.91	6.87	-
Iraq	27.03	31.99	-
Somalia	25.98	10.19	-
Other countries in the M.E.	5.77	13.27	-
Other countries in Africa	19.42	16.35	-
Other countries in Asia	7.87	21.33	-
County			
Stockholm	33.33	32.46	19.87
Skåne	8.14	13.03	10.39
Västra Götaland	17.85	16.35	18.57
Other counties	40.68	38.15	51.17

The dropout rate is influenced by demographic factors such as gender and age at arrival. It is a common finding that females tend to stay in education longer than males in the case of both immigrants and natives in the destination countries (Çelikaksoy and Wadensjö, 2018). However, we do not know whether this is also the case for UMs. We expect that the younger the UMs is at arrival, the better is the educational outcome in the form of attainment of upper-secondary schooling. In addition, the family can be seen as a support system in the lives of refugee children, thus we investigate the role of family reunification for UMs on their dropout behavior. Education and housing for UM is the responsibility of the municipalities. However, in some cases the children have to move several times because of administrative decisions. Thus, we investigate the influence of whether they have moved across counties and the number of times they have moved in addition to where they live. Previous studies show that those UMs who live in the Stockholm region have better employment outcomes compared to those living in other regions (Çelikaksoy and Wadensjö, 2017b). However, we do not know how region lived in influences their educational outcomes.

Unaccompanied minors

Table 6.2 shows the factors that influence the dropout behavior of UMs from the educational system before they have an upper secondary school degree. The marginal effects are presented in all the following tables. The probability of dropout from the educational system before completing upper secondary school is 10.2 percentage points lower for females compared to that of males. It is a common finding for the native population in destination countries that girls have more education than boys do. In addition, this is also found in the case of migrant groups in destination countries. Among all other groups of migrants, migrant girls have more education than boys do (Çelikaksoy and Wadensjö, 2018). Thus, these results show that UMs follow the same pattern. As discussed earlier, we can see in Table 2 that the older they are at arrival the more likely they are to drop out. Early age at arrival has been shown to have a positive influence on school success since it means that they can be a part of the educational system at an earlier age and their exposure time to the Swedish language and culture is longer. Although the registration age is restricted to a narrow age range in this study, we can still see the influence of an earlier age at registration. Another potentially important factor that can influence the academic engagement as well as social bonding in the school environment, thus school success is the stability of the school attendance and the living situation of the UMs. Moving across areas of living, frequent change of living environments as well as schools attended can hinder stability and school success in the lives of UMs. Thus, we investigate two variables to capture these factors. These variables measure whether the individual has moved across counties during the period of the study and the number of times the individual has moved. In this analysis, we do not find significant results for these variables. However, one has to consider that these are crude measures of mobility since it is across counties. Detailed measures of mobility as across municipalities or moves within municipalities may capture such influence.

Family as a support system during the important developmental periods of children have an important influence in their school engagement, continuation and thus their school success. We investigate the influence of family in two ways, one by investigating the role of family reunification for UMs and two by comparing UMs and AMs since one of the main differences between these two groups are whether they arrived with their parents or not. In Table 6.2 we can see that those UMs who are reunified with their families have a lower probability of dropout by 10.6 percentage points compared to UMs who have not been reunified with their parents. This indicates that having their parents in Sweden is a protective factor that facilitates longer educational attainment. Given the current restrictions regarding family reunification in Sweden, this factor needs to be included in the discussions regarding the wellbeing of UMs in Sweden. We can also see that there are differences by country of origin in the dropout probabilities. Those from

118

Iraq and other countries in Asia are more likely to dropout when compared to those from Afghanistan; however, this is not the case for the rest of the

Table 6.2. Factors influencing the likelihood of dropout from the educational system for unaccompanied minors

Variables	
Female	-0.102
	(0.015)**
Age at registration (ref. cat.: 15)	
16	0.387
	(0.043)**
17	0.341
	(0.035)**
18	0.359
	(0.039)**
Moving across counties	-0.026
	(0.020)
Nb of moves	0.012
	(0.009)
Single	-0.011
	(0.015)
Parental reunification	-0.106
	(0.017)**
Place of birth (ref. cat.: Afghanistan)	
Iraq	0.168
	(0.023)**
Somalia	-0.027
	(0.021)
Other countries in the M.E.	-0.065
	(0.027)*
Other countries in Africa	-0.140
	(0.018)**
Other countries in Asia	0.276
	(0.037)**
County (ref. cat.: Stockholm)	
Skåne	0.075
	(0.028)**
Västra Götaland	0.061
	(0.020)**
Other counties	0.008
	(0.016)
N	4.332

* indicates significance at the 5-% level, and ** at the 1-% level.

groups – Somalia, other countries in Africa and other countries in the Middle East. In addition, we investigate whether region lived in Sweden has an influence on dropout behavior of UMs and students in general. We can see in Table 6.2 that those who live in Skåne and Västra Götaland are more likely to dropout when compared to those who live in Stockholm. Similar results have been reported with respect to the labor market as well, where those who live in Stockholm are more likely to be employed compared to those who live in other regions. Thus, in terms of both education and employment living in Stockholm seems to facilitate better outcomes. The first explanation can be related to selection, where those who are more successful and finish high school migrate to Stockholm. A second explanation can be the higher competence of the authorities in Stockholm in both planning and applying support systems for UMs. A third explanation can be related to the higher chances of getting a job in Stockholm, where this motivates the students to put more emphasis on graduating from high school to get a more qualified job.

Comparing unaccompanied and accompanied minors

As a next step, we compare UMs with the AMs to investigate whether there is a significant difference between these two groups as well as to investigate the direction of the difference. Column 1 in Table 6.3 shows that before controlling for any covariates UMs have a 5.9 percentage points higher probability to drop out the educational system before completing high school studies when compared to AMs. Although these are very similar groups, there are still some demographic differences between them, thus we control for these factors. The results in terms of the influence of each factor on dropout behavior are quite similar as in the previous estimation. However, we can see that after controlling for these factors UMs are still more likely to dropout when compared to AMs. Combined with our previous finding, where those UMs who were family reunified were less likely to dropout, this result also supports the importance of family as a protective factor with regard to education. Since the main difference between these two groups is whether they have a family in Sweden or not it indicates the facilitating influence of this factor in terms of education. However, there are also other differences between these two groups as discussed earlier in other studies, such as the extra support UMs receives both during and after reception (Çelikaksoy and Wadensjö, 2017a). However, it is an important question whether these support systems facilitate their employment opportunities or their educational career and in which ways they are supportive of the combination of a continued career in both.

Comparing unaccompanied minors, accompanied minors and native youth

As a final step, we compare the three groups. The first column in Table

6.4 shows that the probability of dropout is 21.4 percentage points higher for UMs compared to the native youth and this figure is 14.9 percentage

Table 6.3. Factors influencing the likelihood of dropout from the educational system for refugee youth

Variables	(1)	(2)
Unaccompanied minors	0.059	0.043
	(0.009)**	(0.009)**
Female		-0.139
		(0.009)**
Age at registration (ref. cat.: 15)		
16		0.056
		(0.015)**
17		0.058
		(0.014)**
18		0.049
		(0.014)**
Moving across counties		0.002
		(0.014)
Nb of moves		0.021
		(0.007)**
Single		-0.023
		(0.011)*
Place of birth (ref. cat.: Afghanistan)		
Iraq		0.112
		(0.017)**
Somalia		0.057
		(0.019)**
Other countries in the M.E.		-0.096
		(0.016)**
Other countries in Africa		-0.067
		(0.015)**
Other countries in Asia		0.181
		(0.022)**
County (ref. cat.: Stockholm)		
Skåne		0.037
		(0.016)*
Västra Götaland		0.042
		(0.013)**
Other counties		0.002
		(0.010)
N	9.047	9.047

* indicates significance at the 5-% level, and ** at the 1-% level.

points for AMs. Once we control for the demographic characteristics the marginal effect for UMs is lower, where they have a higher probability of dropout by 19.4 percentage points compared to the NY, whereas the

121

marginal effects for AMs is almost the same across the two models. Thus, UMs have a higher probability of dropout not only compared to the NY but also compared to their counterparts AMs who are from the same countries of origin and who arrived to Sweden at the same ages even after controlling for a rich set of demographic variables. This result indicates that this group faces unique circumstances that hinders their educational careers even when we compare them to their refugee youth counterparts. These differences are discussed in previous studies and some of them can be listed as the greater degree of financial pressure that UMs face to support themselves as well as supporting their families in the country of origin (Çelikaksoy and Wadensjö, 2017a).

Table 6.4. Factors influencing the likelihood of dropout from the educational system for refugee youth and native youth

Variables	(1)	(2)
Unaccompanied minors	0.214	0.194
	(0.009)**	(0.009)**
Accompanied minors	0.149	0.142
	(0.008)**	(0.008)**
Female		-0.099
		(0.005)**
Moving across counties		-0.039
		(0.009)**
Nb of moves		0.011
		(0.004)*
Single		-0.015
		(0.007)*
County (ref. cat.: Stockholm)		
Skåne		0.035
		(0.011)**
Västra Götaland		0.018
		(0.008)*
Other counties		0.021
		(0.006)**
N	17.077	17.077

* indicates significance at the 5-% level, and ** at the 1-% level.

Our results point to new insights regarding the UMs in Sweden in the case of their dropout behavior from the educational system. However, there are certain factors we would like to point out such as the applicability of our results for the current flows of UMs. Our study focuses on those who were registered during 2003–2005 and follows this group until 2015, thus follow-up studies are needed to see whether arrivals that are more recent follow the same patterns. In addition, some of the measures used in the study are too crude and more detailed measures such as in the case of 'area lived in' as well as other variables such as accommodation type would increase our understanding with regard to the influence of instability and living conditions on educational outcomes (Higgins; et al., 2018).

Our findings point out to the important role of the family as a support system especially during the critical developmental period of transition from childhood into adulthood. Our results show that both within the group of UMs and refugee youth having one's family in Sweden is a protective factor for completing high school studies. The long-term separation from families has an immensely negative impact on refugees in general that adversely affects their integration efforts. Thus, further research is needed to identify the mechanisms behind our findings. Furthermore, it is crucial to investigate further the unique challenges that UMs face with regard to school completion and develop the right support systems that facilitate their continuation in the educational system.

Conclusion

The number of unaccompanied minors and refugee children in Sweden increased much until 2016. Education of this group is a key question for its wellbeing of this group and their adoption to a new life in the destination country. The methods of support and facilitation of a continued and suitable educational process can be different for various demographic groups depending on their life situations. This is especially the case for those who arrive in Sweden at the age of 16 or 17. Thus, in this chapter we investigated the dropout behavior of UMs from the educational system before completing an upper-secondary education, which is one of the key factors for a better labor market career. Furthermore, education is especially important in the lives of UMs as a support system for their wellbeing. Thus, we investigate the factors that influence the dropout behavior of this group. Our findings show that family is an important support system for this group. We find that those who are reunited with their families are less likely to drop out of the educational system before completing an upper-secondary education. Considering these findings and the recent restrictions in family reunification policies in Sweden, the importance of family in the lives of UMs stays as an important area of concern. Thus, fast processing of the asylum claims of the children combined with faster, easier and more flexible possibility for these children to reunite with their parents, which is their basic human right would facilitate stability and security in their life allowing them to continue their education. As discussed earlier, this result also highlights the need for suitable support systems and plans for this group where they have the opportunity to combine work and education in different ways to support themselves and their families abroad without dropping out of the educational system. There are several other factors that influence dropout for this group, such as age at registration, country of origin and county of residence.

To investigate how youth who arrived as UMs are doing in the educational system compared to youth who arrived as minors from the same countries with a parent or other legal guardian (AMs), we looked at the arrival status defined by the Migration Board of Sweden according to UNHCR guidelines. Both before and after controls for factors that influence dropout behavior, we find that UMs are more likely to drop out of the educational system when compared to refugee youth who have arrived as AMs. This can be another indicator showing the importance of family as a support system in the decision to continue one's educational studies. Furthermore, this can also be a result of the different life circumstances of UMs compared to AMs despite the similarity of their demography in relation to migration. Some of these factors have been discussed in earlier studies such as the greater responsibility of UMs to support themselves financially compared to AMs as well as their responsibility to send remittances to families in the country of origin, which influences their dropout behavior (Çelikaksoy and Wadensjö, 2017a, b). Other reasons can be related to the migration patterns of the different groups where the previous educational attainment of UMs could be interrupted in a different way compared to that of those who migrated with their families, thus creating extra challenges in the educational system for this group. Thus, there is a need for further studies to investigate the different patterns and transitions for the groups as well as the mechanisms behind these patterns.

Adjustment refers to a process linking the domains of resilience, access, barriers, achievement, rights and support systems. Thus, investigating and understanding the specific life circumstances of this group is very important for developing support systems that can help this group to stay in the educational system. When we compare UMs and AMs with the native population, we see that by the age of late 20s there is a large gap in educational attainment which shows that the educational attainment of refugee youth is lower due to their specific circumstances and more so in the case of UMs. UMs receive relatively more support from the state during and after the asylum procedure compared to AMs (Çelikaksoy and Wadensjö, 2017a, b). Previous studies argue that this support can also be one of the mechanisms behind their high employment rates. However, this is clearly not the case in terms of their educational careers, which requires further attention. Thus, further research has to take a closer look at the mechanisms behind these outcomes that affect the wellbeing of this group in the short and the long run.

References

Ackerman, X., Dryden-Peterson, S. and Jalbout, M. (2008). A fourth year of war in Syria: What we still need to know about educating refugees. Brookings Institute, 2014/03/14.

Bhanbha, J. (2004). Seeking asylum alone: Treatment of separated and trafficked children in need of refugee protection. *International Migration*, 42(1), 141–148.

Çelikaksoy, A. and Wadensjö, E. (2015a). Unaccompanied Minors and Separated Refugee Children in Sweden: An Outlook on Demography, Education and Employment. *IZA Discussion Paper,* no 8963.

Çelikaksoy, A. and Wadensjö, E. (2015b) The Unaccompanied Refugee Minors and the Swedish Labour Market. *IZA Discussion Paper,* no 9306.

Çelikaksoy, A. and Wadensjö, E (2017a). Policies, practices and prospects: the unaccompanied minors in Sweden. *Social Work & Society,* 15(1), 1–16.

Çelikaksoy, A. and Wadensjö, E. (2017b). Refugee Youth in Sweden who arrived as unaccompanied minors and separated children. *Journal of Refugee Studies.* 30(4), 530–553.

Çelikaksoy, A. and Wadensjö, E. (2018). Sweden: Intergenerational mobility patterns in immigrant and native families, in *OECD Report: Catching up? Country studies on intergenerational mobility and children of immigrants?* OECD Publishing, Paris.

Çelikaksoy, A. and Wadensjö, E. (2019). Unaccompanied refugee minors in Sweden: education and wellbeing in the labour market. (*forthcoming*).

European Commission (EC) (2012). Shaping a common approach on unaccompanied minors. MEMO/12/716, Brussels.

Eurostat (2015). European statistics on migration.

Derlyn, I. and Broekaert, E. (2008). Unaccompanied refugee children and adolescents: The glaring contrast between a legal and a psychological perspective. *International Journal of Law and Psychiatry*, 31(4), 319–330.

Derlyn, I., Broekaert, E. and Schuyten, G. (2008). Emotional and behavioural problems in migrant adolescents in Belgium. *European Child & Adolescent Psychiatry*, 17(1), 54–62.

Derluyn, I. and Vervliet, M. (2012). 'The wellbeing of unaccompanied refugee minors', in *Health inequalities and risk factors among migrants and ethnic minorities.* Vol. 1, D. Ingleby, A. Krasnik, V. Lorant and O. Razum (Eds.), Garant, Antwerp/Apeldoorn pp. 95–109.

Huddleston, T. and Wolffhardt, A. (2016). Back to School: Responding tho the needs of newcomer refugee youth. *Migration Policy Group Report*, MPG 2016.

Keles, S., Friborg, O., Idsoe, T., Sirin, S. and Oppedal, B. (2018). Resilience and acculturation among unaccompanied refugee minors. *International Journal of Behavioral Development*, 42(1), 52-63.

Luster, T., Qin, D., Bates, L., Rana, M. and Lee, J.A. (2010). Successful adaption among Sudanese unaccompanied minors: perspectives of youth and foster parents. *Childhood*, 17(2), 197–211.

Migrationsverket (2015). Aktuellt om ensamkommandebarn och ungdomar. Mars Rapport. (Recent information about unaccompanied children and adolescents).

O'Higgins, A., Ott, E. M and Shea, M W. (2018). What is the Impact of Placement Type on Educational and Health Outcomes of Unaccompanied Refugee Minors? A Systematic Review of the Evidence. *Clinical Child and Family Psychology Review*, 21(2), 354–365.

Ream, R. K. and Rumberger, R. W. (2008). Student Engagement, Peer Social Capital, and School Droput Among Mexican American and Non-Latino White Students. *Sociology of Education*, 81(2), 109-139.

Rodriguez, N., Urrutia-Rojas, X. and Gonzalez, L. R. (2017). Unaccompanied minors from the Northern Central American countries in the migrant stream: social differentials and institutional contexts. *Journal of Ethnic and Migration Studies*, DOI: 10.1080/1369183X.2017.1404257.

Rousseau, C., Said, T. M., Gagne, M. J. and Bibeau, G. (1998). Resilience in unaccompanied minors from the North of Somalia. *Psychoanalytic Review*, 85(4), 615–637.

Seglem, K.B. (2014). Daily hassles and coping dispositions as predictors of psychological adjustment: A comparative study of young unaccompanied refugees and youth in resettlement country. *International Journal of Behavioural Development,* 38(3), 293–303.

CHAPTER 7

ERITREAN UNACCOMPANIED REFUGEE MINORS IN THE NETHERLANDS: WELLBEING AND HEALTH

Anna de Haan, Yodit Jacob, Trudy Mooren and Winta Ghebreab

Introduction

In 2015, 379,766 Eritreans worldwide sought asylum in another country or were on the road (2015, UNHCR). In the last few years there has been a growing number of unaccompanied refugee minors (URMs) from Eritrea. Of the 33,380 Eritreans that applied for asylum in Europe in 2016 (IND, 2017), 2870 applied for asylum in the Netherlands, of whom 773 Eritrean URMs (CBS, 2016).

Of the almost 7000 unaccompanied minors that were under child custody in the Netherlands at the beginning of 2017, three quarters came from Eritrea, Afghanistan and Syria. Hereof, Eritreans were the largest group (Nidos, 2017). Due to the political situation in Eritrea, most Eritrean asylum seekers in the Netherlands are currently being granted a (temporary) residence permit (Pharos, 2016a). However, the recent peace agreement between Eritrea and Ethiopia might influence this, which may lead to a decrease in residence permits being granted to Eritrean refugees. Once URMs have obtained residency in the Netherlands, many hope for family reunification there.

In the Netherlands, the reception, guidance, education and healthcare services for refugees from Eritrea have confronted professionals with new challenges. For instance, the large differences in culture and language between Eritrean URMs and professionals often cause miscommunication, mistrust, frustration and various other challenges on both parts. In response to these challenges, three studies have been conducted in order to tailor strategies to these newcomers. The studies have been carried out by organizations working in the field of (refugee) health care and guardianship. This chapter aims to provide insight into the background of Eritrean URMs in the Netherlands, their reasons for fleeing, experiences during the flight

127

and challenges they face in the host country, including stressors related to the family reunification procedure.

The following research questions will be answered:

- What are the concerns for Eritrean URMs when they start life in the Netherlands, and what are the relevant issues related to health and wellbeing?

- Which factors contribute to the ability to cope with adversity and challenges?

- What are the challenges professionals face when working with Eritrean URMs?

Background information

Eritrea is a relatively small African country that lies between Sudan, Ethiopia and the Red Sea. According to various sources that estimate the world population, Eritrea has a population between 5.2-5.9 million people in 2018 (e.g.; The Statistics Portal, 2018; United Nations, 2018; Worldometers, 2018). It is difficult to get accurate numbers due to limited demographic studies and information available, and fluctuation due to forced migration in Eritrea. The majority of the Eritreans belong to the Tigrinya population and slightly more than half of the residents are Christian (mainly Christian Orthodox and Catholic), the rest are Muslim (Pharos, 2016a). The most important languages are Tigrinya, Tigre, English and Arabic. Slightly more than one fifth of the population lives in cities.

Eritrea has one of the most oppressive regimes in the world. The most common reason for many young people to flee is the endless obligatory military service, which applies to both boys and girls (Amnesty International, 2015), and the threat of being arrested whenever you criticize the regime; there is no freedom of press, or political or religious freedom. Refusing compulsory military service or avoiding it and illegally trying to leave the country are regarded as serious crimes, and human rights violations such as torture take place in prisons (Ministerie van Veiligheid en Justitie, 2014a). That is why the Human Rights Council of the United Nations (UN) adopted a resolution (A/HRC/RES/26/24) condemning Eritrea for widespread and systematic violations of human rights and restrictions on fundamental freedoms. Specifically, the in practice 'open-ended' military service and forced labor during the period of service were mentioned, as well as arbitrary arrests and detention; disappearances; torture and ill-treatment; and restrictions on freedom of expression and on the practice of religion (Ministerie van Buitenlandse Zaken, 2015). Eritreans flee via the neighboring countries of Sudan and Ethiopia, after which most of them continue their journey via Libya, to cross the Mediterranean Sea by boat to Italy (Ministerie van Veiligheid en Justitie, 2014a). From there some travel to Northern

Europe. Within Europe, different routes are being followed to the Netherlands.

The majority of the Eritrean refugees in the Netherlands come from the areas bordering Ethiopia and share the same ethnic and religious background. A smaller part of the Eritrean refugees come from urban areas. Major variances in level of education are seen between Eritreans from rural and urban areas (Pharos, 2016a). Eritreans from urban areas have more years of education than Eritreans from rural areas. While access to higher secondary education and its quality is improved and more facilitated in the last decades, this applies mainly to cities and not to rural areas. According to UNESCO (2012a), on average about 67% of the Eritrean population is literate. Within the group of adolescents (15-24 years), the percentage of literates in 2010 was 89.3%. However, only 53.6% of the rural population was literate, compared to 82.6% of the urban population. In general, boys are higher educated than girls. One of the reasons for the minimum access to secondary education is the socioeconomic unfavorable situation of the parents. The oldest children (both boys and girls) often have to carry out agricultural or other work to financially contribute.

Both adults and children flee Eritrea, not always together, to avoid the obligatory military service. Although boys and girls are obligated to serve in the military from the age of 18, there are many signs of children being kidnapped and forced to serve in the military at the age of 15. It is said that children have been deliberately trying to double classes or drop out of school and hide, both in order not to be called for service. Children who double classes several times or drop out of school face being arrested during local and national razzias, and imprisonment at military camp follows, without any opportunity to continue their education. These factors lead many Eritrean URMs to flee the country prematurely out of fear for the military service. After leaving Eritrea some children spend a few years in a refugee camp before traveling to Europe. Educational services in refugee camps are not or only limited available, resulting in gaps in educational years. All this leads to a lower educational level.

The flight can sometimes take years and has great risks. Refugees run the risk of threats, torture, physical and sexual violence and they are often dependent on people smugglers for their journey to Europe (Ministerie van Buitenlandse Zaken, 2015; Van Reisen, 2016). Human traffickers and smugglers detain Eritrean refugees and, for example, demand a ransom from the remaining family. While men mostly deal with physical violence and torture, women run the particular risk of experiencing sexual violence. Additionally, all refugees have to pay large amounts of money to smugglers to be able to flee. The costs of a journey vary and depend on the travelling route, the means of transport (by plane or by car, boat, bus or train) and the necessary papers (Pharos, 2016a). According to information obtained from refugees, a trip to the Netherlands costs between 5,000 and 15,000 euros.

Family

Few of the Eritrean minors grew up in a traditional household with both parents. The traditional family composition has changed due to the long conscription. Most of the fathers and young adult sons often do not live at home during large parts of the year. This leads to mothers doing the upbringing alone and the absence of a daily 'father figure' in many households. Eritrean young people indicate that growing up without a father has led them lacking an exemplary figure (Pharos, 2016a). They had to bear a lot of responsibility from an early age, especially if they were the oldest in the family. In many cases at least one of the parents of the unaccompanied minors is still alive. If URMs have contact with their family, they usually experience a high level of support, despite the physical absence (Oppedal & Idsoe, 2015). The temporary travel companions that they encountered during the flight, or the villagers or local people with whom they fled, are often important to them (Pharos, 2016a).

Legal guardianship in the Netherlands

In the Netherlands, Nidos Foundation is the guardianship agency which, because of the absence of parents, has the legal custody over unaccompanied minors (both with and without a residence permit) (Nidos, 2018). The guardian accompanies the youngster with his or her asylum procedure and supervises the upbringing and care until he reaches the age of 18 years. The actual legal support is the responsibility of a lawyer. Guardianship also stops when the youngster returns to the country of origin before his 18th birthday, or when a parent arrives in the Netherlands and is able to take responsibility again. As a guardian, Nidos is also responsible for accommodating a child in the right form of reception. The practical and pedagogical daily care is usually carried out by third parties on behalf of Nidos (VNG, 2016). In practice, this is often an organization that also offers regular youth care.

The forms of reception include:

- Reception families: Nidos is responsible for the placement of URMs up to the age of 14. Often the families have a similar cultural background as the youngster.

- Small-scale reception facilities: Nidos is responsible for the placement of URMs of 15 years and older with a (temporary) residence permit. The daily care is carried out by local youth care institutions.

- Small-scale living facilities: COA (i.e., the Central Agency for the Reception of Asylum Seekers) is responsible for the placement of URM's of 15 years and older without a residence permit. COA is also responsible for younger URM's without a residence permit that cannot be placed in a reception family.

Education in the Netherlands

The first period of the stay in the new country is crucial for psychological health and long-term integration of unaccompanied minors (Eide & Hjern, 2008). Schooling is an important developmental task in this respect (Tuk & de Neef, 2015). Like other newcomers in the Netherlands, URMs attend secondary education in the Internationale Schakelklas (ISK). These are classes / departments / schools spread over the country where they mainly learn Dutch. In that ISK period, the URMs usually have contact with other newcomers. Education helps to return to a normal life and to work on a better future. The daily rhythm, a sense of purpose and direction in life, contact with peers, and respect and patience from the teachers all increase self-confidence and wellbeing (Wade, Mitchell & Baylis, 2005). Feeling connected and safety at school leads to less post-traumatic complaints such as depression and anxiety. Therefore, it is really important that the school and accompanying health care organizations work together intensively to ensure that health care can be started in time when needed (Fazel, Reed, Panter-Brick & Stein, 2011).

Methods

The findings presented in this chapter are based on three recently conducted studies in the Netherlands, as well as on literature.

Research questions 1 and 3 are answered using the exploratory study *'Van ver gekomen'* ('Having come from far') (Pharos, 2016a). In this study three focus group discussions were held with 22 Eritrean key persons (Dutch people of Eritrean origin who were themselves professionally involved in the reception, supervision and care for the new group of Eritreans). They speak the language, are affiliated with the background and culture of Eritrean refugees and have a trusted relationship with them. Five Eritrean URMs that recently arrived in the Netherlands also participated in one of these focus groups.

To help answer research question 1, exploratory study *'Welzijn en gezondheid gezinsherenigers'* ('Wellbeing and health of reunited families') (Pharos, 2018) was also made use of. In this study fifteen reunited families were interviewed. In 2016 and 2017 a large number of the newcomers in the Netherlands consisted of family members of refugees who arrived in the Netherlands before them. The fifteen respondent families have different nationalities: nine Syrian families (two of which Syrian-Palestinian), two families from Iraq, two families from Eritrea and two families from Sierra Leone. In most families several people were interviewed. In addition to the families, 25 professionals (e.g., general practitioners, school teachers, mental health care professionals, community health service professionals, and refugee mentors) took part as respondents through participation in local focus group discussions, by filling in a survey or via interviews. In this chapter, only the results regarding Eritrean families will be described. Within both exploratory studies, additional literature research was conducted, and the preliminary results were presented to and commented on by a group of experts.

Finally, results from *'Alleenstaande minderjarigen uit Eritrea in Nederland'* (hereinafter 'The Resilience Study'), which was conducted by Nidos together with Centrum '45/Arq (a Dutch mental health care institution) are used in answering all three research questions. This study was initiated to gain insight in the needs and challenges of URMs to adapt and prosper in a new society, as well as to develop tools needed for professionals in supporting them (Sleijpen, van Es, te Brake & Mooren, 2017). This study combined several methods, among which three focus groups with 18 Eritrean adolescents and interviews with seven mentors and eight legal guardians. For the focus groups, a participatory learning approach was chosen: after the initial focus group discussion, results were presented to the participants, providing them with the opportunity to respond to their accuracy. Proceedings of these discussions and interviews were analyzed using a structured qualitative method. Throughout the project, close cooperation with 'cultural mediators' took place, whom are Dutch of Eritrean origin. They do not only speak the language, but are also able to bridge cultural gaps.

Results

Concerns for Eritrean URMs when they start life in the Netherlands and the relevant health and wellbeing related issues

Adolescence is an important developmental phase in which young people can face complex challenges such as becoming independent and developing their own identity. These challenges also exist for URMs. Some of the tasks, however, are more complicated for them, such as entering into and maintaining friendships and working on their future in a new society (Tuk & de la Rive Box, 2000). Identity formation is complicated by the lack of role models. In addition, although many URMs have shown great autonomy during their flight, it is difficult to match these specific skills with the many rules and intensive guidance which they are faced with in the Netherlands (Sleijpen, van Es, te Brake & Mooren, 2018).

Even though the adolescent phase consists of some universal phenomena, such as biological changes, the psychosocial dimension of this period depends on the cultural context. For example, Eritrean young people come from a large family culture, which means that the family has a big influence on decision making. Families' interests are more dominant or have higher priority than one's own individual interest. In the Netherlands however, adolescents are asked to make their own decisions, to independently shape their own lives and to make choices aimed at their own individual development. This contrast creates an extra burden for these young people (Schippers, 2017; van der Veer, 2002). Thus, Eritrean URMs do not only have to shape their lives again in a strange, new country with a totally different culture and language and without the presence of their parents, family and other loved ones, but they also have to do this during an important developmental phase (van der Veer, 2002).

Education

With respect to education, social and cultural differences play a role. In the Eritrean culture values like respect and patience are really important, while in the Netherlands much more value is attached to assertiveness, something that in Eritrean education is not being encouraged (Ghebreab, 2017). In Eritrean schools there are mainly classroom lessons with little active participation or self-study, while in the Netherlands these two skills are expected from the youngsters especially (Ferrier & Massink, 2016). For instance, in Eritrea students do not question their teachers, as it is considered to be rude in their culture. This is totally different from the situation in the Netherlands, where discussions with teachers are encouraged.

Financial debts

Eritrean URMs in the Netherlands feel great financial responsibility towards their family (Pharos, 2016a). They often want (and need) to financially support their family who stayed behind and the minors are often in large debts as a result of enormous sums of money that parents and other family members had to pay to let them travel to Europe. In addition, family members are sometimes held captive by human traffickers and the URMs are then forced to pay to free these family members (Sleijpen et al., 2017). Furthermore, the minors have little knowledge about the financial system in the Netherlands. The debts incurred by the URMs before and during the trip can have an impeding effect on their participation in Dutch society (Pharos, 2016a). Having debts can lead Eritrean minors to take more risks to get money. This could include getting expensive loans, prostitution, or making arrangements with smugglers.

Sexual and reproductive health

There is little knowledge about sexual and reproductive health among the Eritrean refugees who come to the Netherlands (Pharos, 2016a). Health workers who work closely with URMs have the impression that there are misconceptions about contraception and sexually transgressive behavior. There is now a lack of a strong social control within communities, that used to ensure that boys and girls have limited sexual contact with each other. Virginity for marriage is an important norm, although it is stronger in rural areas than in the city. Most young people start to experiment sexually after they have fled Eritrea (Pharos, 2016a). During the journey, young people are on their own and therefore they draw together. The combination of low (parental) supervision and the fact that they are at the age at which they discover their sexuality may cause problems. Furthermore, in the Netherlands during the stay at a reception location, there is also little supervision and relatively much freedom. High numbers of unplanned pregnancies are seen among female Eritrean refugees (including the unaccompanied minors). In a study among 12 pregnant Eritrean women in the Dutch primary care, half of these women describe their pregnancy as unplanned (Jacob, 2018). These problems are partly related to their low level of education, which often means that they have little basic knowledge about their body, and that they have (limited) health skills which are not always recognized or are of less use in the Netherlands.

Psychological health

Eritrean young people have often experienced much distress, but they hardly talk about it (Pharos, 2016a). Within the Eritrean culture there is a taboo on having psychological problems: people are afraid to be seen as 'crazy'. Their own suffering is put into perspective and compared with the even greater suffering of 'the other'. Sometimes, young people attribute their problems to supernatural powers, such as black magic.

On arrival, many URMs have high expectations of their future. Having success contributes to the honor and wellbeing of the family. Implicit and explicit expectations of the family, such as becoming successful and prosperous, can have a lot of influence on the youngsters. Failure to comply with these expectations can lead to grief, guilt, shame, anger or psychological problems (Bronstein & Montgomery, 2011; Sleijpen et al., 2017). Additionally, because they often feel that they cannot help their family members enough, this leads to feelings of powerlessness. URMs have a higher risk of having psychological problems in the reception countries than other refugees and children with a migrant background, even years after they have received a residence permit (Bloemen & Tuk, 2010; Bronstein & Montgomery, 2011; Derluyn, Mels & Broekaert, 2009; Huemer et al., 2009). These often involve complaints such as depression and anxiety. Research shows that 60% of all the unaccompanied minors need psychological help, while only 10 to 20% of them actually receive it (Bean, 2006).

If psychological problems seriously hamper daily functioning, referral to mental health care may be necessary. However, usually this does not work well. This may have to do with factors such as avoidance as part of traumatization, unfamiliarity with mental health care, the taboo around psychological complaints, and the fear of stigma. In addition, the care offered does not always meet the needs of the youngsters (Pharos, 2016b), and the minors can be distrustful upon arrival in the Netherlands, as distrust may have been functional on the road when they ran the risk of deception, theft, rape and extreme violence (Ní Raghallaigh, 2013). Gaining their trust is therefore essential.

Family reunification

All URMs in the Netherlands whose asylum applications have been granted have the right to be reunited with their parents and siblings (under the age of 18), because this is in the best interest of the child. In general, realizing family reunification is one of the most important goals for URMs in the Netherlands. Eritrean URMs feel a great amount of responsibility towards the wellbeing of their parents, siblings and family members. When successful, it gives URMs a great sense of pride and fulfillment of obligation: a sense of 'giving back'. Being together as family, supporting each other, being complete, is important for integration, as it serves as a powerful protective factor. Especially in the first phase after the reunification, this is tangible: people experience enormous relief and joy to be reunited, and have hope for the future again (Pharos, 2018).

The family reunification procedure can take up all the time and attention of the youngsters and, for example, may seriously impede going to school and learning the Dutch language (Sleijpen, van Es, te Brake & Mooren, 2018). Applications for family reunification of Eritrean minors are by no means always granted. For example, the number of granted family reunification applications for Eritrean refugees has dropped from 50% to 29% between the end of 2015 and the end of 2016 (Pharos, 2018), while this number is around 70% for Syrian refugees in general. In the Netherlands, since 2015, greater importance is attached to the possession of official documents. Because Eritreans often lack these documents, a large part of the applications are rejected (Tweede Kamer der Staten-Generaal, 2017). In addition, some of the family members do not succeed in leaving Eritrea. Thus, many of the Eritreans who come to the Netherlands alone, will not be able to reunite with their family: in 2014 this accounted for 86% of the Eritrean URMs (Pharos, 2018). If reunification is not realized it brings feelings of failure, stress and disappointment.

Eritrean URMs have to deal with a long waiting period in the years prior to reunification. The waiting period produces stress and affects the health and integration of the youngsters. At the same time the waiting time can also have a negative impact on the family members who are not yet in the Netherlands. They often remain in difficult circumstances for a long time, either in Eritrea or in a refugee camp in another country, thereby experiencing insecurity and inadequate facilities (Pharos, 2018). The long and unclear procedure regularly causes mistrust between family members. When family reunification is finally granted, problems sometimes arise (Schippers, 2017). The Resilience Study showed that the family reunification process was of such importance to the Eritrean URMs that they often found it difficult to focus on educational goals or improving self-sufficiency skills (Sleijpen, et al., 2017). The study noted that while Eritrean URMs feel honored for having the opportunity to help their family, the lack of understanding of the process, and the lack of communication with guardians and mentors about this process causes stress. Eritrean URMs felt at times discouraged from undertaking family reunification – this may have been the case as professionals, well-meaningly, thought that the URMs should focus on self-sufficiency first and tried to shelter the URM from the disappointment of the low success rate of the reunification procedure.

In the period prior to family reunification, many URMs will have become accustomed to a certain degree of independence and the much greater freedom compared to what they were used to in Eritrea. In fact, family reunification often means relocating and a break with the network that has been built up and possibly a break with the educational career. Living together again can, in a number of cases, lead to great tensions in the beginning, but also long after family reunification (Schippers & van der Velden, 2016). At the same time, the parents have to get used to their parental role again, while their child has changed (Pharos, 2018). Such situations can lead to parenting problems or to the youngster being overburdened.

Factors contributing to the ability to cope with adversity and challenges

Despite the problems and challenges mentioned above, it is important to realize that URMs are young and resilient and their physical health is relatively good. Factors that have a positive effect on health are: being able to pick up normal life as quickly as possible with a perspective on work, education or other forms of participation, having sufficient social support and networks, clarity about residence, and proximity to close relatives (Naber & Uzozie, 2016). However, unaccompanied minors lack the important protective factor of close parental and family support. Coping mechanisms often utilized include interaction with and peer support from other Eritreans and interaction with their religious institution. Indeed, a remarkable ability amongst Eritrean URMs to support each other in dealing with difficulties was noted by the Resilience Study (Sleijpen, et al., 2017).

The Resilience Study remarked that Eritrean URMs were capable of clearly describing their needs and challenges and the factors influencing their wellbeing and behaviour. They also felt unrecognized as (young) adults who are able to take care of themselves. Often reported complaints were feelings of 'not being heard'. Also, confusion was felt on the part of Eritrean URMs in terms of what is expected from them in the Netherlands, particularly in the shared living facilities (Sleijpen, et al., 2017). Eritrean URMs showed a great sense of responsibility towards family members that were left behind, and towards their education (they showed a high motivation to learn their new host language) and in completing household chores and their daily activities.

Challenges perceived by professionals

Both health professionals and URMs indicate that there are barriers to mental health care services. Indeed, in order to alleviate psychological stress, Eritrean URMs turn to religion and peers as an important coping strategy which reduces URMs' inclinations to rely upon other available mechanisms, thus limiting the opportunity to receive professional help or to adapt to the new host society. Examples of barriers are perceived stigma ("I am not psychiatrically disturbed"), waiting lists and formal intake procedures. Additionally, it is difficult for Eritrean URMs to adapt to the Dutch health care system and to understand how psychological problems are caused and can be treated (Pharos, 2016a).

An adequate preparation for living autonomously after URMs become 18, has been acknowledged as a delicate issue by all mentors that participated in the focus groups. It is difficult to sufficiently prepare URMs to be able to stand on their own two feet once they become 18. Nevertheless, mentors emphasize that they try to encourage school attendance, language acquisition, and realistic expectations from the Dutch society as much as possible. With regard to relationships between professionals and URMs, first of all, guardians and mentors indicate that in general Eritrean URMs need more support, and hence more time from professionals than is available, which often leads to tension between the URMs and their guardians and mentors (Sleijpen, et al., 2017). Mostly, guardians report difficulty in understanding the cultural background of the Eritrean URMs and language barriers complicate communication. These differences between Dutch professionals and Eritrean URMs often cause miscommunication, mistrust, frustration and various challenges on both parts. In general, not sharing the same language hinders being effective in offering help. Professionals report concerns about the quality of available interpretation services, which may also contribute to the distance experienced with URMs.

Also worth to be noted is that URMs, like other young people, want to self-manage and self-direct which, at times, may lead to mutual disappointment and clashes. They miss having a say in important decisions. Eritrean URMs in particular have been travelling from their point of origin alone for lengthy periods, sometimes years, and thus as mentioned before in this chapter have demonstrated a strong ability to operate independently. Furthermore, Eritrean culture and religion sometimes dictate different patterns of socialization, food and organization. For these reasons, the new routines and rules cause confusion and fear among some of the Eritrean URMs causing them to disregard their guardians' and mentors' instructions. Such behaviour would sometimes be interpreted as being obstinate or demanding (Sleijpen, et al., 2017). Guardians and mentors report that having meaningful conversations and getting to know Eritrean URMs under their care was challenging. As a result, guardians were under the impression that Eritrean URMs did not trust them, which some guardians feel is a necessary condition to effectively carry out their work.

Discussion and Conclusion

Explorative studies regarding Eritrean URMs in the Netherlands have contributed to a greater knowledge of Eritrean URMs. The results provide more insight into the socioeconomic and educational background of Eritrean URMs, their reasons for fleeing, the experiences they endured during the flight and the social, educational and health challenges they face in the host country. For instance, family reunification is of great importance for the wellbeing and health of the URMs. Being together as a family, supporting each other, being complete, is important for integration and is a powerful protective factor. It was also shown that the wellbeing of Eritrean URMs can fluctuate and largely depends on factors such as the presence and wellbeing of their family, the quality of services of professionals in the Netherlands, the social environment they live in (e.g., the changing policy towards a less positive political climate and stricter rules and regulations concerning integration) and current events in their country of origin. Understanding how these factors interact with each other and affect the lives of Eritrean URMs, will help to improve their wellbeing.

In addition, the studies provide insight into the challenges professionals face in working with Eritrean URMs and the policy and institutional framework needed to adequately support these minors. Indeed, research has shown that the first period of the stay in the new country is crucial for psychological health and long-term integration of URMs (Eide & Hjern, 2008). Schooling is an important development task in this respect (Tuk & de Neef, 2015).

It should be noted that the time factor is really important. Firstly, in general most Eritrean URMs reach Europe at the age of 16 or 17, meaning that professionals often have less than one year to build trust and achieve the guardianship goals of self-sufficiency. Secondly, the steep increase in the number of refugees arriving to Europe in 2014 and 2015, caused great strains on systems, organizations and professionals (e.g., professionals had less time per pupil) to provide the necessary support. For example, it was found that guardians and mediators had little experience with Eritrean URMs (on average, one-year or less) and that continuity in care could not always be ensured (some URMs had multiple guardians or lived at multiple reception facilities) (Sleijpen, et al., 2017).

Another topic the studies bring to attention is the misunderstanding of cultural norms (including coping mechanisms) by Eritrean URMs and professionals, which is the cause of much miscommunication, and therefore distrust. For instance, is the reliance on religion and religious rituals a healthy coping mechanism or an obstacle for integration? The Resilience Study found that the initial distrust can be rectified by showing genuine interest and cooperating with each other, for example through informal dialogue, so that little-by-little confidence can be gained (Sleijpen, et al., 2017). The active involvement of, and closely working together with cultural mediators or key persons supports this process and bridges cultural gaps, which may be an important step forward to healthy integrative pathways in the new society. For several Dutch institutions that work with URMs, such as Nidos, Centrum '45/Arq and Pharos, working together with cultural mediators and key persons is now an integrated part of their working methods.

References

Amnesty International (2015). Just deserters: why indefinite national service in Eritrea has created a generation of refugees. Index: AFR 64/2930/2015.

Centraal Bureau voor de Statistiek (2016, 30 juni). Alleenstaande minderjarige vreemdeling; nationaliteit, geslacht en leeftijd. http://statline.cbs.nl/Statweb/publication/?VW=T&DM=SLNL&PA=82045ned&D1=0&D2=a&D3=0&D4=0&D5=a&HD=160715-1016&HDR=T%2cG1&STB=G2%2cG3% 2cG4=

Eide, K. & Hjern, A. (2013). Unaccompanied Refugee Children – Vulnerability and Agency. Stockholm. DOI:10.1111/apa.12258

Fazel, M., Reed, R.V., Panter-Brick, C. & Stein, A. (2011). Mental health of displaced and refugee children resettled inhigh-income countries: risk and protective factors. Lancet; 379: 266–82. DOI:10.1016/S0140-6736(11)60051-2.

Ferrier, J., & Massink, L. (2016). Overleven in Nederland. Nijmegen PreciesAdvies.

Ghebreab, W. (2017). Notitie: Wat zou ik moeten weten over onderwijs in Eritrea. Utrecht: Nidos.

Ministerie van Buitenlandse Zaken (2015). Algemeen Ambtsbericht Eritrea, Juli 2015. Beschikbaar via: www.rijksoverheid.nl/documenten/ambtsberichten/2015/07/30/eritrea-2015-07-30

Ministerie van Veiligheid en Justitie (2014a). Kamerbrief, Stand van zaken ontwikkelingen asielinstroom vanuit Eritrea. Beschikbaar via: www.rijksoverheid.nl/documenten-en publicaties/kamerstukken/2014/05/20/stand-van-zaken-ontwikkelingen-asielinstroom-vanuit-eritrea.html (geraadpleegd 07-07-2015).

Naber, P. & Uzozie, A. (2016). Match voor de toekomst?: Een verkennend onderzoek naar de bijdrage van maatjesprojecten aan de maatschappelijke participatie van jonge alleenstaande asielzoekers. Amsterdam.

Nidos (2017). Nidos 2017 Jaarverslag. https://www.nidos.nl/wp-content/uploads/2018/06/Jaarverslag-2017.pdf

Nidos (2018). http://www.nidos.nl/ (geraadpleegd 19-10-2018)

Oppedal, B & Idsoe, T. (2015). Personality and Social Psychology: The role of social support in the acculturation and mental health of unaccompanied minor asylum seekers. Scandinavian Journal of Psychology, 203–211 DOI: 10.1111/sjop.12194

Pharos (2016a). 'Van ver gekomen…'. Een Verkenning naar het welzijn en de gezondheid van Eritrese vluchtelingen. Utrecht: Pharos. http://www.pharos.nl/documents/doc/verkenning%20eritreers%20-van%20ver%20gekomen..-.pdf

Pharos (2016b). Kennissynthese gezondheid van nieuwkomende vluchtelingen en indicaties voor zorg, preventie en ondersteuning. http://www.pharos.nl/documents/doc/kennissynthese%20gezondheid%20van%20nieuwkomende%20vluchtelingen%20en%20 indicaties%20voor%20zorg%20preventie%20en%20ondersteuning.pdf

Pharos (2017). Factsheet Eritrese vluchtelingen. Utrecht: Pharos.

Pharos (2018). Welzijn en gezondheid gezinsherenigers. Een verkenning. Utrecht: Pharos. http://www.pharos.nl/documents/doc/welzijn_en_gezondheid_van_gezinsherenigers-een%20verkenning-pharos.pdf

Schippers, M. (2017). Kinderen, gevlucht en alleen. Utrecht: Nidos.

Schippers, M.T. & van der Velden, M.M.C. (2016). Tijdschrift Jeugdgezondheidszorg, 48: 107. DOI:10.1007/s12452-016-0077-3

Sleijpen, M., van Es, C., te Brake, H. & Mooren, T. (2017). Alleenstaande minderjarigen uit Eritrea in Nederland. Utrecht: Nidos.

Sleijpen, M., van Es, C., te Brake, H. & Mooren, T (2018). Toolkit voor de begeleiding van Eritrese alleenstaande minderjarigen in Nederland. Amsterdam: Arq Psychotrauma Expert Groep.

The Statistics Portal (2018).

Tuk, B & Neef, de, M. (2015). Welkom op School – Docentenboek Mentormethode (vo) en lessen relaties en seksualiteit voor nieuwkomers. Utrecht: Pharos

Tweede Kamer der Staten-Generaal (2017b). Vergaderjaar 2016-2017, Aanhangsel van de Handelingen, nr.2249.

UNESCO (2012a). High level International Round Table on Literacy: 'Reaching the 2015 Literacy Target: Delivering on the promise'. www.unesco.org/new/fileadmin/MULTIMEDIA/HQ/ED/pdf/Eritrea.pdf.

United Nations (2018). https://population.un.org/wpp/DataQuery/

Van Reisen, M. (2016). The involvement of unaccompanied minors from Eritrea in human trafficking. http://www.eepa.eu/wcm/dmdocuments/publications/the_Involvement_of_unaccompanied_minors_in_ht.pdf (geraadpleegd 16-03-2017)

VNG (2016). Factsheet Alleenstaande Minderjarige Vreemdelingen (AMV'ers). Platform Opnieuw Thuis & VNG/OTAV. https://vng.nl/files/vng/20160531-factsheet-amv.pdf.

Wade J, Mitchell F, Baylis G. (2005). Unaccompanied asylum seeking children. The response of social work services. London: BAAF Adoption & Fostering.

Worldometers (2018). http://www.worldometers.info/world-population/eritrea-population/.

CHAPTER 8

SOCIAL INCLUSION PROCESSES FOR UNACCOMPANIED MINORS IN THE CITY OF PALERMO: FOSTERING AUTONOMY THROUGH A NEW SOCIAL INCLUSION MODEL

Roberta Lo Bianco and Georgia Chondrou

Introduction

This chapter describes and proposes a new social inclusion model for supporting unaccompanied minors in becoming autonomous, as they are one of the most vulnerable groups of contemporary migration flows. According to the Committee on the Rights of Children "unaccompanied children (also called unaccompanied minors) are children, [...] who have been separated from both parents and other relatives and are not being cared for by an adult who, by law or custom, is responsible for doing so" (Committee on the Rights of the Child, 2005)[1].

According to the monthly report, "*Unaccompanied Foreign Minors in Italy*", published by the Ministry of Labour and Social Policies (June 2018), 13,151 unaccompanied foreign minors (UAMs) live in Italy. The majority of them are males (92.5% vs 7.5% females) between fifteen and seventeen years old (83.9%). The nationalities represented are over forty, however they mainly come from the western, northern or eastern African countries (over 70%), e.g. Gambia, Egypt, Guinea, Ivory Coast, Eritrea, Nigeria, Senegal, Mali, Somalia. The other countries of origin are Albania, Bangladesh, Pakistan and Kosovo.

Italy was ranked the sixth among the top-ten receiving countries for UAMs in 2015 (with 4,070 applications), while it climbed up to the second position in 2016 with 6,020 UAMs registered (Eurostat, News release,

---

[1] UN Committee on the Rights of the Child (CRC), *General comment No. 6 (2005): Treatment of Unaccompanied and Separated Children Outside their Country of Origin*, 1 September 2005, CRC/GC/2005/6, p., 5 available at: https://www2.ohchr.org/english/bodies/crc/docs/GC6.pdf [accessed 5 February 2019]

80/2017). In 2016, a total of 13,862 UAMs lived in Italy (Ministry of Labour and Social Policies, August 2016). The areas the most affected by the arrivals also host the largest number of UAMs; 43.3% of them (5,699 minors) live in Sicily. The others are distributed, e.g., in the region of Lombardy (7.5% of the population, 980 minors), Lazio (7%, 921 minors), Emilia Romagna (6.6%, 862 minors) (Ministry of Labour and Social Policies, June 2018).

According to the report "*Il Modello Palermo: la presa in carico delle ragazze e dei ragazzi stranieri non accompagnati*" (The Palermo Approach: Dealing with Unaccompanied minors) published by the Municipality of Palermo, 90 minors were hosted in Palermo in 2013, and the number increased to 1,300 in 2016 (Comune di Palermo, 2018). As of July 7th, 2018, the Municipality accommodates 300 unaccompanied minors whose statistics are in line with the national context. These fluctuations can be explained with the changes in migration policy (Scherer, 2018), as increasing restrictions were posed on rescue ships. In addition, many UAMs progressively reached the age of 18, so they are no longer considered as minors in official statistics.

As the number and share of UAMs in migration flows increased in importance in the past few years, the need for new approaches, programmes and inclusion policies has risen (Giovannetti, 2017). Furthermore, due to their life stories and cultural backgrounds, UAMs might feel and act like adults (Rania, et al., 2014; Novara et al., 2016). For this reason, it does not seem adequate to apply the same approach and facilities used with Italian children in foster care system to UAMs, as these two vulnerable groups have different material and emotional needs. In addition, researchers agree that Italian reception policies are mainly focused on the material wellbeing of UAMs, as inclusion-oriented measures have a secondary role (Catarci and Rocchi, 2017; Rania et al., 2018). Moreover, most reception centres in Italy are located in remote places, far from relevant facilities (e.g. youth centres, recreational facilities, migrant associations etc.), which are necessary to include young people within the society effectively. As a result, UAMs' inclusion process is not very efficient (Catarci and Rocchi, 2017).

It is also possible to distinguish between a structured inclusion process (i.e. guided by social workers, outlined in a policy paper) and a 'spontaneous' one (resulting from informal encounters with fellow migrants, especially from the same cultural background). Melossi and Giovanetti (2002) state that these encounters "are a key factor for the success or failure of a migration project". Therefore, the initial influences on the newly arrived UAMs are crucial and determine their path in the host country, their relationships with the law and their inclusion process (Giovannetti, 2017).

Rania, Migliorini and Fagnini compare three intervention and integration projects carried out in Sicily, Tuscany and Veneto between 2014 and 2016 and conclude that, even though these programmes sought to provide UAMs with more effective inclusion measures, they managed to reach only a small portion of the overall UAM population (Rania et al., 2014; Novara et al., 2016). These projects did not have great impact because they were not incorporated into the state's reception policies.

We can deduce that a structured inclusion model was needed to reach a greater number of UAMs arriving in Italy and help them become part of their hosting communities. This chapter describes a holistic social inclusion model implemented in the city of Palermo, which strives to accompany UAMs towards autonomy. It presents its methodology and the holistic learning processes targeted at UAMs to promote a better inclusion of the minors. The results of the project show that for social inclusion interventions collaboration between the private and public actors is necessary. Moreover, it is essential to work with the vulnerable groups concerned, to create effective models and approaches that can answer all their needs. We advocate this model to be implemented in other contexts.

In what follows, we first give some background information that enables a better understanding of the context in which the project in Palermo was established. Then we describe the project.

Background

Motives for migration and experiences during the journey

Minors decide to undertake the migration journey for multiple reasons, and it is impossible to gain a comprehensive insight into their motives. UAMs often come from conflict-affected countries, sometimes ruled by dictatorship, where they see few opportunities of escaping poverty and going after their dreams (REACH, 2017).

Research, carried out by Demurtas et al. shows that for some of these minors, the decision of undertaking the 'journey' to Europe is taken together with their families: an investment to improve their living conditions and go after a better future (e.g. Demurtas et al., 2018) In other cases the influence of peers or family members that have already moved to Europe seems to play an important role, as they decide to migrate without taking into consideration the dangers and hardships that the journey itself entails (e.g. INTERSOS, 2017).

Being confined in migrant detention centres in Libya, final departure point of the central Mediterranean route is among the most violent experiences with a deep physical and emotional impact on the life of these UAMs, which has frequently been observed when they finally reach the Italian coast (OXFAM, 2018).

It is important to note that UAMs are mostly unaware of the challenges they would face upon their arrival in Europe (Demurtas et al, 2018), as they do not even have a clear idea of the European geography. Those who already have a destination country in mind, based on the presence of family or friends would usually try to escape the reception system and travel to the desired country, as family reunification procedures take a long time to be completed (Zandonini, 2017).

Italy tends to be the destination of those who lack this kind of family ties and hope to find educational and professional opportunities there, which would allow them to support their families and create their new home. In these cases, the reception system plays a crucial role in determining the speed at which they adapt to and become active members of their new local community.

Accommodation and Care System of Unaccompanied minors

Once the identification process has been finalised, UAMs access the accommodation and care system. Initially, they are hosted in First Reception Centres (Centri di Prima Accoglienza, CPA) managed by the Ministry of Interior (MI), or in Temporary Reception Centres (Centri di Accoglienza Straordinaria, CAS). In both centres, professionals carry out relevant procedures in order to define the legal position of migrants and start processing international protection claims. Their stay in these centres is limited to the time strictly necessary for the applicant to be transferred to second reception centres (Colombo, 2017). The first and temporary reception facilities do not offer inclusion programmes to their residents.

Second-line reception is managed by municipalities and funded by the Ministry of Interior. UAMs are accommodated in small-scale facilities provided by the System for the Protection of Minor Asylum Seekers and Refugees (SPRAR Minori) such as community housing (where also local disadvantaged children are hosted) and apartment-sharing groups. In second reception facilities social workers help minors set up their 'Individual Educational Plan' (*Progetto Educativo Individualizzato*, PEI) (Servizio Centrale SPRAR, 2017), after having assessed their educational and social needs, in order to initiate their path towards an autonomous and active life in the hosting communities. These programmes offer vocational training, career guidance and school enrolment. Even though this framework is outlined by relevant legislation, individual educational plans are not always as effective as they should be, since they are not based on children's actual goals and motivations.

In case of unavailability of places in second reception facilities, which frequently occurs in Sicily, minors are hosted in CAS. In these structures, minor migrants can wait for an indefinite amount of time for their inclusion process to start, and they often age out of the system without having been able to set up their educational plan.

Asylum Procedure and residence permit for minor age

According to Italian legislation, in the aforementioned reception facilities migrant minors could be assigned a guardian who will support them in regularising their stay and becoming more autonomous. Guardians act as a point of reference in unknown territory.

Minors have two possibilities to regularise their stay: Non-asylum-seeking unaccompanied minors, supported by their guardian or the head of the reception centre they live in, can ask the public authority to issue a residence permit due to being a minor. All minors have the right to apply to the state in which they are, to obtain a residence permit for being a minor[2]. The legislation foresees that for the acquirement of the residence permit for minor age, identification papers, such as the passport from the country of origin, is not necessary[3]. When the migrant turns 18, the social services of the Municipality, the guardian, the manager of the facility where the minors lived, or the minors themselves may submit a request to the Juvenile Court so that it can decide on the so-called *prosieguo amministrativo (administrative follow-up)*. With this, ex-minors can keep relying on the social services they have been provided with, up to 21 years of age and complete the inclusion process they had started[4]. After having turned 18, non-asylum-seeking minors who could not apply for this measure, (Prosieguo Amministrativo), could apply for a residence permit for studies or work purposes.

Secondly, asylum-seeking unaccompanied minors can apply for international protection to regularize their stay. Such applications are examined by the Commission for the Recognition of International Protection. If UAMs are granted refugee status, they receive a 5-year renewable residence permit. If the asylum application is rejected, the minor has the right to appeal once. Most of the legal procedures last months as a result of which the minor reaches the age of majority and is no longer protected under the status of a minor. In cases where the person does not win the appeal[5] and has already reached the age of majority, the police office gives them a 'sheet of road' (7 days paper) but does not force repatriation due to the absence of bilateral agreements with many countries from which minors arrive.

In cases when the asylum application is rejected, the Territorial Commission, entitled to process the asylum application, may still decide to issue a 2-year residence permit on humanitarian grounds in order to allow those unaccompanied children to build up an inclusion process and access educational and professional opportunities.

---

[2] The asylum application is a procedure that can be applied for simultaneously.

[3] This right has often been denied because the police requests for an identification proof, thus requiring for the passport, which has led minors to directly apply for asylum.

[4] More information on the topic can be accessed at : http://www.tavolonazionaleaffido.it/2018/09/16/prosieguo-amministrativo-e-msna-una-delibera-regionale-del-fvg/ (in Italian)

[5] Before Minniti-Orlando Law came into force, minors were entitled to a second appeal. More information can be accessed at: https://openmigration.org/en/analyses/why-the-new-italian-law-on-immigration-and-asylum-is-not-good-news-at-all/

Recent changes in legislation and bottlenecks in implementation

On April 7th 2017, Law no. 47 (the so-called Zampa Law after the Italian politician Sandra Zampa who drafted the bill) came in to force. This legislative measure can be regarded as the first attempt to improve the reception system and protection mechanisms for UAMs in Italy as it put together and harmonised existing legal provisions. Italy became the first European country to legislate a comprehensive framework for protecting unaccompanied children (Lelliott, 2018).

The Zampa Law introduced new tools to improve the living conditions of UAMs, and among others, addressed serious gaps in the reception system.

For instance, before this law came into force, minors could not start the proceedings to regularise their stay in Italy, unless a guardian was appointed. Such process could take several months as the guardianship system was extremely congested, causing migrants who turned 18 to lose special protection benefits connected to their status (Rozzi, 2017). In compliance with the new regulation, the legal representative of the reception centre can serve as a guardian and help the minors submit their asylum application or a request for a residence permit due to minor age. In addition, people coming from civil society can apply and become 'volunteer guardians' selected and trained by the Regional or Metropolitan Ombudsperson for Children (FRA, 2018). Volunteer guardians may take care of maximum of three minors, in order to individually assist each of the minors throughout the process[6].

In spite of the new protection measures introduced, the Zampa Law faces bottlenecks in implementation, especially in the effective management of unaccompanied foreign minors in Italy.

Most UAMs are still forced to stay longer in first or temporary reception centres due to the lack of accommodation in housing communities under the SPRAR system. The major part of the UAMs turn 18 while waiting for their inclusion process to start (Zandonini, 2017). Another problem, which has not been addressed by recent legislation, are the conditions of reception centres that are often overcrowded or exceed the limit of their capacity. This scenario is quite common in the region of Sicily where the largest percentage of UAM population resides.

Moreover, it is common for UAMs to be relocated from one facility to another, which in most cases also means they need to move from one city to another, mainly due to administrative issues (e.g. limited availability of places,

---

[6] As for the reception system, Law no. 47/2017 has reduced the duration of stay in first reception centres from sixty to thirty days. This change was implemented in order to improve UAMs living conditions considering that in most cases minors could spend up to one year in first reception facilities (Colombo, 2017).

closing housing communities), regardless of the results they had achieved in their path towards inclusion and autonomy. This precarious condition hinders the continuity of their learning path, which might affect their psychological wellbeing.

Developing Innovative Practices – The *Ragazzi Harraga* Project

Having observed the local reality of UAMs, a group of NGOs and associations joined forces to develop the *Ragazzi Harraga* project[7] in order to answer local needs, ensure the inclusion of UAMs and promote active citizenship. The project proposal was conceived in 2016 when Italy (and Palermo) faced a high influx of unaccompanied minor asylum seekers. The aim of the project is to strengthen, test and evaluate innovative pathways to sustain unaccompanied minors' transition to adulthood, by offering them a series of educational experiences such as training opportunities and work placement, as well as independent housing solutions. The innovative project uses a more 'local inclusion-oriented approach' instead of the one based on 'material wellbeing of migrants'.

Methodology for Defining an Effective Inclusion Model

The *Ragazzi Harraga* model was built on a thorough analysis of the needs of the unaccompanied children and the weaknesses of the services provided. The proposed holistic model of inclusion aimed to take over the complexity of the process and tests innovative pathways towards autonomy, linking different actions and connecting all the social actors involved in the life of these unaccompanied children. Specifically, it provided for a closer collaboration and co-creation amongst private and public sectors.

The thirty-month long project that started its first activities in 2017, identified three challenges as priorities and consisted of five actions (see Figure 8.1 for an overview of the actions).

The following paragraphs outline and describe these challenges and actions developed by the partners.

As mentioned previously, each minor accessing a second reception facility should initiate his/her individual educational plan (PEI) which serves as a tool for planning and implementing the inclusion process. However, the application of the PEI is not always guaranteed due to a lack of continuity,

---

[7] The name of the project reflects migrants' life experiences. In fact, the Arabic word harraga means 'those who burn': 'harraga' boys and girls symbolically burn the borders, put their whole existence at risk in order to change their lives. The *Ragazzi Harraga* project was coordinated by CIAI (Italian Centre for Aid to Children) and was implemented in cooperation with nine stakeholders. The project is funded through 'Never Alone, per un domani possibile' - an Italian initiative aimed at building pathways to autonomy and inclusion targeted at unaccompanied minors, so as to create a new culture of reception which respects and promotes children's rights.

causing a fragmentation of these pathways and exposing the fragility of the entire procedure.

Figure 8.1: List of actions featured in the inclusion model

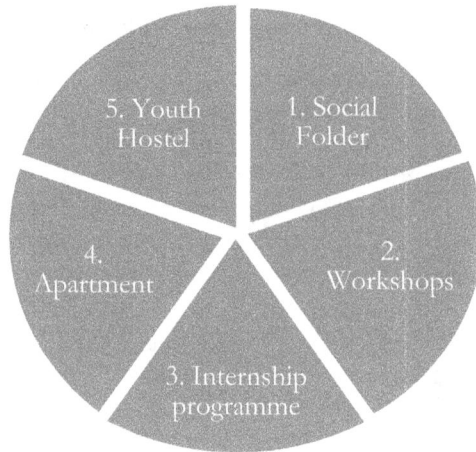

First Challenge: Lack of Tracking Tools for UAMs' pathways

PEIs are often standardized and not based on individual competences and expectations. Moreover, the absence of connections and the lack of communication between different actors and institutions working on the minor's inclusion process, the inadequacy of training offered to professionals, contribute to system fragmentation and convey a sense of disorientation to minors.

In order to address this challenge, the *first pillar* of the model provides for the creation of a digital social folder for each unaccompanied minor, including personal data, information concerning the reception and inclusion process initiated, as well as notes on professional, transversal and basic skills acquired. These data are uploaded in a database and should be constantly updated by social workers of the municipality of Palermo. In this way, they can trace the path, stages of reception and the individual training plan of the child and promote relevant actions in order to enhance it, since the paper documentation might often get lost.

The digital social folder also prevents different social workers asking the same questions to minors (e.g. concerning their studies in their country of origin, the activities they are participating in, the diseases they had, etc.) which may sometimes cause emotional distress. Furthermore, when UAMs are transferred from one reception centre to another, the managers can already access their files containing important information regarding their inclusion path. The efficacy of the solution suggested by *Ragazzi Harraga* partnership is demonstrated by the decision of the Italian government to include this procedure in the provisions of Law no. 47/2017 (Blangiardo et al, 2018).

Second Challenge: Need of Self-Awareness and Work Experience

The transition to adulthood means accessing the job market. However, migrant minors have to deal with a reduction of their career opportunities due to the lack of appropriate collaboration between Provincial Centres for Adult Education (CPIA), secondary schools, vocational training and guidance courses. In general, UAMs' vocational training is weak, and they are unaware of labour market dynamics. In addition, they are not accustomed to reflecting on themselves and on their skills or to elaborate long-term career plans. The persistence of negative stereotypes, connected both to the age and the origin of minors, aggravate their situation. The absence of a parental and social network also plays an important role, exposing them to the risk of failing to access the labour market and being exploited. Since the Italian model of integration is focused on entry into the labour market (Allsopp, 2017), unaccompanied minors need to deal with and understand the importance of finding a job.

The *second pillar* seeks to change these dynamics by helping unaccompanied minors strengthen and develop their soft skills through a series of workshops. The partnership agreed to devote these series of workshops to three different topics (see Table 8.1). The general aim of the workshops was to provide UAMs with different skills at the end of each cycle. In addition, these workshops targeted to create opportunities for young Italians and UAMs to meet and get to know each other, raise awareness of their personal characteristics and identify their life goals. In this way, minors are given the opportunity to develop tools for making autonomous and informed decisions concerning their personal and professional lives.

The aims of the specific workshops provided were as follows:

The intercultural workshops among others, aim to help youngsters familiarise themselves with values and traditions of the different communities living in Palermo, understand the culture of the host society, and the essence of encounters between different cultures and religions. Such awareness would allow minors to trust the city and its people.

The workshops on rights and active citizenship (2) aim to make the minor understand that they have an active role in the city and that being citizens is contributing in the well-being of the society. Meeting, discussing, and creating personal connections are ways to find a place of their own in the city.

The theatre workshop is an opportunity to learn about new forms of self-expression and to manage one's emotions by exploring other kinds of interpersonal relationships, and on the other hand, video-making workshops aim at helping minors to develop hard skills while looking at the reality from another perspective, by increasing the attention towards oneself and the outside world.

Table 8.1: List of workshops provided within the *Ragazzi Harraga* project (Action 2)*

Topic	Duration	Description
Intercultural, non-formal education workshops.	240[8] hours (80 hours per cycle)	The intercultural workshops deal with topics such as: intercultural awareness; Palermo and its cultural life; stereotypes and prejudices; interreligious dialogue; verbal and non-verbal communication; body language as a means of intercultural
Rights and active citizenship workshops aimed at strengthening children's awareness of the cultural and social life	240 hours (80 hours per cycle)	Rights and active citizenship workshops start from an analysis of the concept of citizenship and allow participants to reflect on the opportunities and the risks of their new community, as well as on the
Theatre and video-making workshops aimed at developing and strengthening UAM's relational skills (communication, interpersonal relationships, collaboration, group dynamics, etc.).	Theatre :140 hours (70 hours per cycle) Video-making: 100 hours (50 hours per cycle)	Thanks to theatre workshops, participants can improve self-awareness and explore different ways of expressing themselves. Moreover, they experiment new ways of connecting with other people, increase their self-confidence and develop teamwork skills. Video-making workshops allow participants to familiarise themselves

Ragazzi Harraga, application form, 2016

The **third pillar** of the model provides for the development of an active policy aimed at including migrant children into the Italian labour market. In order to achieve this goal, the partnership designed an internship programme, offering co-curricular and extra-curricular work placements and on-the-job training mainly in the hospitality industry. Internships are on-the-job training opportunities that allow the minors to understand the labour

---

[8] The hours of instructions allocated to each topic were determined after having sought advice from experts and validation groups and assessed learning needs and potential outcomes. For instance, as participants needed also to rehearse for their final performance, the partnership decided to allocate additional hours to the theatre workshops.

market and its rules. UAMs can put themselves to test and understand if these occupations are in line with their aspirations. In addition, traineeships facilitate entry to the labour market because they allow minors to demonstrate their skills and to demolish prejudices and stereotypes that employers sometimes have.

Along with the second pillar, UAMs reinforce and develop their soft and professional skills, improve self-actualisation and self-esteem, and learn to identify and recognize their own skills and talents.

Third challenge: Barriers to Independent Living and Autonomy for UAMs Ageing Out of Special Reception Systems

In their path towards autonomy, unaccompanied minors also need to deal with housing issues, as leaving the second reception facilities when they turn 18 can be extremely critical. Most of the time, if transferred to second reception structures it is very likely that they will be located in other cities due to unavailability of places in centres managed by SPRAR. In other cases, they are forced to return to first reception centres, temporary reception centres or to low- threshold reception facilities. It is extremely difficult for them to find accessible and sustainable housing solutions, both because of the aforementioned stereotypes and because of the costs they have to bear (Allsopp, 2017).

The **fourth pillar** of the project tries to address this issue. It includes the opening of a temporary self-sustaining housing solution available for unaccompanied migrants who have turned 18 and stopped benefiting from the UAM reception facilities. As a matter of fact, many UAMs spontaneously decide to give away their place in reception facilities in order to avoid being transferred to another city and undermining all their efforts. After a round of applications, eight ex-UAMs were selected and were granted the opportunity of being hosted in Foresteria Santa Chiara[9] for one year. Living for a year in a house where they neither have to pay rent nor housing expenses, provides these youngsters with the opportunity to keep building their paths towards autonomy, to find a job or to continue with their studies.

Finally, the **fifth pillar** provides for the creation of a youth hostel in the premises of the guesthouse, ensuring its sustainability at the end of the project. This tool will also be used to raise awareness about the project and encourage people to support and promote its actions and activities aimed at creating an intercultural community. Moreover, it provided a job opportunity for three of the unaccompanied minors who have turned 18 and have participated in *Ragazzi Harraga* activities. This solution allows for the sustainability of an affordable social housing solution.

---

[9] More information can be accessed to: https://www.foresteriasantachiara.com/

A Reflection on the Provisional Results

It was expected that 336 UAMs would be involved in the activities of the *Ragazzi Harraga* project. In order to approach and register the UAMs multiple methods are used, but they mainly include the use of social media and the promotion of the project inside reception facilities through social workers, volunteer and legal guardians. At the time of writing this Chapter, *Ragazzi Harraga* had entered its second phase of implementation. Table 8.2 summarizes the results achieved so far regarding some of the key performance indicators.

Table 8.2: Key performance indicators of the *Ragazzi Harraga* project (latest updates: 30/10/2018, edited by the authors)

Pillar	Action	Goal	Results Achieved	Comments
1	Launch of the platform which hosts the social folders of the unaccompanied minors	1	1 (100%)	The platform has been launched and social workers are uploading the digital social folders of each unaccompanied minor living in Palermo.
2	Number of unaccompanied minors supported by the project (participating in the workshops offered by the project)	**240**	**107** (44.6%)	The workshops are in their second implementation phase, which attracted an increasing number of participants. The last cycle of workshops started in January 2019. The reported figure refers to minors who have participated in at least 50% of the sessions and obtained the skills portfolio.
3	Number of unaccompanied minors who have participated in the internship programme.	**85** (50 C) (35 E)	**62** (72.9%) (35 C) (27 E)	'C' stands for *Co-curricular internships*, which coincide with school hours and last up to one month. Interns do not receive a grant. 'E' stands for E*tracurricular internships*, this kind of internships is not connected to the formal educational system and last up to 9 months. Interns receive a 300-euro grant.

3	Number of unaccompanied minors who have participated in the internship programme and were offered a job.	**13**	**12** (92.3%)	12 unaccompanied minors of those that participated in the internship program were offered to sign an employment contract at the end of their internship.
4	Number of migrants, ageing out of UAM's reception facilities who had access to the apartment for one year.	**8**	8 (100%)	The apartment opened in May 2018 and it is hosting eight 18-year old boys.
5	Number of migrants who now work in the youth hostel.	**3**	3 (100%)	The youth hostel opened in June 2018 and 3 adult migrants (18-19 years old), 2 boys and 1 girl have started working there.

The combination of all these actions conveyed a sense of belonging to the participants who have had the opportunity to develop key skills leading towards autonomy. The partnership has carried out follow up meetings in order to observe the life paths of the minors who participated in *Ragazzi Harraga* activities. They noticed that these youngsters are more capable of making informed decisions concerning their future, are more self-aware and autonomous. Moreover, they finally feel part of Palermo city life.

Since the beginning of the project, *Ragazzi Harraga* has involved already around 200 people, both foreigners and locals, in its activities, fostering the creation of a special community in the city of Palermo and increasing the interaction among young people from different backgrounds. Consequently, the impact of the project goes beyond its target group, since it seeks to open a dialogue between various stakeholders that cooperate to the reinforcement of an intercultural city.

Strengths of the Model

In order to develop its actions, the project partnership resorted to a 'validation group', consisting of eight unaccompanied minors, who were contacted at different stages of the project to give feedback on ideas, activities and ways for encouraging the participation of youngsters who live in Palermo. Their feedbacks allowed the partners to co-create activities that would effectively answer the challenges they also face. Therefore, *Ragazzi Harraga* is not a project created for the UAM but with them.

As for the workshops and career guidance sessions, linguistic/cultural facilitators and peer tutors have been employed; they were selected among 18-21 years old migrant youths; some of them had also participated in the project, through which they were provided with direct and indirect job opportunities.

A high number of extracurricular internships turned into job contracts highlighting how those opportunities have been crucial for guaranteeing UAMs and migrant adults' access to the job market.

Another strength is the establishment of a network of partners, stakeholders, volunteers, and volunteer guardians who now represent a strong social network for these youngsters. These people have become a genuine point of reference and encouraged UAMs to play an active role in the hosting community.

Considering the complexity of the project, the involvement of diverse experts within its activities has allowed the partnership to achieve high quality results, also regarding the methodologies included, the analysis carried out, and the different perspectives presented.

The connection *Ragazzi Harraga* created between private and public sectors, as well as among associations and civil society, allowed the partnership to overcome bureaucratic issues and promote cross-agency collaborations.

Bottlenecks in implementation

The inclusion initiatives and autonomy-supportive interventions mainly targeted at UAMs, proved to be an inefficient strategy. That is why the second pillar of the project aimed at involving young locals to create an intercultural environment. However, it was hard to reach and attract young locals during the implementation phase due to the fact that in the beginning the whole communication strategy was mainly targeted at unaccompanied minors and not at local youth who wanted to get new experiences and develop their skills, regardless of their origin.

Another challenge has been the involvement of unaccompanied minor girls, even if their number is significantly inferior compared to the boys; partners had to overcome many obstacles to reach them and enable their participation. The results have not been satisfying, despite the efforts made in order to sensitize girls and encourage them to take part in the activities or apply for the internships. This outcome might be explained with girls' mistrust and indifference towards locals, including professionals. Moreover, the reception centres in which they reside usually have strict rules that also discourage them from attending activities in Palermo due to their manifold vulnerability as UAM, women exposed to trafficking and migrants.

Despite the fact that UAMs feel a sense of belonging to the city, the lack of opportunities to participate in the city life does not allow them to become visible and interact with actors and subjects who are not aware of or work in the field of migration.

Suggestions for Wider Implementation of a Holistic Inclusion Model

Regarding the inclusion paths of UAMs, it is necessary to adopt a holistic model that takes over the complexity of the processes and delivers diverse methods of inclusion, which enable migrants to achieve independence. This is why it is important to understand how multiple actions answering diverse needs under a common framework allow to create connections among different stakeholders, foster continuity and strengthen new pathways to UAMs' autonomy.

In order to create links between the local community and minors, it is important to find occasions where both groups interact to move towards a more intercultural society. Creating opportunities to share and get to know each other is an antidote to negative and racist narratives concerning migrants. Taking the actions within the project into account, the workshops to develop the 'soft' skills of the UAMs (pillar no. 2) and the internship programme designed to include the minors into the Italian labour market (pillar no.3) seem to be intertwined. The workshops aim to involve UAMs in learning paths that foster their self-confidence and self-awareness, distracting them from the concerns of their daily lives and preventing them from associating with organised crime. At the same time, internship schemes, either co-curricular or extracurricular, reinforce and develop their soft and professional skills, improving self-determination, self-esteem and self-awareness. This connection should be supported by the construction of the skills' portfolio together with UAMs. It is essential to follow this procedure at the end of the learning paths and before the internship to allow UAMs to reflect on their competences and get prepared to enter the labour market with a clearer understanding of who they are and which career pathway they would like to pursue.

Regarding the process-oriented aspects, the following points should be taken into consideration to implement a holistic model of inclusion.

The model proposed may have a stronger impact on smaller cities, where migrants tend to live in a central neighbourhood, facilitating the establishment of accessible points of reference. In the case of bigger cities, it seems important to identify 'hubs' which enable to create comfort and protected space where the UAMs may develop a sense of belonging.

In the establishment of a local partnership, it is crucial to involve organizations (CSOs, reception centres, local authorities, etc.) that have already expertise in the field and carry grassroots daily work with the target groups. Community based organizations would provide different points of view and approaches, widening the array of solutions.

One of the success factors that might foster the implementation of such a model would be the close collaboration between private and public sectors, having the civil society sharing responsibility and creating social networks around the UAMs. This connection should encourage them to define common objectives and expertise and reach an understanding concerning the essential needs of the community. As *Ragazzi Harraga* was funded thanks to the contributions of several private foundations, it is crucial to underline the importance of accessing independent resources that will ensure more flexibility for cooperation initiatives that would be more adaptable to local needs and to the methods used by community-based organizations.

Local cooperation shall always start from a needs analysis in order to adapt the model after having identified relevant actions. In the case of *Ragazzi Harraga*, the creation of a temporary self-sustaining housing was an answer to the increase of UAMs' arrivals in the city and the lack of facilities. Thanks to this initiative, the partnership showed public authorities managing the reception system that it is possible to find alternative and sustainable solutions.

Concerning financial sustainability, large-scale projects should find new self-financing schemes so that their impact is not restricted to the years of direct funding. The suggested model is characterised by a great flexibility and presents good strategies. For instance, the creation of a hostel in Palermo is not only a means of dialogue, but also an answer to the increasing tourist flows gravitating towards the city. Accordingly, the creation of a restaurant or a youth centre could be an answer to the needs of other cities.

In order to apply the model in a wider context, the partnership of *Ragazzi Harraga* project suggests following one rule: to apply bottom up approach, which means - co-create projects *with* unaccompanied minors not for them. Such approach guarantees: (1) a very detailed analysis of the UAMs' needs and values, (2) the effectiveness of the actions proposed, (3) a stronger cooperation of the beneficiaries and a better and lasting impact on the local community.

Disclosure Statement

No potential conflict of interest was reported by the authors.

Acknowledgements

The authors would like to thank CESIE, Jelena Mazaj, representative of its Competence Cell, Maria Luisa Cerniglia and Maryna Manchenko who contributed to a special revision of the actions with their feedback; CIAI, *Ragazzi Harraga* project coordinator Alessandra Sciurba, and its local partners: Municipality of Palermo, Associazione Santa Chiara, Cooperativa Libera…mente, CPIA Palermo, Libera Palermo, Nottedoro and SEND, with which we are promoting a significant social change in the context of socio-labour inclusion paths targeted at UAMs living in Palermo.

Additionally, we would like to thank the contributors Moussa Ben Said, Numu Touray, Gulzar Hussain, Njfon Mouhamed Chamwil, Magasouba Gassimou, Bassirou Dembele, Alhagie Sankareh, Khaoussou Diassigui, whose support in the the *Ragazzi Harraga* activities has been fundamental for their role as intercultural bridges between the UAMs and the experts.

References

Allsopp, J. (2017). *Unaccompanied Minors and Secondary Migration between Italy and the UK*. Becoming Adult Research Brief no. 8, London: UCL *www.becomingadult.net*.

Blangiardo, G., Valtolina, G., Zanfrini, L., Codini, E., Pasini, N., Santagati, M., Bosetti, E., Locatelli F., & Cesareo, V. (2018). *The Twenty-third Italian Report on Migrations 2017*. Fondazione ISMU.

Catarci, M., & Rocchi, M. (2017). ALIA. The Inclusion of Unaccompanied Minors in Italy. *Education Sciences & Society-Open Access Journal, 8*(2).

Colombo F. (2017, August 2). *Il sistema di accoglienza dei migranti in Italia, spiegato per bene*. Retrieved from https://www.lenius.it/sistema-di-accoglienza-dei-migranti-in-italia/. Accessed: 18.3.2019.

UN Committee on the Rights of the Child (CRC), *General comment No. 6 (2005): Treatment of Unaccompanied and Separated Children Outside their Country of Origin*, 1 September 2005, CRC/GC/2005/6. Retrieved from https://www2.ohchr.org/english/bodies/crc/docs/GC6.pdf. Accessed: 18.3.2019.

Comune di Palermo. (2018, July 10). *Il Modello Palermo: la presa in carico delle ragazze e dei ragazzi stranieri non accompagnati*. (in Italian).

Demurtas, P., Vitiello M., Accorinti, M., Skoda, A., & Perillo, C. (2018, April 6). *In Search of Protection: Unaccompanied Minors in Italy*. Center for Migration Studies. Retrieved from: *http://cmsny.org/publications/2018smsc-cse-uam/*. Accessed: 18.3.2019.

Disposizioni in materia di misure di protezione dei minori stranieri non accompagnati. Law no. 47, 7 April 2017. (in Italian). Retrieved from: http://www.gazzettaufficiale.it/eli/id/2017/04/21/17G00062/sg. Accessed: 18.3.2019.

European Union Agency for Fundamental Rights. (2018) *Guardianship for Unaccompanied Children in Italy: Update after the adoption of Law No. 47 of 7 April 2017 and Legislative Decree No. 220 of 22 December 2017*.

Eurostat. (2017, May 11). *News release 80/2017*. Retrieved from: https://ec.europa.eu/eurostat/documents/2995521/8016696/3-11052017-AP-EN.pdf. Accessed: 18.3.2019.

Giovannetti, M. (2017). Reception and Protection Policies for Unaccompanied Foreign Minors in Italy. *Social Work & Society, 15*(2).

INTERSOS. (2017). *Unaccompanied And Separated Children along Italy's northern borders*. Retrieved from: https://www.intersos.org/wp-content/uploads/2018/02/UASC-along-Italys-northern-borders.compressed.pdf. Accessed: 18.3.2019.

Lelliott, J. (2018). Italy's' Zampa'law: increasing protection for unaccompanied children. *Forced Migration Review*, (57), 79-81.

Ministero del Lavoro e delle Politiche Sociali. (2017). *La presenza dei migranti nella città metropolitana di Palermo*. (in Italian).

Ministero del Lavoro e delle Politiche Sociali. (2016, August 31). *Report Mensile Minori Stranieri Non Accompagnati (MSNA) in Italia*. (in Italian).

Ministero del Lavoro e delle Politiche Sociali. (2018, June 30). *Report Mensile Minori Stranieri Non Accompagnati (MSNA) in Italia*. (in Italian).

Ministero del Lavoro e delle Politiche Sociali. (2018, June 30). *Report di Monitoraggio: I Minori*

Stranieri Non Accompagnati (MSNA) in Italia. (in Italian).

Novara, C., Serio, C., & Moscato, G. (2016). Unaccompanied foreign minors in the Italian context: From legal order to networking in educational services. *Turkish Online Journal of Educational Technology, 2016,* 1229-1235.

OXFAM. (2018). *Libia, l'Inferno senza fine.* (In Italian). Retrieved from: https://www. oxfamitalia.org/wp-content/uploads/2018/01/MediaBrief_FINAL_OK.pdf. Accessed: 18.3.2019.

Rania, N., Migliorini, L., & Fagnini, L. (2018). Unaccompanied migrant minors: A comparison of new Italian interventions models. *Children and Youth Services Review, 92,* 98-104.

Rania, N., Migliorini, L., Sclavo, E., Cardinali, P., & Lotti, A. (2014). Unaccompanied migrant adolescents in the Italian context: Tailored educational interventions and acculturation stress. *Child & Youth Services, 35*(4), 292-315.

REACH. (2017, June). *Children on the move in Italy and Greece –Report June 2017.* Retrieved from: http://www.reachresourcecentre.info/system/files/resource-documents/reach_ita_grc_report_children_on_the_move_in_italy_and_greece_june_20 17.pdf. Accessed: 18.3.2019.

Rozzi, E. (2017). *The new Italian law on unaccompanied minors: a model for the EU?.* Retrieved from http://eumigrationlawblog.eu/the-new-italian-law-on-unaccompanied-minors-a-model-for-the-eu/. Accessed: 18.3.2019.

Scherer S. (2018, October 1). *Italy's closure to rescue ships drives up sea deaths: think tank.* Reuters. Retrieved from https://www.reuters.com/article/us-europe-migrants-italy/italys-closure-to-rescue-ships-drives-up-sea-deaths-think-tank-idUSKCN1MB353. Accessed: 18.3.2019.

Servizio Centrale SPRAR. (2017, December 13th). Percorsi e strumenti per l'accoglienza integrata dei MSNA. Rome. (in Italian).

Zandonini G. (2017, February 8). *The long wait of young unaccompanied migrants in Italy.* Open Migration. Retrieved from *https://openmigration.org/en/analyses/the-long-wait-of-young-unaccompanied-migrants-in-italy/.* Accessed: 18.3.2019.